Ambiguous Selves

New Jewish Identities

Melanie Fogell

To Dayle,
Something
witty. Thank
you for coming.
Love
Melanie Fogell

DETSELIG
ENTERPRISES LTD

Ambiguous Selves: New Jewish Identities
© 2006 Melanie Fogell

Library and Archives Canada Cataloguing in Publication

Fogell, Melanie
    Ambiguous selves : new Jewish identities / Melanie Fogell.

Includes bibliographical references.
ISBN-13: 978-1-55059-327-3
ISBN-10: 1-55059-327-7

    1. Jews--Identity. I. Title.
DS143.F58 2006   296.3'6   C2006-904078-8

Detselig Enterprises Ltd.   www.temerondetselig.com
210, 1220 Kensington Road NW   temeron@telusplanet.net
        Calgary, Alberta   DETSELIG   Phone: (403) 283-0900
                T2N 3P5   ENTERPRISES LTD   Fax: (403) 283-6947

We acknowledge the support of the Government of Canada through the Book Publishing Industry Development Program (BPIDP) for our publishing program.

We also acknowledge the support of the Alberta Foundation for the Arts for our publishing program.

SAN 113-0234
ISBN 1-55059-327-7   978-1-55059-327-3
Printed in Canada   Cover Design by Alvin Choong

In memory of my father, David Fogell.

Contents

Acknowledgments

Although the gestation period of this book has been my entire life, it began to take written form as a doctoral dissertation at the University of Calgary. I was fortunate to have Dr. Hans Smits as my advisor in the Graduate Department of Educational Research. He encouraged me to write and to keep writing. It was largely because of his gentle and generous guidance that such a project came within the scope of my abilities.

Before getting to the doctoral level I received invaluable support from several of my earlier professors. Dr. Ron Glasberg was truly an inspiration; his excitement for teaching and learning helped to launch what was to be a long journey for me. I am thankful to have the chance to work with Dr. Elly Silverman, my Master's advisor at the University of Calgary. She encouraged me to explore and write my history, and she helped me see that women's history is important. Additionally, I also thank Dr. David Taras for his consistent mentoring over several years.

I owe a great debt to the women who participated in my research for allowing me into their busy lives, as well as my family, friends and colleagues – who bolstered my confidence along the way. In particular, I am grateful for my mother's constant interest and support; I felt her love urging me to keep going. She has always been a source of strength for me although there have been many times in the past when I did not fully appreciate her endurance.

It is also important for me to mention my gratitude to my publisher, Ted Giles, at Detselig Enterprises Ltd. for taking a chance on me. My book addresses many sensitive issues that other publishers likely wanted to avoid. I also thank Leif Baradoy, my editor, for his valuable comments and help in completing this project. Special thanks is also due to Linda Lentz for her careful reading of my manuscript.

Finally I would like to thank Ken Goldstein for being a constant source of patience and support in all areas of my life. He believed in me even when I did not believe in myself, and his insistence that I finish the book was an invaluable gift.

Preface

The self-consciousness and self reflection that essay writing demands cannot help but have an influence on the personal essayist's life . . . The essay is an enactment of the creation of self.

– Phillip Lopate

In this book I explore the doubts and ambiguities of identity – principally Jewish identity. Although I document this investigation primarily in the form of personal essay, I synthesize research narratives, academic theory and community discourse to show how identity changes and emerges. The broad range of topics that inform this project each represent ways that I link myself to the world. My hope is that, in this era of fragmentation and chaos, others may benefit from the discoveries of my conflicted journey.

For many reasons I have had difficulty finding a comfortable place for myself in the world. I suspect that many people share this feeling. I wonder how I am connected to the world? Am I important? Does it even matter what a person remembers of his of her life? For me, it has made a difference. Memories may or may not be reliable, but they are worth exploring in an effort to find meaning in life. I have the luxury to search for meaning, and some of my findings appear in this book.

During my research I had the privilege of hearing the stories of Israeli women, who explained their Jewish identity. How is that identity connected to Israel? How is my identity linked to Israel? What does it mean to live as a Jewish woman in Canada? Although names and details have been changed to protect these women's privacy, I have attempted to record their feelings and thoughts accurately – always remembering that I am interpreting words and events from my own location in the world.

In the chapters that follow I will address many issues concerning Jewish identity. Chapter One covers describes my discomfort in the world and looks at some details of my background, information about Israel, as well as some of the theories of identity. Chapters Two and Three explore the construction of identity in the public world and thoughts about being judged by others. These chapters also introduce most of the Israeli participants whose stories are woven throughout the rest of the book. Chapter Four examines how people see themselves in the world, by drawing from Richard Kearney's work and feminist theory. Chapter Five concerns the judgment of others and the difficulties involved in moving to a new community. Chapters Six and Seven go in to a detailed discussion of Zionism from several perspectives, including Michael Barnett, Yael Zerubavel, Melanie

Kaye/Kantowitz and others. In Chapter Eight I continue to focus on some of the scholarly interpretations of Zionism as it pertains to identity. Chapter Nine continues the discussion of identity, this time focusing on boundaries and Jewish self-hatred. In the final chapter I bring together the ideas raised throughout the book in an attempt to reconcile some of the identifiable conflicts raised; here, I summarize what I have learned in the writing of the book.

I wonder about the ideas I passed on to my children and what they will pass on to their children. In this way I see myself as a part of history. More specifically I feel a stronger connection to the past, present, and future of the world. My education in public schools left out the history of the Jews. I have attempted to fill in a few of the gaps; I hope other writers will continue this process. In writing this book I have come closer to finding out what goes into the construction of a Self. I look at how we are created by society and how we create society for ourselves. Assuredly, this project will lead to larger questions about the kind of world in which we want to live.

The journey of writing my history has given me the courage to ask new questions of myself and of the world. Moreover, it has inspired me to make changes in my life.

One

Fear of Strangers

Even before the events of 9/11, the Hebrew school that my youngest daughter attended in Calgary employed security guards for all the doors. In May 2002, a letter was sent to parents of children at the Hebrew school explaining that classes would end a week earlier in June. For my daughter this was cause for celebration. The reason given for the early dismissal date was that the school security guards were required at the G-8 conference in Kananaskis, Alberta in June, 2002, and the school officials thought that the lack of security was a hazard to the children at the school. Anti-Semitism continues to be a threat for Jews all over the world.[1] Although it is possible for some Jews to hide behind a light skin tone, fear does not easily disappear.

Although my family was in Canada throughout the Holocaust, they were very aware of Hitler's "Final Solution"– the plan to eliminate Jews.[2] I was born in 1951, a few years after the end of World War II, and Jews all over the world were still reeling in shock at the atrocities of the death camps. The aftermath of the war left many Jews with a pervasive sense of fear. As I grew up, I was often reminded by my parents how fortunate it was that my grandparents had the strength and foresight to leave Eastern Europe before World War II. My parents would regularly tell me that if the Nazis ever came again, they would take us all to concentration camps to be gassed and burned. There would be nowhere to run or hide. This particular phrase was very useful when they wanted to discourage me from dating non-Jewish boys. They warned that even if I was married to a non-Jew, the Nazis would find me anyway. "The Nazis will take you away. Be ready to leave everything and run for safety, and by the way, don't marry a non-Jew." Although it may seem ridiculous that my parents would actually say these things to me, they probably felt that these warnings would somehow protect me. Their warnings actually did have an enormous impact on me. When I dated non-Jews I felt guilty about it – as if I were betraying my parents. I have been married twice, each time to a Jewish man. With my own children I was conscious of trying not to be like my parents, but it seems they still got a similar message but perhaps not as clearly.

I lived in a middle-class suburb in Winnipeg, Manitoba from 1951 until we moved to Vancouver, British Columbia in 1966. In Winnipeg, at that time, it was not uncommon for people to leave their doors unlocked. In contrast to the omnipresent fear that my parents and other Jews experienced concerning anti-Semitism, living in the suburbs during the 1950s there was also a secure and easy feeling that all was well in our little corner of the world. As a child I roamed from one friend's house to another without having to check in with my mother. In contrast, my own children were taught never to open the front door, which is always locked, to anyone. Later, I gave them cell phones so they could always inform me of their whereabouts.

The conflicting themes of safety and danger were in constant juxtaposition as I was growing up. Although the setting of my childhood appeared safe, my parents' constant reminder of the danger for Jews was always lurking beneath the surface. I attended a Hebrew school twice a week in the late afternoon after public school and again on Sunday mornings. The need to be on guard was also reinforced there. At the time I attended Hebrew school, during the 1950s, the importance of Israel to the survival of the Jews was paramount. The curriculum included history, Hebrew language, and most importantly, education about the newly formed State of Israel. Part of the classroom time was taken up with writing letters to our pen pals in Israel. We wrote to them in Hebrew and they responded in Hebrew. They enclosed Israeli coins and dried flowers in their letters. As a child I had an image of a biblical scenic country filled with dried flowers. I am sure that there must have been an important reason for these enclosures. Perhaps the flowers were symbolic of new growth and the coins a symbol of success. Whatever the reason, these memories have stayed with me and have played a part in my early connection to Israel as a second home where Jews were free to be openly Jewish.

There were other ways to link young minds to Zionism. We were always encouraged to donate money to Israel. This was accomplished by the virtual planting of trees. We could purchase a printed picture of a tree with empty leaves which needed to be filled in with stamps and the completion of tree page was accompanied by much praise. We would then receive a certificate – the official documentation of the tree we had planted. Building a strong connection to Israel also included showing students – as young age seven – documentary footage of dead emaciated Jews being shoveled into mass graves. We were warned to "never forget." I never did.

This legacy instilled a sense of fear and distrust that still lingers. Even with Canada's policy of official multiculturalism, I am not comfortable about being different; I still have the sense that I do not quite fit in and often feel that I need be silent about the fact that I am Jewish. Although my parents were born in Canada and English is my first language, I have a sense of not belonging. It is probably not unusual for a person from a minority group to experience a sense of feeling different because that is the reality of the situation.

Unfortunately, this constant reality can be accompanied by anxiety and uneasiness, instead of a celebration of uniqueness.

Being the third generation of East European Jewish immigrants, I grew up hearing stories of the pogroms in Russia and Poland that my grandparents survived. Other stories etched in my childhood memories were those about Jews who had to leave their homes because they were hated by everyone (I never really understood why they were hatred). The Holocaust and the murder of six million Jews was also a common topic in our home, especially when my brothers and I complained about having to attend Hebrew school after a long day at public school.

For many years, I thought my parents and grandparents were exaggerating about the existence of anti-Semitism. Why would they be afraid of Nazis when it happened, in my mind, so long ago? It was difficult for me to believe that our kindly non-Jewish neighbors next door might not like us because we were Jewish. Now I realize that my parents fears were well-founded. Historian, Laurence Rees, discusses the sense of betrayal that a Holocaust survivor, Toivi Blatt, experienced during World War II:

> Before the war, Blatt's hometown had contained around 3 600 jews. There was little overt anti-Semitism, especially for Toivi as he grew up. His father had fought in the Polish army and had been wounded, and that gave the family a certain status in the town. Once the German army arrived, however, Toivi witnessed an immediate change: "The [Polish] population noticed that the Jews are second-class and you can do with them whatever you want....In the end I was more afraid of my neighbors – Christian people – than of the Germans, because the Germans didn't recognize [that I was Jewish] and my neighbors did."[3]

I use this particular example because my father's family came from Poland. As I grew up I came to understand more about my parents' attitudes. Although they wanted to be modern and liberal-minded, they had grown up with blatant anti-Semitism and they passed their fears down to me. While my parents often voiced their concerns about non-Jews, they also explained that many immigrants came to Canada to escape persecution. Canada was a tolerant country where anyone could live free of persecution. Persecution against Jews is usually referred to as anti-Semitism. Even during the Spanish Inquisition, Jews could simply convert to Christianity, thereby avoiding exile or death. But after the Holocaust anti-Semitism took on a new meaning. Hitler's goal was to eliminate a race of subhumans. Conversion was no longer a choice in avoiding execution. The message was confusing to me because some people still argue that being Jewish is 'just' a religious or cultural choice. The question of 'who is a Jew?' still goes unanswered.[4]

During the post-Holocaust period of the 1950s, my upbringing and education were imbued with Zionist ideals, so I feel a strong (albeit confused) connection to Israel. The State of Israel is a symbol of Jewish strength and hope for the future. I learned as a child that the existence of Israel would always protect Jews from annihilation. After the Holocaust, the founding of the State of Israel in 1948 promised Jews all over the world a safe haven. It promised that the Jewish people would be like other people. There would be a place where persecution was no longer a danger. Yet, this promise has not materialized and the level of conflict has grown over time. For those Jews who live in Israel there has never been a time of total peace.

Much has been written about Jewish migration that focuses on the historical necessity of being a nomadic people due to religious persecution. In a recent book on Jewish migration, historians Daniel J. Elazar and Morton Weinfeld discuss the extent of this geographic movement.[5] They explain that the Jewish people have more experience with migration "than any other people, and certainly more than any other that has positioned itself in the center of many civilizations"; "Jews have always been on the move."[6] Jewish communities exist in every part of the world and their mass migrations have affected Jewish and world history. For example, there is a history of Jewish movement at the time of the Roman Empire. The Spanish Inquisition resulted in Jewish migration from Western and Central Europe to Eastern Europe. There was also movement to North and South America. And, of course, there was the post-war movement of Holocaust survivors and North African Jews to Israel, France, the Americas, Australia, and South Africa.[7] Yet, in this recent and comprehensive treatment of Jewish migration almost nothing is said about Jews who have left Israel. The topic of Jews leaving Israel and migrating to the Diaspora is a disconcerting idea. With the establishment of a national home in Israel, Jews no longer had to flee to all corners of the earth. The relationship between Israeli Jews and Jews in the Diaspora is often difficult and confusing. Before investigating this relationship, an explanation of Diaspora is necessary.

The word *diaspora* is derived from the Greek verb *speiro* (to sow) and the preposition *dia* (over). Robin Cohen explains in *Global Diasporas*:

> The ancient Greeks thought of diaspora as migration and colonization. By contrast, for Jews, Africans, Palestinians, and Armenians the expression acquired a more brutal meaning. Diaspora signified a collective trauma, a banishment, where one dreamed of home but lived on in exile.[8]

James Clifford, another expert in Diaspora literature, discusses the difference between immigrant populations and Diaspora populations. In his description, "Diasporic populations do not come from elsewhere in the same way that 'immigrants' do."[9] The distinguishing factor for

Clifford is that "immigrants may experience loss and nostalgia, but only en route to a new home in a new place."[10] He is referring, in particular to the American national ideology that aims to assimilate immigrants. He contrasts the situation of immigrants to Diaspora as "peoples whose sense of identity is centrally defined by collective histories of displacement and violent loss [which] cannot be 'cured' by merging into a new national community."[11] Although Clifford is using the American example as a host society, some of his points are relevant for Canadians. Israeli Jewish immigrants coming into contact with the North American Jewish Diaspora provide an ambiguous and complex example of ethnic identity to ponder – for Israelis in Israel, for Israeli emigrants, for the Jewish Diaspora, and for the host society.[12]

Even the question, "who is a Jew?" is a contentious issue among Jewish people, because it is difficult, if not impossible, to find consensus on the definition. Meryl Hyman, a specialist in Jewish history, explains:

> Israel's 1950 Law of Return, under which every Jew in the world has a right to immigrate, and the Citizenship Law of 1952 under which all Jewish immigrants have a right to Israeli citizenship, did not initially define a Jew. An immigrant had only to declare himself a Jew to be granted citizenship and enjoy the specific rights of Jews in the new homeland. In fact, Israel's standard of Jewishness and conversion was so much more lenient than the Orthodox standard in the Diaspora that some people who married into Jewish families and were denied conversion in the Diaspora came to Israel to be certified as Jews.[13]

As the flow of immigration to Israel increased, the laws became stricter and Orthodox Jews became more firmly entrenched in Israeli politics. By 1959, new guidelines were issued which stated that "a Jew was a person whose mother was a Jew or one who had been converted according to the orthodox *halachik* (Jewish law) standard, which requires circumcision for males, immersion in a ritual bath for males and females, and most important, a promise to live by Orthodox rules."[14] Although these guidelines became law in 1970, the controversy continues. As Hyman describes, "the political games over the issue have been intense. They have brought down politicians and governments, and thrown seemingly immovable blocks between the Diaspora and the homeland."[15]

The Jewish Diaspora refers to all Jews living outside of Israel. Many Jews in the Diaspora support Israel financially and even show support by making *aliyah* (relocating from the Diaspora to Israel). But, when Jews leave Israel it conflicts with the story that Israel is the Jewish homeland. In other words, the emigration of Jews from Israel raises questions concerning identity for Diaspora Jewry as well as for Israeli Jews in Israel.

One of the many layers of complexity I will address in this book is the way in which the discourse of Zionism has an impact on Israeli migrants as well as on Jews living in the Diaspora. In his seminal work on Israeli emigrants in New York, *Children Of Circumstances*, Moshe Shokeid cites the *Harvard Encyclopedia of American Ethnic Groups* in its short reference to Israelis in the United States:

> Israeli immigrants pose a problem for the Jewish community: they have chosen to leave the land that every Jewish American has learned to regard as a haven, the guardian of Jewish survival, and the center of Hebraic culture. The ambiguity toward *yordim* . . . has expressed itself in the absence of formal recognition of the Israelis as a Jewish immigrant group.[16]

The Hebrew word *yordim* refers to those whose have left Israel. As Linn and Barkan-Asher (1996) explain, *aliyah* (immigration to Israel) usually has positive connotations, while *yerida* (emigration from Israel, the emigrant being a *yored* – plural *yordim*) implies a rejection of Israeli life. *Aliyah* translated means to go up, while *yerida* means to go down. Sociologists, Linn and Barkan-Asher also point out that "every loss of a citizen through emigration is conceived as a weakening of the defense of the country" and that emigrants are "acutely aware" that "the term *yordim* has a pejorative connotation . . . and are consequently subject to feelings of vulnerability and guilt."[17] Thus, Israeli emigrants are subject to suspicion from Diaspora Jews as well as feeling insecure about their position in a new society

As a child I did not give much thought to idea of Israelis leaving Israel. It was rare that I would have any contact with Israelis except for the few who were teachers at the Hebrew school. I had no contact with Israeli children except for the pen pal correspondence mentioned earlier. The whole idea of Israel, to me, was part of an epic story of the Jews. It did not seem any more real than the biblical stories I heard. The first time I actually met young people from Israel was at summer camp. One section of the camp was set aside as Hebrew immersion. In that section the campers only spoke Hebrew. The camp counselors were often from Israel. It was like a completely separate camp, and they always seemed to be having more fun than the rest of us. They had more *ruach* (spirit or vitality). It was not until I reached adulthood that I had any real contact with people from Israel. I found that they too had a vitality I did not see in Canadians.

When my children were young I began to have more contact with Israeli immigrants because our children would attend school together as well as take part in activities at the Jewish Community Centre. During that time I started to become aware of a sense of unease between Israeli Jews and Canadian Jews. The Israeli Jews stuck together and usually spoke to each other in Hebrew. The Canadian Jews, for the most part, kept their distance from Israeli Jews. There were times when I heard Canadian Jews mutter negative comments about Israeli Jews. There was a sense that somehow they were taking advantage of Canadian generosity and hospitality.

Zvi Sobel, an Israeli scholar, stresses the importance of immigration and emigration for Israel in very strong terms. He contends that "each immigrant is considered a victory" and that emigration is seen as "a challenge to the inner viability or worth of those staying."[18] Some Israelis see emigration as a condemnation of their own decision to stay in Israel and view emigration as a form of desertion.[19] Thus Israelis who return to Israel after living away are not viewed in a positive way. Gold and Cohen argue that emigration from Israel stigmatizes Zionist ideologies which encourage immigration to Israel. In their study they found that those Jews who leave Israel develop "a myth of return which defuses the guilt of departure and authenticates the status of permanent expatriate" and that "it is this myth that contributes to the social construction of a distinct Israeli ethnicity."[20] From what I have seen in Canada, it seems that Israelis who leave Israel cannot win. In Israel they are often viewed as betrayers, and, in their new homes in the Diaspora, the unspoken message is that they will return to Israel. Their departure from Israel often causes discomfort among Diaspora Jews.

Israeli Jews in Canada can be considered a separate ethnic group from Jews born in Canada or anywhere else in the Diaspora. Canadian statistics on the number of Israelis residing in Canada are difficult to know because census forms allow Israelis to identify themselves as Canadian, Jewish, or Israeli when recording one's ethnic group. This means that Israeli Jews have three choices in answering the question of ethnic group so that the numbers can be confusing.[21]

The whole concept of migration can also be seen as a metaphor for making changes in one's life – moving on. It is not necessary to travel to the other side of the world to experience change. Migration can be also be envisioned as a coming into awareness from one state of mind to another. This changing of thought as it affects identity can be viewed as a kind of migration. Put in these terms, migration is something that most people experience. To physically move one's complete life to "a new setting and society is one of the most drastic social actions people may take during their lifetime."[22] However, the notion of migration itself has changed with globalization. Elazar and Weinfeld point out that "the entire paradigm of migration has . . . shifted dramatically in the second half, and even faster in the second quarter, of the twentieth century."[23] In the old pattern of migration it was more difficult to make return visits to relatives. In addition, "immigrants were generally ready to give up their Old World loyalties and become citizens of their new country." Elazar and Weinfeld contend that the present situation is very different. Immigrants can remain connected to all elements of their country of origin through regular visits to and from the old country, telephone and email, and up-to-date radio and television shows dealing with the homeland.[24] In the 1990s, when I returned to university as a graduate student, the new attitude towards immigration became clear through my interviews with Israeli women who were living in Calgary. Many of the women I spoke with are in touch with their families in Israel on a daily basis. Now, when someone chooses to migrate they do not say goodbye forever.

Displaced Jews spread out all over the world in search of a safer life, especially after World War II. For many Jews there was the promise of beginning a new life in North America both before and after the Holocaust. My own family is an example of those who escaped before the Holocaust. But beginning a new life is not the same as starting with a clean slate. Physically leaving a place does not somehow magically change who we are. And the stage set constantly changes. Minnie Bruce Pratt, a black feminist writer, comments in *Identity: Skin, Blood Heart*, on the difficulty in making changes.

> Each of us carry around with us those growing up places, the institutions, a sort of backdrop, a stage set. So often we act out the present against a backdrop of the past, within a frame that is so familiar, so safe that it is terrifying to risk changing it even if we know our perceptions are distorted, limited, constricted by that old view.[25]

We carry our past with us in the present and into the future; although this may work for a while, it is necessary to recognize the need to become something different. As circumstances change we are changed by the situations we find ourselves in, but we can choose to make changes. Moving from one place to another is an extreme example of a time in life when change may be necessary; however change, and the need to change, are lifelong processes. Often, we only become aware of the changes after they occur. And we do not always have a chance to rehearse for our new roles. In my own life the set has changed several times and each time I bring with me old feelings and memories.

For the last thirty-five years I have carried with me a recurring dream – actually more like a nightmare – that reflects the turmoil of ongoing change. The dream has many variations but the theme is always the same: my home is taken away. In one variation, the house burns down and I bravely try to salvage what I can and move to another house. Other times the house is unrecognizable. I find rooms that I have never noticed in the past, and, when I open the doors, the rooms are in a state of ruin – there are holes in the walls or the ceiling is caving in, or there are stairways I had never seen before that lead to menacing dilapidated upper floors. In this particular version, my home is lost to me because I do not recognize it and I am disturbed by what I find. In my most frequent night journey, my home is sold without my knowledge. I arrive home only to find that it has been sold and there is a new family living there. In this version I am not left completely homeless because there is always a replacement house usually just a few streets away, but it is a shabby slum often infested with mice and rats. Stoically, I walk past by my expropriated house every day in the dream. Although I desperately miss my old home, I try to find something to like about my new home. Perhaps it can be renovated; I always try to adapt. The rest of the dream usually involves surviving my new situation, which is filled with insurmountable obstacles. When I wake up from these dreams, sometimes in tears, I am incredibly relieved to be in my own bed. I have this dream about once a week.

Yet the nightmarish quality of this dream does not echo my life experience. Although we did in fact move to three different homes when I was a child, each new house was always an improvement over the previous one. The transitions of moving were difficult but not the high drama of my dreams. There is nothing in my lived reality to suggest the intense suffering I experience in these dreams. Certainly I missed my friends when we moved from Winnipeg to Vancouver, but we visited frequently, and I loved living in Vancouver. I admit it was difficult to start over with new friends at a new school but this was not the kind of experience that might scar one for life. When I moved to my current city, Calgary, as an adult the migration was not due to any sort of hardship, yet same dream continues.

Whether or not they are based on real life experiences, these dreams have become part of my identity and also seem to be part of a collective Jewish narrative of exile. The house dream conjures up all of the tragic stories of Jewish persecution throughout history – the stories of displaced persons with no homes and the sense of fear and loss have found a place in my recurring dream. The promise of having a safe place to live is broken because the house is either burnt down, unrecognizable, or sold. The shock of losing my safety is the central trauma in this dream. Something has been taken from me and I am not ready to let go. The wound caused by the loss of my home is unable to heal because I am faced with it every day in the dream. The promise of happiness becomes more distant each time I remember my old home in the dream. In this recurring dream I make an effort to heal my wounds and I try to adjust to the new situation, but I cannot escape the sense of betrayal.

The sense of loss that haunts my dreams may symbolize unresolved problems in my life. Even when I am awake I do not feel that I have ever been home. What I mean by home is having a sense of safety and security, feeling at home in my own body, and having an identity with which I am comfortable. Many women share these feelings of insecurity and self-doubt. I became more aware of this when I moved to Calgary at the age of thirty-one. Although the Jewish community was warm and welcoming, I found that I was drawn to and felt comfortable with Israeli immigrant women. Like them I was in search of a new identity and a new way to become part of Jewish community in a city where I had no past. Several years later I explored these Jewish identity issues further in my graduate research.

I moved to Calgary in 1982 and I felt connected with the Jewish community almost immediately. I mention this immediate connection because it occurred under unusual circumstances, and I had not experienced a positive connection to the Jewish communities in Winnipeg or Vancouver. The reason for my move to Calgary from Vancouver was to marry a Jewish man who was committed to living in this particular city. A year earlier, my husband's brother and his wife, along with another Calgary couple, were killed in a car accident in Las Vegas, Nevada. My husband's brother and sister-in law left two children, aged three and one. The other family left three children. My husband needed to stay in Calgary in order to fight for custody of the children. When I married him I knew that I would be raising these children. The Jewish community in Calgary is tightly knit and the whole community was devastated by the loss of the four young Jewish people. When I arrived a year later, I was welcomed by a warm community still grieving over this tragic loss. I was highly visible partly because the community was interested in the well-being of our newly-formed family. There were also many who were simply curious and it took us a while before we determined who we could trust.

In Calgary I was thrown into the middle of a story already in progress. I stepped into other people's lives. This process is not unique. We are all born into a pre-existing story that began before we were born and will continue after we die. This fact goes unnoticed when we are children, but as an adult in a new situation I gained a new per-spective on the construction of identity.

In this book I have included several stories, my own and those of the Israeli women participants in my research. The focus of the stories is the ambiguous nature of Jewish identity. My place in the Jewish community, as well as my perception of self, changed drastically when I left Vancouver, the Shangri-la of Canada. Every year on the Jewish holiday, Passover, which is a celebration of freedom and a reminder of suffering, we hear the phrase "next year in Jerusalem" conveying a wish for future happiness, freedom, and fulfillment. What does it mean then when Jews leave the Promised Land? I felt that in leaving Vancouver I was also in exile from a promised land, so I had something in common with the Jewish Israeli women in my study. This was further complicated by my own emotional attachment to Israel. Over the years I have become aware of the similarities and contradictions existing between the Jewish communities of the three cities in which I have lived, so I was eventually compelled to dig beneath the surface. I have become aware of my own conflicts concerning Israel and how these feelings affect my relationship to the Jewish community. It is my hope that in an effort to look further, my fear of strangers may begin to dissipate. I am looking for a place, even if it exists only in my own mind, where I can finally feel at home.

[1] Rees, *Auschwitz*, xii.
[2] Ibid., ix.
[3] Ibid., 199.
[4] Ibid.
[5] Elazar and Weinfeld, *Still moving: Recent Migration in Comparative Perspective*, 3.
[6] Ibid.
[7] Ibid.
[8] Cohen, *Global Diasporas*, ix.
[9] Clifford, 283.
[10] Ibid.
[11] Clifford, "Diasporas," *The Ethnicity Reader*, 283.
[12] Ibid.
[13] Hyman, *Who is a Jew?*, 12.
[14] Ibid, 13.
[15] Ibid.,19.
[16] Shokeid, *Children of Circumstances*, 4.
[17] Linn and Barkan-Asher, "Permanent Impermanence: Israeli Expatriates in Non-Event Transition," *The Jewish Journal of Sociology*, 38 (1), 5-6.
[18] Sobel, *Migrants to the Promised Land*, 17.
[19] Ibid.
[20] Gold and Cohen, "The Myth of Return and Israeli Ethnicity in Toronto," 180.
[21] Torzymer and Brotman, *Weaving Diverse Strands: Demographic Challenges Transforming the Fabric of Jewish Communal Life in Calgary,*15.
[22] Gold, 412.
[23] Elazar and Weinfeld, 6.
[24] Ibid.
[25] Minnie Bruce Pratt, "Identity: Skin, Blood, Heart,"17.

Two

Making Something of Oneself

The focus on individualism and accomplishment is a common theme in Western society: we must make something of ourselves. Richard L. Ochberg, writer and professor of psychology, explains that "to 'make something' of oneself means colloquially, to be successful."[1] He explains that making something of oneself is an evaluative process and there is "effort that goes into maintaining a positive self-image" and he describes the process as "work" that is "continual."[2] In other words, through this constitutive activity it is possible for individuals to "continually rediscover themselves in new situations in which they may be unmade."[3] According to Ochberg, one must be vigilant in this continual creation of the self to avoid being "revealed as flawed."[4] As he describes, this work is accomplished "via narratively structured and publicly performed action."[5] This way of interpreting individual narratives takes into account the effort expended in the continual process of creating and performing the self as well as the effort involved in avoiding being judged as flawed by those around us. I have always known that a big part of my sense of well-being depended on what others thought of me, but moving to a totally new situation in Calgary emphasized my insecurities to the point that they interfered with my coping skills.

Until the time that I moved to Calgary, I assumed that I could direct my life no matter what was happening around me; that was how I was raised. In elementary school the principal regularly lectured us about being part of the "Second Milers Club." To be a member of this elite club we were expected to go that 'extra mile' scholastically. Those who made it were rewarded with a special colorful school crest with wings on it. "You can achieve whatever you want as long as you try hard enough." These words still echo in my head. I like to think of myself as a second miler. That is also what I wanted other to think of me.

Concentrating on achievement at school gave my life much needed predictability that was missing at home. My parents had a very volatile relationship. There was never any question that they loved each other, but there was a great deal of high decibel arguing on a regular basis. As the story goes, at one time, when my parents were living in Vancouver before they had children, they had an idyllic existence. They had eloped to get married in Vancouver and they spent several years there before returning to Winnipeg. My maternal grandfather in Winnipeg had offered my father what seemed like a very good job in the clothing manufacturing business. Unfortunately the job turned out to be one of the many topics of discord. By the time my father decided to quit, my brothers, Wayne and Mark, had been born. The three of us were very close in age, each only twenty months apart. My father's new job was also in the clothing business, this time as a manufacturer's agent. This position entailed a great deal of travel which left my mother at home with three young children.

Like many people, my mother came into the marriage with her own personal problems. Combined with the stress of being alone at home in a challenging situation, she had what was known at the time as a nervous breakdown. During the 1950s the remedy for this was apparently to be found at a hospital in Chicago. Although my memory of that period of time is not very clear, I know that she was sent to Chicago for treatment that lasted several months. My brothers and I were only told "your mother is not well." My father hired a full-time babysitters to look after us. In those days, the word nanny was unknown, at least in Winnipeg. I remember the whole time as being extremely chaotic. I was approximately five years old and I walked to school everyday. I remember feeling a tremendous relief as soon as I walked out the door of what seemed liked a madhouse. There was always a lot of crying and screaming, which was probably just the normal behavior of young boys at the age of one and three. Although my mother was gone for only a few months, to me, it seemed like years. Eventually when she did come home she seemed very fragile.

My father warned us that if we did not behave, my mother would become ill again. I remember trying to be a perfect child. In the mornings before I left for school, I used to climb up onto the kitchen counter to make percolated coffee for my mother in the hope that she would be in a good mood by the time I got home for lunch. I tried to always be a 'good' girl. Her moods were quite unpredictable and I craved a peaceful existence. I managed to find the stability I needed by maintaining high grades at school. My brothers were too young to come up coping strategies and, as a result, they have each been affected differently. I am not really sure if the situation improved or if I just got used to my home life. In any case, some times were better than others. Overall, I do not have memories of having a terrible childhood. I do remember that there was a great deal of love and that there was more laughter than tears.

I learned that to survive in the world I would have to be good and that meant that I needed to do well at whatever I attempted. Not only did I excel at school but I also did well at piano, swimming, art school, and anything else I attempted. The relentless pursuit of achievement became an indispensable survival skill. However,in 1982, at the age of thirty-one, I arrived in Calgary to begin my life with few of the skills that I actually needed. Although I had been married briefly once before, that was during my early twenties and there were no children. In Vancouver I had been living a rather Bohemian single life for the previous seven years and during that time I taught piano lessons, at first in a rented studio and later in my own home. Because my students were mostly children, my working hours began at about 3:00 p.m. and continued until 8:00 or 9:00 in the evening. My social life began after 9:00 pm and I had a wide network of friends, many of whom were also single and working in arts related jobs. I was not involved with the Jewish community except to attend synagogue on the Jewish New Year with my parents. I enjoyed being on what I saw as the fringe of society. I did not fully consider the metamorphosis required in order for me to adjust to a completely different life-style in Calgary.

My family was not particularly religious although we observed many of the cultural customs and traditions. As a child, I went grudgingly to Hebrew school at the end of a long day at public school. As an adolescent, I was outright rebellious when it came to any Jewish involvement. By the time I moved to Calgary I had drifted away from most things Jewish. However, I still felt the expectation to accomplish great things and to assimilate into Canadian society. One of the messages I received as a child was that, as Jews, we would have to work harder than average Canadians if we wanted to be successful. I still have this expectation of myself.

During the year before I moved, I had a long distance relationship with my husband-to-be, Ken. We met in Winnipeg at my best friend's wedding in the summer of 1981. I had never met him before although we had both grown-up in Winnipeg. At the wedding party we were among the few singles flirting, and after the party, we ended up talking for most of the night. He told me the tragic story about the recent deaths of his brother and sister-in-law. It had happened only three months earlier when they had been on vacation in Las Vegas. They were in the way of a high speed police chase and were killed instantly. I had never met these people but hearing the story from Ken left a profound effect upon me. He told me about the phone call he received relating the terrible news and then about the horrific task of having to tell his parents. I encouraged him to tell me everything. At the time of the wedding, he was in the process of uprooting his life in Winnipeg so that he could move to Calgary to take care of his brother's two young children. I had no idea that listening to his story would also change my life.

Since he would soon live in Calgary, and I lived in Vancouver, I did not expect that we would see each other again. Nevertheless, it had been an intense evening and I felt honored that he had shared his story with me. I was surprised when he offered to drive me to the airport a couple of days later. We said our goodbyes and I wished him luck in his new life. Usually I do not remember friends' or relatives' birthdays, but for some reason, I remembered Ken's birthday a week after I got home to Vancouver. I thought about phoning him to wish him a happy birthday. I knew he was still in Winnipeg tying up the details of his old life and I was more worried about his vulnerability than my own. I argued with myself about making the call. I knew it could mean much more than just a friendly or kind gesture. I was not sure if I was ready to potentially become involved in such a complicated and sad situation. In the past, I might have been more impulsive and considered only protecting my own feelings, but I knew this was different. It felt dangerous; perhaps that was part of the attraction.

After that, we continued to communicate by phone, which quickly became a daily occurrence. Ken kept me up-to-date about his attempt to gain custody of the children, including the difficulty experienced with the maternal family's unwillingness to accept him. After the accident, the children, Carie (age three) and Daniel (age one), were living with their maternal grandparents, Belle and Al Viner. The grandparents were reluctant to place the two orphans with a single man that they did not know very well. There were also several members of the extended family on the maternal side living in Calgary, who were unwilling to accept him. He went to see the children in their grandparents' home each evening to read them bedtime stories. It was this sense of responsibility that I found most attractive. In the past I had dated men who avoided even the hint of commitment. Ken and I began visiting about once a month. He would come to Vancouver or I would go to Calgary. We had met in August of 1981 and by December of that year, it was clear that we were headed towards a committed relationship. He invited me to Winnipeg to meet his parents and the rest of his family and I was very pleased that he asked me. I had not been expecting to meet his complete extended family on the evening that I met his parents. They had all come to inspect me as a prospective wife for Ken, as well as a mother for Carie and Daniel. The experience was overwhelming. It was then that I realized just how deeply I had gotten into the whole situation and some doubts started to creep into my mind about my ability to meet everyone's expectations. I was happy to return to Vancouver – a more comfortable distance from the reality.

I was surprised to learn that my parents were not particularly happy about my new involvement. I thought they would be pleased with the idea that I was finally settling down with a Jewish man. However, they knew it would mean a move to Calgary and they had a more realistic idea of what I was getting myself into. My father likened it to "getting onto a sick bed." I felt that they were overreacting and that they should be excited for me. By March of 1982, Ken and I decided to marry. I was delighted with this decision and could barely contain my excitement although my friends and family were not particularly forthcoming with positive feedback. They found it hard to believe that I would actually leave the beautiful city of Vancouver and change my relatively carefree life for one of intense responsibility. They warned me that my life would be extremely difficult. I saw the situation differently. I was already thirty years old and had pretty much given up on the idea of getting married or having children. I was thrilled that I would become the mother of two beautiful healthy children and, as a bonus, I would not get stretch marks!

Even before we announced our engagement, it had been determined that Ken would get custody of the children. The fact that he would be marrying in the near future only strengthened his case. During our long distance conversations he often warned me that it would be like living in a fishbowl in Calgary. He said people in the Jewish community would be watching us. I really did not take the warnings very seriously. Vancouver, a larger city, has a more assimilated Jewish community than Calgary so I was used to being anonymous and I really could not anticipate anything else. I would be the same person except that I would live in Calgary and be married with two children. I would continue to teach piano lessons and my life would continue, only in a different setting. I was that naïve!

Our wedding date was set for September 5, 1982, approximately one year after we had first met in Winnipeg. It was small by Jewish standards – about one hundred guests. I would have been happy to be married by a Justice of the Peace, but it was Ken's first marriage and he looked forward to a happy occasion after many months of mourning. I moved to Calgary in July. I rented my house in Vancouver, said good-bye to all my students, and packed everything (including my two pianos) into a moving van. Considering the enormity of the change, I was very calm about the whole experience, at least at that point.

After the first week of life in Calgary, the reality of my new situation began to set in. Until then, Ken and I had only spent short periods of time together and it had been romantic and filled with dreams for the future. In Calgary, Ken was working everyday and I was left on my own to discover my new surroundings – which felt like a huge wasteland. There was no ocean. I had no friends. Each evening when Ken returned home I expected that we would go out for a roman-tic dinner. Instead, he was tired and was happy to stay home and watch television. I began to panic, thinking I had made the worst mistake of my life. I phoned my mother and told her not to send out the wedding invitations. My good friend Susan came from Vancouver to try and help me calm down. She helped remind me why I had thought this was a good idea in the first place. After Susan left, Ken and I saw a therapist who helped us to look closely at some of the issues we were about to face. The wedding invitations did go out and we were married by a rabbi at my parents' home in Vancouver. After a short honeymoon we returned to Calgary. With the help of the therapist, we had decided that it would be best to wait at least six months before the children moved in with us and during that time they would stay with us on weekends. I would pick up Carie from preschool and take her to swimming lessons and ballet lessons. I began to meet other mothers. This was a new world for me and I found it difficult to fit in.

I went from living a single life on the periphery of the society to being an average, married Jewish woman driving children to lessons. I was not used to being average at anything. During that time I advertised for piano students and began to build up my teaching clientele again. It was September, a perfect time for students to register. Once I started teaching I began to feel more like myself, although I was not sure who that self was anymore. Ken had been living in Calgary for a year, and as a result, he had made quite a few friends. They were all receptive and kind, and they went out of their way to make me feel welcome. But I missed my own friends and missed the cultural pulse of Vancouver. I missed everything. Most of all, I missed the person I used to be. I finally recognized that I was indeed beginning a new life and that I would have to make some changes. At that point I was not aware of how much I would have to change.

One day I went out grocery shopping and ran into the wife of one of Ken's friends. She asked me how I was doing and I started crying in the frozen food aisle at Safeway. She started crying too. After that we became good friends. She was also a newcomer to Calgary and she was interested in who I was rather than what I was supposed to be. My life improved greatly after meeting Sherrill that day. I no longer had to pretend that everything was wonderful and I afforded her the same freedom. We remain friends to this day, partly because we allow each other to keep changing over time.

Six months passed and the children moved in with us. Their grandparents were not in very good health and it had been a strain for them to care of two young children, even with a full-time nanny. They were heartbroken and yet, at the same time, relieved. The children were familiar with our home because they had spent a lot of time there over the past six months. Their nanny, Linda, came too. In a very short time both Ken and I had gone from being single and alone to being married with two children and a live-in nanny. The nanny had been with the children even before their parents were killed so the whole situation was certainly not easy for her. We stumbled along trying to become a family.

The only model I had for family life had been my own, and Ken had grown up with a different model in his own family. Now here we all were: two orphaned children, a nanny from the Philippines, and Jewish newlyweds in their thirties. From the outside we did look like a family, but for each of us the experience was something completely new. The fact that I was now a visible member of a Jewish community affected me much more than I had expected. I had thought I would be the same somewhat oddball person in a different location; instead I was now an upstanding member of the Jewish community by virtue of the fact that I was the new mother of the orphaned children. It seemed that everyone in the community knew who I was and everyone had an opinion of how I should act. Many of the people I met had known the children's parents, Robin and Allen. They were probably well inten-tioned when then described how Robin and Allen used to do this or that, but what I heard was that I was expected to do the same. Ken had warned me about this but I had not taken him very seriously. The fact that I had chosen to keep my maiden name, Fogell, rather than take my husband's name, Goldstein, was not well-received by the people I met in the Jewish community in Calgary. Most people ignored it and called me Melanie Goldstein. Even Ken had been a little shocked that I did not plan to take his name but he never made it an issue. I felt that my name was the only thing I had left of my own identity. I did not realize at that point that hanging on to name would not be enough of a foundation on which to build a new life.

Although being Jewish was always prominent in my sense of myself, it took on a new importance in my life in Calgary. Carie had been attending preschool at a Jewish day school so she continued there. I had also attended a Jewish preschool so that part was not strange to me. By the first grade I was attending public school and as an adult I thought that it was narrow-minded and constraining to keep a child at a Hebrew day school. But, in Calgary, that was how things were done. I was now part of the Calgary Jewish community and so I waited everyday with the other mothers who were picking up their children from preschool. We would make small talk concerning our children. They would invite Carie to come and play with their children. Unfortunately, I did not understand the rules of child networking. I thought these women actually wanted to get to know me and that I would make friends. What they really wanted was for me to be involved in the play-date network. It took me a while to understand the rules. When I had been single and living in Vancouver, I had friends based on mutual interests and affection. At least half of the relationship was about me. But the play-date network foregrounds the socializing of children. Any relationships with the children's parents are in the background. I was unsure of how to behave in this new social situation.

When discussing the self in community, Calvin O. Schrag, a scholar who writes about the self in postmodernity, maintains that "community is constitutive of selfhood" and that "it fleshes out the portrait of the self by engendering a shift of focus from the self as present to itself to the self as present *to, for* and *with* the other."[6] Not only is the self connected to community, but it is called into being by community.

Although I did not know it at the time, Schrag's description seems to fit what I was experiencing when adjusting to life in Calgary and my new situation. It felt as though the community was calling upon me to become the perfect Jewish wife and mother. Scholars such as Paul Ricoeur discuss this community-driven change process in terms of narrative. The sharing of experience and language only takes place with the presence of other people. In other words, Ricoeur is saying that because human beings have experiences, they need language to talk about them and when those experiences are shared, a narrative identity emerges.[7] In telling my own story I am creating a narrative specific to a particular time and place. Schrag expresses this idea somewhat differently: "the self that is called into being through discourse is at the same time called into being within a community."[8] The sharing of experience through language is part of what makes up discourse and in this process the narrative emerges within the horizon of community. Several questions are raised when looking for connections between self and community. How does one belong to a community? In what ways does the community define the self and in what ways does the self define the community? It took me a while to figure out that these were questions I needed to face.

Schrag also addresses questions about the other people we meet and with whom we interact. He contends:

> Responsibility, nurtured by the call of conscience, supplies the moral dimension in the narrative of self in community. To be in community is to recognize the requirement not only to respond to prior discourse and action but to respond to it in a fitting manner.[9]

In order to live in a community it is necessary to make definite choices about the ways in which the self lives with others. As a single woman in Vancouver I had tried to abstain from taking any responsibility for my role in the Jewish community. For example, in my late twenties I broke up with a Jewish man with whom I had been quite serious (disappointing both his parents and mine) and moved to a very non- Jewish part of Vancouver. In fact it was the Italian area in the east end of the city on Commercial Road (before it became trendy). I rented what I thought was a fabulous apartment on the third floor of a three-story walk-up. It was $175 per month, which was inexpensive even then. The actual apartment was huge and the ceilings were high and I was even permitted to have my piano there. My father helped me to move in and I remember him saying how depressing he found the building and the whole area. It reminded him of where he grew up during the Depression era. He could not believe that his daughter wanted to live there. I could not admit that I had my own doubts and that I was afraid of being alone in a part of the city with which I was unfamiliar. People rarely came to visit me because I lived so far out of the way.

There was no buzzer entry system in my building so if people wanted to visit they had to call first and this was before cell phones became common. For this reason I was completely confused when I heard banging on my door one night at 1:00 a.m. I recognized the building manager's voice shouting that there had been an accident and could I open my door. Being half asleep I unquestioningly opened the chained door. Through the space I could see the building manager, and with him were two huge scruffy looking men. I panicked at once. They said they were the police, but they did not look like policemen to me. They did not wait for me to unchain the door. They just pushed in the door breaking the chain while one of the men took hold of my arm and dragged me into the living room. During this time I was screaming in a voice that I did not recognize as my own. I thought this would attract the attention of my neighbors but I was wrong. I was kicking and punching but the man was holding me off with just two fingers.

After about fifteen minutes of screaming I realized they were not killing or raping me. They showed me a warrant. As it turned out, they had the wrong address for a drug bust. They apologized and left. They actually came back later to apologize once again but by that time I was so traumatized that I would not open the door. I called my ex-husband, a lawyer, to see if I had any grounds for a complaint. He said the police would just get a slap on the wrist so I decided to try and put it out of my mind. I could not discuss it with anyone because I would become anxious all over again. Also, it seemed to me that it would be like admitting defeat. What was a nice Jewish girl doing living in that part of town anyway?

Shortly after that incident I borrowed funds from the bank and bought a tiny house much closer to where I felt I belonged. I advertised at the Institute for the Deaf to find a tenant for my basement suite. In that way, I could play the piano at all hours of the day and night. I moved my piano studio from downtown to my own home so I would not have to pay extra rent and was really quite pleased with myself. By the time I met Ken I had been living in my own house for about a year. He must have seen me as an independent, strong woman although the incident with the police had definitely left a chink in my armor. An alarm system was installed in my new house. When Ken came to visit he saw a successful, strong single woman running her own business out of her own home. That was how I tried to see myself but I also liked to envision myself as being on the periphery of mainstream society. When I moved to Calgary there were life choices to be made that I had managed to avoid in the past. Several years later when I met and interviewed Israeli immigrants I found that I was not alone in facing unexpected life choices about how to live in a community as a Jew.

Schrag explains that "'community' is not a pure, value-free description of a societal state of affairs."[10] Moreover, the self that exists in community is also, in part, created and judged by the community. He talks about a "grammar of community" that develops "as a mixed discourse of the descriptive and the prescriptive."[11] He explains:

> There is no purely descriptive fact of being-with, no value neutral intersubjective state of affairs. The 'sociality' of being-with is always already oriented either toward a creative and life-affirming intersubjectivity or toward a destructive and life-negating mode of being-with-others.[12]

The power of the community to define the individual is exactly what Ken had been referring to when he warned me that we would be living in a fish bowl. It is impossible to claim that an individual description of living in a community is real or truthful because all the players involved have their own version of the community's values and they each interpret the other's actions in a particular way. As Schrag puts it, "there are no facts without interpretation. And interpretation is always the work of a community of interpreters."[13] We are engaged in being-with-others whether we agree to it or not. However, there are occasions when "our roles in ongoing stories are not always self-chosen" and further, that "we are recruited into them by virtue of our membership in the community."[14]

I take responsibility for choosing to move to Calgary, to get married, and become the mother of two children. However, once I was there I did feel as though I had been recruited into action. And much of the action felt as though it was beyond my control. Luckily there were some familiar signposts for me to follow. It seemed appropriate for me to meet Carie while she was in preschool – the time when she was becoming an individual with an awareness of the world around her. I could relate more easily to a child of that age than to a baby. The earliest memories I have of myself as a person in the world are of attending a Jewish nursery school. According to my mother, I was hyperactive before nursery school and, as the story goes, I was a difficult child. At the age of two I entertained myself by throwing my mother's shoes out of the apartment window. My mother had to get special dispensation from the rabbi to allow me to register in nursery school at the age of two instead of waiting until I was three. Thus my life as a person-in-the-world-with-others began in the basement of the Shaarey Tzedek Synagogue, Winnipeg, in 1953. Most of my memories of that year are vague. It was the accepted practice in the 1950s for Jewish parents to send their children to nursery school by taxi cab. There were no seat belts then, which meant that the taxi could accommodate many children. So everyday I went to my school in a cab just as my father went to work in his car. The nursery school was a Jewish institution maintained by the community; it was here that I first encountered the public sphere. On Fridays, *Shabbat* (the Jewish

Sabbath), one girl in the class was chosen as the *ima* or mother. It was the mother's duty to make the home Jewish which included lighting the *Shabbat* candles –since *Shabbat* begins at sunset – and singing the blessing. It was made very clear in nursery school and in kindergarten what our Jewish roles in life would be. One of most important roles was lighting the Shabbat candles. Beginning at an early age, we learned Hebrew, sang Hebrew songs, said Jewish prayers, and followed the Jewish lunar calendar, which differs from the Christian calendar. We observed the holidays just as the ancient Jews did. Years later, the curriculum at Carie's school was very much the same as it had been for me.

I had not lit candles for *Shabbat* since I had been in preschool, but when Carie and Daniel moved in, we started to have Friday night dinners, with candles and all. It seemed logical to aim for consistency. My own mother lit candles when I was young, probably for the same reason. Different habits crept into my everyday life, which, after a while, I did not even notice. When I lived alone I rarely cooked at all. I used my oven for storage. Once the children moved in I started cooking meals. When I was growing up we always had live-in help. In those days they were not referred to as nannies. They were usually poor farm girls who wanted to get away from home and they did the work in exchange for room and board and a very modest salary. In any case, it did not seem strange to me to have a non-family member living in the house and eating meals with us. Much of my new life seemed to be within my realm of experience.

Growing up, I lived with my family in one of the two Jewish areas in Winnipeg, but there were very few Jewish children in my classroom at public school. Over the years, more Jewish people moved into the south end so there were some more Jewish faces at school, but not many. Some parents chose to send their children to one of several Hebrew day schools where students studied English half of the day and Hebrew for the other half. My parents told me that it was too expensive to attend the Hebrew day school and that they wanted me to have a more well-rounded education. Quite simply, I had to learn how to assimilate at an early age.

My father often told my two younger brothers and me compelling stories about how he was beaten everyday on his way to Hebrew school. My father always was the champion in these stories, but the message that came across was that non- Jews were dangerous and that they did not like us. I had difficulty believing this and I thought my parents were exaggerating. It was not until junior high school that I realized my parents might have been correct. I was not invited to the homes of some classmates and they did not attempt to hide the fact that it was because their parents did not like Jews. In fact, some of my classmates belonged to a country club that did not allow Jews. I thought that I must be missing something wonderful, so I was hurt. I did not want to believe that this made any difference to my school friendships. In retrospect, it probably did make a difference. I felt somehow diminished. Once in a while in junior high school, Jewish children were beaten after school dances. Some were even locked in their lockers, but I did not take this very seriously. It was more important to me to believe that I was well liked by everyone than to think that I might somehow be unacceptable.

Being well liked and accepted by everyone seemed to be an obvious goal during adolescence and I assumed that it was everyone's goal in life. I saw my parents interact with the non-Jewish community and they seemed to be accepted. I never saw any of the anti-Semitism that my parents insisted was always under the surface. Since my parents did not allow me to date non-Jewish boys, I would regularly point out that they were hypocrites. Their response was to remind me about the concentration camps. I thought my parents were unreasonable because I could not imagine my non-Jewish friends persecuting me.

Every Sunday, my father took my brothers and me to our grandmother's house in the north end of Winnipeg. It was very different from the new development where I lived in the south end. On my grandmother's street the houses were small and very rundown and the trees were huge. Everyone spoke different and strange sounding languages. My father spoke only Yiddish to my grandmother. Each Sunday my father would tell us a different exciting story about how he was persecuted as a Jewish child. His father had died when my father was seven years old and my father was compelled to be the man in the family. They were extremely poor, but his mother managed to raise four children under very difficult circumstances. She was religiously observant and maintained a Jewish environment for her children. She had come to Canada from Poland with her husband and daughter to escape the pogroms. Each week we heard another installment of this history and it became our history too, at least on Sundays.

The Sunday stories usually cast my father in the hero's role, always saving the day, and his mother was the strongest, kindest, most self-sacrificing woman in the world. His eyes would light up when he told these stories of his past. He still likes to tell the same stories and I still enjoy hearing them. While I was not aware of it at the time, those Sundays became a significant part of my identity. I loved my grandmother and I wanted to be a saint like her. I wanted my father to admire and love me as much as he loved his mother. I knew my father loved my mother, but it was clear that she was not in the same category as my grandmother. My mother also came from the north end of Winnipeg – her parents were immigrants from Russia – they lived only a few streets from my grandmother and were considered wealthy. Apparently my father was not considered to be good enough for my mother. There was a different set of stories that vilified my maternal grandparents. These were often bedtime stories – about how my father was too poor, and not good enough, for my mother. But in the end, the pauper got to marry the princess. In fact, to make it even more magical, they eloped to get married!

My grandparents were much more observant as Jews than my parents. My father's mother was strictly kosher and followed every rule. My mother's parents, although they had heavy accents, were much more modern. They travelled the world, went out for dinner (strictly kosher Jews would not eat in a restaurant), and were more cosmopolitan. My grandfather was an ardent Zionist and he donated large sums of money to Israel. Many people in Winnipeg knew who my grandfather was and still remember him. It felt good when people of my parents' age would say, "she's Shia and Becky's granddaughter." My grandparent's stories became my stories.

There were other stories that also stayed with me. I received the message that my father's mother was wonderful because she kept a Jewish home even through great adversity. There was also another set of more somber stories about how my dad joined the Air Force during World War II and he managed to get posted close to Winnipeg, as his mother was a widow. He told me that the Jews were usually the first to be sent overseas. According to my father, the Jews were always the first to die because they were put on the front line. One of his closest friends, Archie, was sent overseas and, as my father tells the story, when Archie returned from the war he said, "it's a good thing you weren't there Fogell because you would have been standing next to me and the guy standing next to me was killed." In his Air Force stories, my father always outsmarted the non-Jewish officers. I loved these stories and I wanted to believe they explained who I am.

In my new Calgary situation I soon began to understand that I would be instrumental in providing family memories for Carie and Daniel. Previously, I had not considered how much of my identity had been ready-made; I thought I had created my own reality. Before coming to Calgary I had not truly considered that my life would no longer be just about me, at least not the "me" that I was before. I felt myself putting up boundaries to protect that old self. Often times I would revert to my 'wild girl,' artsy persona. It only served to alienate the new people I met and wish I could still be that person. This made the transition more difficult but it was the only tool I had at the time.

Looking at boundaries on a different level, Kaye/Kantrowitz, a Jewish feminist writer, suggests that the unclear boundaries between self, family, and community many be dangerous for Jewish women. For women the "fuzzy boundaries" raise difficult questions. "How do I live my life if it is not my own?"[15] She points out that there are "injunctions" directed at the Jewish woman "as a Jewish member of a larger entity, the Jewish people; as a female member of this same entity; and as a woman"[16]. Speaking as a Jewish woman, Kaye/Kantrowitz argues that all of these entities agree on one point: *"Everyone else is more important than I am."*[17] She also maintains that while many ethnic minorities experience the blurring of boundaries between the self and community, "the issues of boundaries or their lack seems particularly acute for Jews." These include "boundaries between the self, the family, and community. Between the generations. Between history and the present. Between national identity and identification across national lines with the Jewish people." She suggests that the existence of these various boundaries is "perhaps . . . why much of the Jewish religion . . . involves drawing boundaries – between secular and sacred; between acceptable and non-acceptable food."[18] She suggests that the lack of boundaries between community and self can be damaging for women. I had never really considered that the lack of boundaries between self and community could be damaging for me. My thought was that I could somehow keep myself separate and, although I was Jewish, it did not mean that I was necessarily defined, or even influenced by, the community.

Kaye/Kantrowitz suggests that to move forward Jewish women need to struggle with many conflicting feelings. Speaking for herself and other Jewish women, Kaye/Kantrowitz argues:

> As we define our relationship to Jewishness we confront our relationship to and role in the family. For Jews who felt constrained by the growing up demands of their family of Jewish community, who may have created some freedom through distance, the thought of engaging with any level of Jewishness will feel like rejoining the family, with all the attendant conflict.[19]

To some extent I had managed to avoid confronting these difficult issues. By moving to Calgary and becoming more visible in the community than I had been in the past I was suddenly faced with a host of identity questions that I had previously pushed into the background. In Calgary I was becoming part of a new family. Although I felt strongly about my Jewish identity, I experienced a conflict as well. I remember that I had felt constrained by the Jewish communities in both Winnipeg and in Vancouver but I thought I could just reject those problems through avoidance.

Several years later – doing the research for my doctoral dissertation – I noticed that the Israeli women in my study were more aware of the adjustments required when entering a new community. At that point in time I had a limited experience Israel and Israelis; I had only visited Israel once in 1995 on a Jewish Federation tour. In Calgary I was acquainted with a few Israeli women through my children's friends. I found the participants for my research by advertising in the local Jewish newspaper. That is how I met Orit. At that time, she had lived in Canada for almost two years. Through her job she had daily contact with Canadian Jews. I asked her how she was treated by

Canadian Jews and she admitted "it's hard when I'm talking to you because I know you are a Canadian Jew." I tried to push her on this point by explaining that this was exactly the type of information I was interested in knowing, and so she continued.

> I'm going to be totally honest with you. Because I think we do come from a different culture. We do come from a different country, and as much as Canada is a country of immigrants who are supposed to accept different persons, so why can't they accept us as we are? Why are they like that? What is it in them that we can maybe adopt? I adopt many people's things that I think are nice and good and maybe we should learn from it.

Orit was painfully aware that she was not accepted by the Canadian Jews with whom she has had contact, but she was willing to try and be more like them. I pursued this topic by asking "how do you get this message?" She explained that some Canadian Jews seemed to think that Israelis were just using Canada, even though she pointed out, "I don't even use Canada or use what it has." She then continued to tell me how she believed Canadian Jews perceive her.

> Also we're more barbaric, the way we speak, the way we talk, the way we behave. Our demands are sometimes not logical even, even in terms of education. We're not supposed to educate kids in terms of behavior or manners.

At this point I was having difficulty understanding what she meant so I asked how she got this idea.

> I notice by the attitude, by the way I am judged. My work is judged. By the way they would look at my car that stands out in the parking lot. By the way they would, when I tell them where to come to my house for my son to play with or where she lives, they wouldn't take a step further.

Orit noticed that Canadian Jews treated her as if she was somehow inferior to them. Her car was not expensive enough and she did not live in what might be considered a desirable Jewish neighborhood. She felt judged by her own people. Maybe they thought that she was too Jewish or maybe not Jewish enough. I could understand her words because I was also aware of being judged by the Jewish community and I found that several of the women I interviewed felt they were being judged unfavorably by the Jewish community.

For some Israelis, Canadian Jews have made them feel that they are not entitled to enjoy the riches of living in Canada – that they should have stayed in Israel. As Orit pointed out "the feeling they give you is that you are barbaric and uneducated." Devora, a woman I met at the university, reiterated Orit's ideas. Like Orit, Devora sensed that Canadian Jews somehow feel threatened by Israeli Jews; they "feel as if we have come to take away their security, take away their positions." Devora was surprised when I gave her a lead on a job. She told me that many Canadian people would not be so open.

Morny Joy, an expert in religious studies and philosophy, prefers the term strategic identity to Ricoeur's term narrative identity. She explains the term:

> [Strategic identity] alludes to the fact that to narrate one's life is always an interpretation, situated at the confluence of many influences. It thus makes provision for the fact that a life can be viewed as a composite of many plots, not just as one major theme in the service of a master plot or ideal. At any one time, then, I could be trying to grasp or make sense of a particular episode that has affected my life, in relation to other plots, rather than an all-embracing panorama that incorporates every facet of my existence.[20]

Joy believes that "in thinking of the narration of one's life as a composite of many factors we are able to gain partial, contextual, or relative insight (in a larger context of shifting frames)."[21] In this way she accounts for Ricoeur's, statement that "we can learn to become the narrator of our own story without becoming the author of our life."[22] Joy reinforces the potential for agency in narrating one's life. Her view of strategic identity makes room for flexibility and change that may provide a tool by which an individual can better cope with a particular situation. I like Joy's interpretation because it allows for a sense of individuality in combination with social construction. As she explains,

> Each plot lends cohesion and coherence to the manifold influences that ceaselessly threaten to overwhelm us. So it is a particular plot that is constructed by a person in response to a particular situation or experience that needs clarification. This plot can help a person establish a bridgehead from which he/she can thematize a set of events that may otherwise be either too chaotic or too distressing.[23]

Joy follows Ricoeur's notion of narrative identity as "constitutive of self-constancy" as well as including the capacity for "change and mutability . . . within one lifetime."[24] This perspective endows the individual with a nominal amount of agency. Ricoeur's version of "self-constancy refers to a self instructed by the works of a culture that it has applied to itself."[25] There is a continual interplay between the self and cultural discourse. I find the combining of individual ability to act in the world with the forces of societal recruitment to be more reasonable than one explanation alone.

The awareness of being called into being or calling others into being is especially beneficial for educators and for parents. What role do educators and parents play in the constitution of agency? Are they aware that they do have a role? This kind of awareness has the potential to gain insight into why we perform our lives in a particular way. Without this awareness there is little hope for change.

Anna Neumann, a writer and philosopher, describes a process that is very similar to my own experience. She has spent most of her academic life interviewing others thinking that she was gaining an understanding about others and for others. When she wrote about her own father's life, she began to realize how much of herself was invested in another person's narrative. This is also true for me. In describing her feelings and thoughts about interviewing her father, she explains:

> While I reached for his story – accessible to me only in partial form . . . I have been able to discern that story only on my own terms – only in the image of who I am, where and when I am, and what I seek out. What I discern of his story, what I remember of it, and what I then retell is not his experience as such. Rather, it is what I, with my inclinations and needs and understandings, imagine his experience to be. What I heard, what I saw, and what I felt *then* as I listened, were *about* him. But they were less *of* him than myself. Searching for his story, I created the beginnings of my own.[26]

My father's stories were part of my story as well. My retelling of the participant's stories is also in large part, about myself. Although I recorded and transcribed every word, I heard them in a way that made sense for me. I was searching for a resolution for conflicts in my own life through other women's stories. I heard their stories on my terms. This has implications for understanding the ways in which the individual and society interact in the construction of narrative identity. We may then be better able to understand how viewing identity narratively offers insight in terms of self-understanding in the world.

Paying more attention to the notion of being provides an opportunity to understand our own ways of being-in-the-world. We can ask who is doing the calling and why we are answering these calls. We can also look at our own role in naming others. This is particularly relevant to those who find themselves in positions of power. Parents and teachers can become more responsible through awareness of how they constitute a child's being in a particular way. By recognizing the discourses of which we are a part, we can possess the possibility of choice in the way we configure and refigure our lives. We have the possibility of agency rather than simply living out the scripts written by others.

[1] Ochberg, 143.
[2] Ibid.
[3] Ibid.
[4] Ibid.
[5] Ibid.
[6] Shrag, 78.
[7] Ricoeur, 245.
[8] Schrag, 77.

[9] Ibid., 100.
[10] Schrag, 88.
[11] Ibid.
[12] Ibid.
[13] Ibid., 93.
[14] Hinchman and Hinchman, xxiv.
[15] Kaye/Kantowitz, 14.
[16] Ibid., 13.
[17] Ibid., 14
[18] Ibid., 13.
[19] Ibid., 16.
[20] Joy, 37.
[21] Ibid., 38.
[22] Ibid.
[23] Ibid.
[24] Ricoeur, 246.
[25] Ibid.
[26] Neuman, 434.

Three

The "Right" Kind of Jew

The conflicting messages I received while growing up contributed to my confusion about whether or not it was a good thing to be Jewish. Within my family and my community I was encouraged to be proud of my Jewish heritage. Yet the family and community also consistently warned me about the dangers of being Jewish and the history of Jewish suffering. I was never really sure why I should be proud to be one of God's chosen people; it seemed arrogant. I was also taught that in Canada everyone was equal, so therefore the notion of being special seemed wrong. And if being Jewish was so wonderful, why is there such virulent anti-Semitism? The answers I received usually had something to do with the need for scapegoats on which to blame the ills of society and, since the Jews were different, we made the perfect targets. I did not really understand this as a child and I am still puzzled by it as an adult. I did not see myself as being so different than the rest of Canadian society. It is difficult to form a positive and coherent sense of one's sense of identity if being Jewish is seen to be negative by the dominant society and even by Jews themselves.

In *The New Anti-Semitism*, Phyllis Chesler, a Jewish feminist writer, provides a comprehensive history of anti-Semitism.[1] She begins with what she calls "the old anti-Semitism" describing the persecution of the Jews as "a complex psychological phenomenon."[2] She argues that "one of the most prominent and credible theories is that the Jew is the scapegoat of the world."[3] Expanding on the notion of the scapegoat she comments:

> Perhaps someone of a different race or religion might better serve as the scapegoat, the one who must suffer and atone for the people's sins. Perhaps perpetual evil may be perpetually embodied by one group in particular, a group that seems to exist everywhere but does not really fit in or belong; a group that resists fitting in, rejects belonging, prefers its own ways, its own kind; an indigenous nomadic group – secretive, strange, different, but worldly wise and well-traveled. Smart. Monied. Filled with ideas. Who better than the Jews?[4]

Chesler claims that "the old anti-Semitism" extended until the end of World War II. According to her, as the facts of the Holocaust became known, "the period immediately after World War II was one of unprecedented worldwide sympathy for the Jews."[5] However, she also points out that even during what looked like a "quiet period," from "1948 to 1968," persecution of Jews continued. She then divides anti-Semitism into two broad categories, modern anti-Semitism before 9/11 and "new anti-Semitism after 9/11."[6] Chesler argues that anti-Zionism and anti-Semitism became one and the same and that the two have been collapsed into anti-Jewish feeling up until the present. She contends that after the events of 9/11 a "new anti- Semitism" emerged. The difference, she explains, is "that acts of violence against Jews and anti-Semitic words and deeds are being uttered and performed by politically correct people in the name of anti-colonialism, anti-imperialism, antiracism, and pacificism."[7] As an academic she finds this change particularly disturbing. My own situation as an academic is similar.

The "quiet period" to which Chesler refers, coincides with my early childhood. I was born in 1951 and by 1968 I was seventeen years old and almost with finished high school. By the time I was born, many of the horrific details concerning the torture and slaughter of the Jews during the Holocaust had become public knowledge. There was widespread support for the new state of Israel. Chesler goes so far as to call this time a "brief honeymoon period between the world and the Jews."[8] She then goes on to discuss specific Arab attacks against Israel during the same time period explaining that it is a mistake to think of that time period as "the best of times" for Jews. For me, Chesler's discusion of this quiet period sheds light on the mixed messages I received about being Jewish. While life in Canada was peaceful, even idyllic, during the 1950s and 1960s, Israel was in a constant state of war for survival. We were made to feel that we were doing our part as good Jews, just by supporting Israel ideologically and financially.

I was aware that anti-Semitism existed, but it seemed to me that the world was on the same side as the Jews. The International Military Tribunals in Nuremburg which began in 1946 recognized the crimes of the Third Reich.[9] I was ten years old in 1961 when Adolf Eichmann, a Nazi perpetrator, was tracked down in Argentina and then put on trial in Tel Aviv, Israel. It felt to me like the Jews who had perished in the concentration camps were being avenged. However, historian Laurence Rees tells us that "out of the 6500 or so members of the SS who worked at Auschwitz between 1940 and 1945 and who are thought to have survived the war, only approximately 750 ever received punishment of any kind."[10] It was more comforting to think that the world was on my side, but, underlying that false sense of security, fear was always lurking.

Living with conflicting messages has had a profound impact on how I see myself and how I behave in the world. As a very young child I loved to sing Israeli songs and dance Israeli dances. I loved the celebration of the many Jewish holidays and the traditional foods. As

I became older and more aware of anti-Semitism, I became more apprehensive about discussing this part of my life with anyone who was not Jewish. At public school I enjoyed taking part in Christmas and Easter festivities. I remember coloring printed pictures of Santa Claus and drawing pictures of decorated Easter eggs. I enjoyed being included and never thought to ask why Jewish holidays were never mentioned. I knew all the words to every Christmas Carol. I sang in the school choir and often played Christmas Carols on the piano at home. My parents never discouraged me from taking part in these activities. I did not expect Santa to make an appearance at my house even though my father took us to the annual Christmas Parade, and we a sat on Santa's knee at the department store to tell him what we wanted for Christmas. My father made it clear that we were just taking part in a local custom and that Jewish people do not celebrate Christmas.

I do not remember any resentment on my part. However, I remember being secretive about being Jewish in situations where I thought the information would not be well-received. It was difficult to know exactly when these situations occurred unless someone made an obvious anti-Jewish comment. As a result I felt an underlying anxiety in places with which I was unfamiliar. One place where I did feel a sense of safety was the Young Men's Hebrew Association (YMHA), the Jewish equivalent of the Christian association. I spent almost every Saturday afternoon there from the time I was nine years old until I was approximately eleven years old. I joined various clubs and took part in sports activities. The children I met there were Jewish and from different areas of the city. Sunday mornings were spent at Hebrew school with children that I did not see during my regular week at public school. I never talked about this Jewish part of my life with non-Jewish friends. Although I do not remember anyone telling me to be quiet about my Jewish identity, the message must have been there. When I was young I did not expect that anything should be different than it was.

On Mondays and Wednesdays I also attended Hebrew school after public school. I was very private about not wanting the non-Jewish students to see the strange writing in my Hebrew notebook. Once in a while a Jewish student might blurt out a Hebrew word at public school. For the student speaking in Hebrew this was cause for great embarrassment because the other Jewish students in class would just about fall off their chairs with laughter. The non-Jewish students just gave us strange looks. I took the bus to Hebrew school along with a few other Jewish students and I remember that there were students who would tease us and throw rocks or snowballs at us when they found out where we were headed. Instead of waiting at the bus stop directly outside the public school, a few of us would walk back a few bus stops to avoid being teased. I never thought to tell my parents about these events. I just accepted that being Jewish meant I was different. My father had often told me stories about how he had been beaten up everyday by Jew-haters when he walked to school, so I thought my experience was normal.

At Hebrew school and at the YMHA there was a certain level of comfort in knowing that being Jewish was not only accepted, but valued. But I do not remember actually enjoying these times. I remember vividly that I did not have to pretend who I was. The problem was that it was more fun to pretend. The older I got the more difficult it became to live in two very different worlds, but that did not mean that I stopped trying. I did not look very closely at the incongruities in my sense of self until much later as an adult. As the wars in Israel continued I felt a vague connection to my people. The unrest in Israel was regularly discussed in our home; however, I never felt connected enough with the nation to discuss Israeli issues outside my home. Until I had children of my own, I really did not feel the need to confront these difficult issues. Having to make life choices for others forced me to look more closely at my own choices as well as my avoidance of choices. When I started looking for answers I found that many Jewish authors had struggled with similar issues. Much of what Phyllis Chesler writes about coming to terms with being Jewish resonates with my own experience but not in the way I expected. I see myself in those whom she criticizes. I feel that I have somehow been disloyal by not educating myself more fully on Jewish issues. It is a gap I am now trying to fill.

As if to convince herself, Chesler lists many of the anti-Jewish terrorist acts around the world. She seems convinced that these acts are perpetrated by Palestinian and Islamic terrorists.[11] I do not intend to argue who is at fault. I mention the attacks and the Middle East conflict only to point out that there has been more world attention on the Israelis and the Palestinians than before 9/11. For people of Middle Eastern heritage and those assumed to have connections with the Middle Eastern conflicts, visibility has increased to an uncomfortable level. There have been numerous reports of anti-Muslim behavior in North America since 9/11 and some efforts have been made to address anti-Muslim feelings. Many universities have added a study of the Qu'ran to the requirement for first year students. "In the fearful aftermath of September 11th, Attorney General John Ashcroft vowed to use the full might of the [American] federal government and 'every available statute' to hunt down and punish the terrorists among us."[12] This announcement was followed by the arrests of Arabs and Muslims. "Many of the Arabs and Muslims caught in the government dragnet . . . spent up to seven months in jail before being cleared of terrorism ties and deported or released."[13] The panic that set in after 9/11 pushed the limits of civil liberties.

There have also been more anti-Semitic incidents in Canada since 9/11.[14] Bernstein of the *New York Times*, like Chesler, suggests that world criticism of Israeli attacks on Palestine can be interpreted as a resurfacing of anti-Semitism. He raises the question:

> Does ferocious moral condemnation of Israel mark a recrudescence of that most ugly of western diseases, anti-Semitism? Or is it legitimate, if crude, criticism of a nation's policies? Where does one draw the line? And how does one judge?[15]

For Diaspora Jewish supporters of Israel, this criticism is also sometimes seen as anti-Semitism rather than simply a criticism of a nation's policies. A recent headline in a Canadian national newspaper announced "Academics Attack Israel for 'Atrocities.'"[16] In this article, Sherene Razack, director of The Centre for Integrative Anti-Racism Studies at the Ontario Institute for Studies in Education, part of the University of Toronto, sent out a letter through university email denouncing Israeli "crimes against humanity."[17] A spokesman for the Canadian Jewish Congress, Simon Rosenblum, "condemned the resolution as a 'prejudicial, inflammatory and highly biased view' of the Middle East conflict that pays no attention to Israel's attempts to achieve peace nor Israel's legitimate need for self-defense."[18] These political matters have translated into anti-Semitic behavior in the universities. In the same article of the *National Post* Turley-Ewert reports that "many Jewish students have said they no longer wear yarmulkes [scull caps] on campus for fear of reprisals."[19] Although it is possible that these university-related articles have been sensationalized, the increased appearance of this type of reporting is disconcerting, especially for those like me who are already fearful of anti-Semitism. Even before 9/11, I was not usually forthcoming about being Jewish, especially in academia. I noticed that if people found out they were not outwardly hostile, but they were overly interested. I was expected to be the expert on all things Jewish. After 9/11, I was much more careful.

Any sort of calm discussion about Israeli policy was no longer possible. Even though I do not agree with all Israeli policy I felt as though it was assumed that because I am Jewish I would automatically be ready to defend any Zionist policy. When asked about my research interests at university, I would usually say something about identity issues and multiculturalism, leaving out the word Jewish. I noticed a more receptive reaction when I omitted my interest in Jewish identity. A discussion of identity issues in the context of multiculturalism was much safer ground. After 9/11, with the mention of the word Jewish, all pretense of neutrality disappeared.

Within the Jewish community the notion of having a simple discussion concerning Israel also changed drastically. The Calgary Jewish community has always been pro-Israel and not surprisingly became even more so after 9/11. Expressing any sort of disagreement with Israeli policy could be interpreted as betrayal of world Jewry. Through my children's attendance at Hebrew school I came into contact with several Israelis living in Canada. Some were parents of students and some were teachers at the school. They all had relatives living in Israel, so I would hear about suicide bombs and other attacks on a daily basis, and it had an impact upon our own much more sheltered daily lives. For many Jews underlying fears about anti-Semitism surfaced during that time. For me, the feeling that I needed to be hyper-vigilant has not subsided. It also made me realize that this is not a new feeling for me – it was just more intense.

Living my life in a muffled state of fear has been alienating. It is a lonely place to be. About ten years ago I discussed Canadian anti-Semitism with a visiting Israeli professor. He had never really noticed the existence of anti-Semitism in Canada. He came to Calgary almost every summer to teach the history of the Jews or Middle Eastern politics, and he had no qualms about making known to his students the fact that he was an Israeli Jew. When I sat in his class as a student, I felt like hiding and this was a wake-up call for me. I had never really admitted to myself that I had a problem with being Jewish and after that summer class I began to face my embarrassing fears. I continued to research Jewish identity. Almost every paper I wrote had something to do with the struggle to come to terms with being Jewish. After all this time it is still a struggle but one that I am finally willing to look at. What I found particularly interesting was the lack of self-consciousness and fear on the part of the Israeli professor. Several years later I explored this theme further when I interviewed Israeli women as part of my doctoral research and, again, I noticed in them a pride and self confidence that I see lacking into myself. Before I could make any comparisons between my own Jewish identity and what I perceived as a contented and fearless sense of Israeli Jewish identity I had to look more closely at myself. What exactly was I hiding? And why did I feel the need to hide?

It was difficult – if not impossible – to shield myself from the stereotypical images of Jews that abound. One of the many stereotypes about the Jewish people is that they are "a devilishly cunning, parasitic, malevolent 'race'."[20] According to the stereotypes, Jews also have a different appearance than other people.[21] I was often told that I looked very Jewish and I did not take that as a compliment. What did that mean? Did I have horns? Did I have a long hooked nose? I have what some people referred to as "olive colored" skin, and, apparently, that makes me look exotic. Sometimes people like to guess that I am Italian or Spanish. When I say that I am Canadian, they are clearly disappointed and they often press further saying, "but what is your background?" I usually do not want to tell them that I am Jewish.

My youngest daughter, Kylie, has red hair with green eyes and very white skin. She lived a fairly sheltered life during elementary and junior high school having attended a Hebrew school. When she went into public school in grade ten, she came home and told me that many students told her that she did not look Jewish. She really had no idea that Jews were supposed to look a certain way. I considered telling her that at one time her red hair and white skin might have saved her life, but I worried that I would be forcing my own paranoia on her. Laurence Rees recounts the travesty of the 1942 Nazi policy to separate children from their parents.

> In the wake of the Paris round-up of July 1942 and the expulsion of the children, there was considerable protest from Church leaders about the actions of the French political leadership. The archbishop of Toulouse ordered a pastoral letter of protest to be read out in his diocese on August 23, and the archbishop of Lyons told Laval when he met him on September 1, that he supported both protest action and the hiding of Jewish children by Catholics. But all this was too late to affect those taken in the Paris sweep that July.

After reading this passage I could not stop myself from thinking that my own daughter would have blended well into a Catholic setting.

Adolescence is often a time when young people experience tremendous anxiety about the way they look. During my teenage years, I was certainly concerned about my looks. Fitting in with the others takes on a supreme importance. As I remember, the 1960s was a time when having perfectly straight long blond hair like the girls in California was the secret to happiness for young women. It was a bad time for chubby, Jewish girls with dark frizzy hair. Some of my friends received a nose job as a sixteenth birthday present, which was not considered unusual in the Winnipeg Jewish community – it was almost a rite of passage! I wondered if I needed a nose job. Even though my family and friends assured me that my nose was fine, that is, not too Jewish, I was not convinced. After their surgeries, the girls who had nose jobs apparently had more self-esteem. I really did not give the issue much thought until I was older and pregnant with my first child. I thought back to my friends with their new noses. Would their children need nose jobs too? I soon found the answer. My youngest daughter told me, in hushed tones, that a girl she knew had recently had a nose job. My daughter's friend's mother had also had some 'work' done. She carried before and after pictures of her daughter's nose and showed them to anyone who would look. A non-Jewish mother of a child in the same group of friends commented to this particular mother that she had always considered her daughter to be very beautiful, and she wondered why the mother would put her daughter through such an ordeal. The mother said "it's a Jewish thing." I was horrified when I heard this story. The non-Jewish woman then asked me if this type of surgery really was a Jewish thing. I explained to her that "of course it is not a Jewish thing!" – too embarrassed to tell her how commonplace the nose job really was. Secretly I wondered exactly how 'bad' a nose should look before going under the knife. This was only the tip of the iceberg when it came to Jewish self-hatred.

Evelyn Torton Beck, a professor of Jewish Studies and Women's Studies, describes some of the stereotypes of Jewish women. She particularly focuses on the Jewish American Princess.[22] The traditional anti-Semitic image represents the Jew (most familiar as Shakespeare's Shylock) as manipulative, calculating, avaricious, materialistic, sexually perverse, ugly (hook-nosed), and foreign in speech. In the Jewish American Princess these same characteristics are combined with misogynist stereotypes associated specifically with women, to create a Jewish female who is manipulative (of men), calculating (to obtain the men's money), materialistic (focussed only on clothing, furniture, and looks), vulgar (sports designer clothes, furs, and conspicuous jewels) and ugly (needs or has had a nose job). She is both sexually promiscuous and frigid – the male Jew is accused of being both a communist and capitalist – while she is accused of trading sexuality for goods.[23] I have made a conscious effort to separate myself from the stereotype of the Jewish American Princess. In doing so I am placing a boundary between how I see myself and those women who might fit the description of the Jewish American Princess. When I get angry with my daughters, they know that if I say, "you're acting like a princess," that I must really be upset with them. I do not like the stereotype, but by making the effort to distance myself from it, I am contributing to perpetuating the stereotype. Not only am I maintaining the stereotype but I am passing it on to my children. In some of the interviews with Israeli women, their descriptions of Canadian Jewish women sounded like the Jewish American Princess. I remember hoping that they did not see me in the same way. Beck sees the Jewish American Princess stereotype as anti-Semitic and she is correct in her assumption. This stereotype does promote hatred of Jews. By perpetuating the stereotype I am engaging in self-hating behavior. But even having this awareness, the accompanying feelings do not disappear.

[1] Chesler, *The New Anti-Semitism.*
[2] Ibid. 26.
[3] Ibid. 26.
[4] Ibid. 28.
[5] Ibid.
[6] Ibid.
[7] Ibid. 88.
[8] Ibid. 43.
[9] Goldensohn, *TheNuremburg Interviews*,vii.

[10] Lasik, "The Apprehension and Punishment of the Auschwitz Concentration Camp Staff," in *Auschwitz 1940-1945* (Auschwitz State Museum 2000), 5:99-119, in Laurence Rees, *Auschwitz: A New History*, 2005, 285.

[11] Ibid. 72-75.

[12] Liptak, Lewis, Weiser, 1.

[13] Ibid. 16.

[14] League for Human Rights B'nai B'rith Canada; Blackwell and Arnold, 1.

[15] Berstein, *The New York Times*, 14, section 1.

[16] Turley-Ewert, A4.

[17] Ibid.

[18] Ibid.

[19] Ibid.

[20] Daniel Jonah Goldhagen, *Hilter's Willing Executioners*, 29.

[21] Evelyn Torton-Beck, 23.

[22] Ibid.

[23] Ibid.

Four

Mirror, Mirror on the Wall

In the fairytale "Sleeping Beauty" the wicked and jealous Queen obsessively gazes into the magic mirror in order to be reassured that she is "the fairest in the land." Although we are supposed to hate and fear the evil Queen most people understand her constant need for approval. By examining my own Jewish identity I desire the assurance, not that I am "the fairest in the land," but that being Jewish is, at least, not despicable. Much as I abhor the idea of being judged by others, I find that I am doing the same thing to both others and myself. It is exhausting. If I am acceptable today, does that mean I was also acceptable in the past or that I will be in the future? The mirror on the wall can never really be trusted to reflect the world accurately.

On one level I feel that I am the same person that I remember growing up, but on other levels I am no longer that person. I am not even the same person I was yesterday. Richard Kearney, a professor of philosophy, maintains that we have a sense of our selves that "perdures" over time.[1] Most of us have a sense of something like a core self that we remember as our identity from time we were children. But there is also a sense of ourselves that is forgotten. Paul Ricoeur explains that the temporal component of identity "rests upon the ordered series of small changes, which taken one by one, threaten resemblance without destroying it."[2] The minute daily changes of everyday life go unnoticed as far as shaping how we see ourselves. In the daily unfolding of one's life, the question, "who am I?" rarely emerges. In my daily life I do not see myself emerging as a different person with each passing moment. It would be unbearably confusing.

Drawing on Ricoeur's work, Kearney explains that, "our existence is already to some extent pre-plotted before we ever seek out a narrative in which to reinscribe our life as life-history."[3] We are all born into an existing situation, which includes anything that might help to shape our identities such as family traditions, cultural history, gender, education etc. At some point we begin to tell our stories in a particular way depending on the ways in which we have interpreted the experiences in our lives. Thus we are both shaped by others and shaped by ourselves. When people are contentedly engaged in the familiar activities of their lives then there is no need to raise the question of "who am I?" When our lives are played out in the expected manner, we usually do not feel the need to question everything. Anthony Paul Kerby points out "we are supported by our ongoing practices, our established meanings. It is often in light of a possible or impending future, or a problem in the present that the question of 'who?' is seriously raised."[4] He continues, "memorial experience (recollection) is not simply the past; it is . . . the past for me now."[5] In other words, the individual tells her story in a way that works to explain and rationalize the present. It may feel like a betrayal when life does not unfold in the anticipated way. Professor of sociology, Erving Goffman, observes that we do not become aware of these expectations or "demands . . . until an active question arises as to whether or not they will be fulfilled."[6] Migration to a new country and culture would be one such occasion when questions about the self may arise, but there are other major life changes that cause identity issues to surface.

Having had some time to reflect on the research I did, I realize what a difficult task I set for myself and for the women I interviewed. Going back to the theme of gazing in the mirror, the discomfort of looking at one's past self became even clearer to me when I telephoned and sent out letters to each participant before I printed the final draft of my Ph.D. dissertation. Most of the Israeli women participants in my research were able to look at the transcripts of their original interviews from an earlier time and able to recognize a resemblance of themselves while still acknowledging the changes. Others could not bear to read their own words. Although I had their consent at the time of the interviews, I sent them an addendum to the consent form. Along with the letter I printed out each individual's quotations, descriptions, and pseudonyms. They had the opportunity to revisit what they had said two years earlier and one of the participants decided to withdraw completely. A few wanted some minor changes to clarify what they meant. Some were embarrassed about their grammar mistakes. One participant sent me a letter explaining how strange it was for her to read her words from two years earlier, but she thanked me for sending her the copy. Looking in the mirror of even the recent past was a challenge for many.

I was surprised at my own reaction to the one participant, Yahav, who withdrew completely: I took it personally. It was as though I was seeing my own reflection through her eyes and I wanted her to like the way we both looked in print. I had spent so much time listening and going over her transcript that to me it seemed that we had a close relationship. Then she cut me off. She did not return any of my phone calls. Maybe I will talk to her in the future, but for the present I can only speculate about why she decided to withdraw. At first I thought that she was angry with me, but I realized that she probably did not feel anger in a relationship that only existed in my mind. It is more likely that she did not want to be the person in the transcript. She had been very angry at the time and perhaps she did not want to be that angry person any longer. It is possible that Yahav could not be, or did not want to be, the person she saw mirrored in the transcription. I can only hypothesize.

Meshi, another participant, also had difficulty reading her own words from an earlier interview. Meshi eventually contacted me and we discussed the part of the interview she wanted changed or deleted. She felt that she came across as being quite bitter about some of her experience in Canada. She did not want to have anything included that came across as a criticism of the Calgary Jewish community. She did not want her reflection to portray a bitter and ungrateful person. Since the time we spoke, two years earlier, she has come to understand Canadians a little bit better. Like several of other participants she had difficulty understanding the polite attitudes she encountered among Canadians. She explained that if someone behaved in the same polite manner in Israel, they would assume that the person wanted something from them. Other participants found the politeness cold or even dishonest. Many participants simply did not trust what they described as politeness. Meshi explained that for a long time she wondered what was behind the politeness. Eventually she realized that they wanted nothing from her. I wondered if she was afraid that she might be recognized if anyone in Calgary happened to read her words. It would not surprise me if she did not trust me or other Canadian Jews. Her distrust made me ask myself, "what did I want from her?" The answer I now realize is that I was looking for part of myself in her.

I am not sure how I would react, or if I would recognize myself, if I were confronted with a transcript of my own words from the past. I have noticed that a similar process happens with photographs, both old and recent. When I look at some pictures, even recent ones, I do not recognize myself, whereas I think other photographs are a very good likeness of me. I might even ask someone, "do you think this picture looks like me?" I am surprised if they do. If I think the picture does not look like me and the other person does, I experience a combination of feelings ranging from, "oh no, that's what I look like?" to "This person is an idiot and obviously does not know me very well." My point is that it can be difficult to see or even imagine oneself as others do. We have the choice to recognize our past selves or not. In this same way we choose the narratives of our lives – sometimes with awareness of doing so and sometimes without. When we choose a personal narrative without awareness we are often surprised what is reflected back to us. The stories or images that we have concerning ourselves are the ones that work best for us to make sense of the present. When I moved to Calgary to begin a new life my own stories about myself and who I was in Vancouver were not a match with my new life in Calgary. It has taken many years to fill in the missing spaces.

When moving to a new culture, the participants I interviewed had to make sense of unfamiliar Jewish stereotypes. This is not to say that stereotypes do not exist in Israel, but they are different stereotypes. Kaye/Kantrowitz describes some of the disturbing Jewish Diaspora stereotypes that add one more level of conflict concerning Jewish identity. According to Kaye/Kantrowitz, the main issue has to do with power. As she points out "Jews are supposed to be all-powerful: controlling Wall Street, the world's money, media, colleges – the world itself."[7] Returning to the myth of the all-powerful Jew there is "the Israeli, the soldier, the one who breaks the hands of Palestinian children; inherently worse than other soldiers, worse than other men; the one who justifies hatred, is pointed proof of the problem: you see what they're like?"[8] There are also stereotypes that depict the Jew as powerless. "Tucked under the myth of the all-powerful Jew is the victim Jew, the old-world Jew, the shlep [slob], the nebbish [loser], and – somber but receding into the vague undifferentiated past – the Holocaust Jew."[9] It is not surprising that one would want to distance oneself from these negative stereotypes. I know the discomfort of feeling this way. It is a fear that I will be judged along with the stereotypical Jew. It is a double-edged sword. I feel guilty for being disloyal as a Jew, for being ashamed of other Jews; and I dislike myself for having these conflicting feelings.

To continue on the subject of the Diaspora, the stereotypes of Jewish men are different than, but related to, the stereotypes of Jewish women. Describing the perplexing situation of Jewish women in the Diaspora, Kaye/Kantrowitz points out that "as a Jew, she's assumed to have so much power already."[10] However, in the category of woman, she has very little power and any power that she does have is considered "excessive."[11] She explains:

> Stereotypes of Jewish women combine with prejudice against powerful women, pressuring us to cloak our strength lest we be seen as pushy; hide our desire, lest we be deemed oversexed (or fuck on demand, lest we be considered frigid); mute our feelings, lest we be judged overemotional.[12]

She asserts that "Jewish women are asked to sit on [themselves] lest [they] seem too powerful ... for men."[13] According to Kaye/Kantrowitz Jewish women are "too powerful" for men and women, Jews and non-Jews."[14] This imagined power makes Jewish women "too powerful" even for themselves. The notion of being too powerful for oneself is somewhat confusing. I have felt this myself, particularly in situations where I feel judged by others. Even in today's world Jewish communities still expect women to be the main caregivers in the family and maintain responsibility for keeping a Jewish home. Although many Jewish women are also expected educated and have well-paying jobs, the care of the family is still thought of in a traditional way. Drawing attention to oneself is acceptable only where it benefits the community, such as in volunteer work. When I moved to Calgary I was very visible to the community because of the situation with the children. Even by doing nothing I had already attracted too much attention. It did not help that I kept my maiden name and returned to school. It is this imagined power that caused me to feel too powerful for myself. I felt that I had to keep it hidden.

Kaye/Kantrowitz tells us that Jewish women are seen as *"aggressive, bossy, tense, driven, difficult,* not to mention *loud and pushy."*[15] Jewish women do not want to be thought of this way, nor do they want other Jewish women to embarrass them by behaving in this way. Consequently, there is a system of surveillance in place in Jewish communities. Jewish women judge themselves and they judge other Jewish women. It is difficult to live with the constant feeling that one is being held up to some sort of standard, especially if one is not always sure what that standard is or if the measuring stick has somehow changed. For example, several years ago, while my children were in the elementary grades at the Hebrew school, I was waiting with the other mothers to collect our children at the end of the day. One acquaintance mentioned to me that she had heard I had gone back to school and she inquired about what I was studying. She seemed genuinely interested and excited for me. At that time I was an undergraduate in the department of Women's Studies. In an extremely judgmental tone she exclaimed, "you're not interested in that feminist stuff are you?" I replied that yes, in fact, I was very interested. The sound of her judgmental voice even now keeps ringing in my ears. The underlying message that I heard was that by being different I came across as intimidating and that was unacceptable. Obviously I did not mirror back a pleasing image. After that day when I would pick up my children I was more cautious in my interactions with the other mothers. I even started waiting in the car for my children to avoid talking with the other women. Perhaps I was feeling too powerful even for myself. I needed to downplay the fact that I actually did have issues concerning my own power.

In one interview the theme of looking in the mirror came up again when the subject of Jewish people in the community watching each other was raised. Devora felt othered by many of the Canadian Jews she met, but she insisted that it was not a negative experience for her. She made it sound more like an adventure. She seems to enjoy seeing herself as an observer, an outsider. When I asked if she was bothered by being the other, she replied:

> No. I love it. And maybe with it, unless you create close relationships, it becomes a sense of superficiality. I can explore then disconnect. I don't need to take that responsibility, so I often, if I establish a close relationship with that person, the lack of difficulty stems from my natural, whatever 'natural' means – a

natural inclination to engage, with a tendency then later to back off.

I then asked her if the people with whom she engages see her as an anthropologist. Because she is not an anthropologist, this question seemed to take her slightly aback. She responded:

> I'm not sure. On occasion a person or two would say, 'You ask very interesting questions. Why do you want to know that?' . . . So some would recognize it occasionally, but not as an umbrella term as you just presented it. There might be a problem, you know, now that you've said it, I'm thinking, imagine being with friends and their thinking, 'Oh, she's observing us and she — what is she doing? I need to be careful here,' you know? And smile or it's like a camera Right? This woman is like a camera.

My response was, "it's possible." In this exchange we both became aware of our behavior as performances. When she told me the way she approached people, I then became aware that she was closely observing me. Devora seemed genuinely shocked that her friends might have this opinion of her. She became aware of her performance. Her face tightened with tension and I became uncomfortable. She probably noticed a change in my demeanor as well. I had the feeling that she was rethinking her own position as other and perhaps it no longer sounded like so much fun. Rather, it indicated that she does not trust people and it is quite possible that people do not trust her. When we began the discussion of being an outsider, Devora acted as though being an outsider gave her a certain amount of power that she enjoyed. Towards the end of the conversation she was no longer sure about who had the power. I noticed that many Israeli women are not afraid of seeming powerful. I could almost see Devora's mind in action, reassessing the situation almost as a matter of survival. It seemed as though she was experiencing self-doubt concerning what she perceived as being more powerful since she was considered outside of the Calgary Jewish community. She took pride in being different. During our conversation I sensed that she was now questioning the power that she thought being an outsider had bestowed upon her.

Devora's experience of being an outsider is very different than what Kaye/Kantrowitz describes some of the conflicts and challenges that Jewish [non- Israeli] women may face in a Diaspora community.

> She wants to feel proud of her Jewish tradition, but she finds elements she is not proud of, and this it seems is what non-Jews know best....On the one hand, she may feel profoundly threatened by the legacy of hate that haunted , at least her grandparents; probably her parents; possibly herself. On the other hand she may feel profoundly ashamed of, and oddly responsible for the oppression visited by Israelis on Palestinians and masquerading as a defense of the Jewish people. About the Holocaust legacy: Is she paranoid or foolishly off guard? About Israel: the same question.[16]

A Jewish Israeli woman faced with a particular discourse in the Diaspora may not have experienced the same challenges although it is likely she will have dealt with other conflicts. Kaye/Kantrowitz's description above could have been written about me. She refers to Jewish women who move in "progressive circles" which also applies to me. Doing research and teaching at a university is considered by many to be "progressive." Kaye/Kantrowitz adds, "she may discover that she cannot say she's a Jew without being called to account for the Israeli army."[17] Also like me, "she may be shocked by the animosity" provoked by any discussion of the Middle East. At a family gathering she may be accused of being too young to really know about what is real in the realm of persecution. Thus it is difficult to be Jewish and progressive. "Either way, she risks anger, dislike, alienation."[18] Kaye/Kantowitz maintains that it does not matter to what degree a Jewish woman is assimilated because at some point "she will grapple with her Jewishness or she will be split from herself." The idea of "splitting from oneself"' feels very familiar to me. Confusion about where one fits within a society can be the cause of anxiety. If a woman is unclear about her relationship to an existing discourse, trying to make sense of her place within social relations is extremely difficult. I found it very demanding to behave in the correct way at the correct time. I was never absolutely sure what the correct behavior was. At the university I did not want to appear too Jewish but in the Jewish community I needed to be careful that I did not give the impression of rejecting the Jewish community. Splitting from oneself can be played out in both a physical and emotional manner. I remember feeling that I was not meeting anyone's expectations, especially my own. At the same time I could not really pin down exactly what those expectations were.

Issues concerning the body have long been a feminist topic. A woman's feelings about her body and her sexuality have a significant impact on her sense of self.[19] Rachel Josefowitz Siegel maintains that "conversely, a woman's sense of self . . . can significantly affect her feelings about her body and her sexuality."[20] She also points out that culturally transmitted messages about the female body "in the case of the minority group, are conveyed by the host culture as well as by the minority group's own cultural, historical and religious customs."[21] This double interference can result in a damaging effect for women in minority groups.

> The negative attitudes and biases of a host culture are frequently expressed by means of stereotyping the physical attributes and sexuality of the more marginal group. Such caricaturing, when directed at women is likely to be more socially acceptable than when it is directed at men.[22]

Siegel makes it clear that negative stereotyping affects all ethnic and minority women. She acknowledges that Jewish men are also the target of "anti-Jewish body stereotyping."[23] However, her particular interest is Jewish women in the West. She has not studied the topic of body image among Israeli women who she says "are not exposed to the forces of a differing host culture."[24] This remains a area to be explored.

The Israeli women in my research may be subjected to the same negative stereotyping as women in the West when they leave Israel and come to Canada. As Siegel points out, "women of all ages, Jewish and non-Jewish, are preoccupied with looks and body image."[25] In spite of feminist attempts to draw attention to "the tyranny of this pervasive over-investment in how women look, most women are still caught up to some degree in wondering what they can do to become more attractive."[26] Although women's appearance was not the main focus of my research, I am certainly aware of my own over-investment in this area. There is a connection between feeling safe and secure and at home with a sense of comfort inside one's own body.

In one particular interview I was very much aware of the time and energy invested in the relentless pursuit of being attractive. I am always conscious of the ways in which I present myself in the performance of being a woman. Although I am a feminist, I also consider my looks and attire important. With each passing year it takes more time, energy, and money to maintain the appearance I want. I had hoped that as I grew older concern for my exterior image would subside; this has not happened yet. The interview I refer to now made me aware of the performativity of appearance in a way I had not thought of before.

Leora, unlike the others, did not want to meet with me in her home. Instead we arranged to meet at a place she chose. When I asked how I would recognize her she hesitated for a moment and then told me what color wig she would be wearing that day. She told me that she was very religious and wore a wig because Orthodox married Jewish women keep their heads covered. A married woman should not draw attention to her appearance and wearing a wig is supposed to accomplish this. When we did find each other she wanted to eat lunch first and she thought I would be able to interview her during lunch. The restaurant was far too noisy to get a good quality recording so I suggested that after lunch we could try to find a quieter place in the building.

During lunch we had a chance to get to know each other. I really felt as though she was interviewing me. She still was not sure that she wanted to be part of my study. This extra time gave me a chance to really observe her without the stress of the interview. And I knew she was observing me. I noticed that even though she was wearing a wig, which is a symbol of modesty for religious Jews, the wig itself was beautiful in a sexual way. Her wig was shoulder length and looked like real hair. Had she not told me about the wig, I would not have noticed it. She also wore expertly applied makeup. She was sending rather contradictory messages with her appearance. On the one hand, the wig signified her modesty and adherence to Orthodox Judaism. On the other hand, the style, quality, and color of the wig, along with her makeup and clothing, sent a message that she wanted to be noticed as an attractive woman. So before we even began the interview, Leora's appearance told me that part of her story included Orthodox Judaism and that she wanted to stand out from the collective narrative. I was confused about the message she was sending. Seigel suggests:

> Since 'Jewish traits' have negative or ambivalent connotations in predominantly non-Jewish countries, the Jewish woman has the additional burden of wondering whether her appearance conveys an image that is 'too Jewish' .... She wonders if she will be avoided by others because her looks convey ethno-religious messages.[27]

I saw Leora's light-colored wig as an attempt to blend in with such a diverse culture. This is another example of unclear boundaries. Although Leora tried to separate herself from non-Orthodox Jews and non-Jews, her careful attention to her appearance allowed her to blend in anywhere. This interview forced me to take a closer look at the effort I put into my own appearance and the messages I convey.

I was reminded of my mother's weekly visit to the hairdresser during my youth. Friday was the day that "everyone" seemed to get their hair done. Over the years my mother's hair went from her natural color brown, to lighter and lighter shades of blond. Perhaps this was her way of disguising her Jewish appearance. I often feel over concerned with my appearance; in part, this focus issues from the messages that media transmit to women about youth and beauty, but for me there is also the extra concern with blending in – not looking too ethnic.

Many Jews, both men and women, manage to avoid grappling with their Jewishness until they are actually called into being Jews by the dominant discourse. If a Jewish person has managed to live without confronting any Jewish stereotypes then they may have no awareness that a certain discourse (and its ensuing conflicts) exists. Only once the subject perceives that she is named as particular kind of Jew can she react to that imposed identification. The confusion and splitting from oneself begins to happen when one cannot reconcile how one is called into being in discourse with one's own naming of the self.

Because of the situation with the adoption of my children, I had the sense that the community was watching me. My awareness of this surveillance was confirmed when rumors concerning my family and me reached my ears. I have an awareness that many people in the community know who I am and what is going on in my life. Well-meaning friends sometimes tell me when someone asks about me or thinks I am a bit weird. I did not become fully aware of my own conflicting Jewish issues until I moved to Calgary and my presence was known in the Jewish community. I became aware that others were talking about me – particularly in relation to becoming a mother to Carie and Daniel.

This attention caused me to feel a need for privacy and a sense of loneliness and isolation.

Kaye/Kantrowitz discusses several issues that she believes are "especially intense for Jewish women, or have a particularly Jewish slant to them."[28] These include children and family, money, alienation, and the question of who is the Real Jew. Family concerns and the decision whether or not to have children is an important issue for many people. Kaye/Kantrowitz maintains that "these issues have particular weight in the Jewish community, as in many other minority communities, especially those subjected to attempted genocide."[29] The survival of the Jewish people has depended on having a strong family so "women's reproductive performance" becomes more significant than it might be among minorities who have not been threatened in the same way.[30] For Jewish women, being a good Jew for the benefit of the community is an added dimension in the decision to have children. Unfortunately, my sense of being on display interfered with my enjoyment of becoming a new mother.

Continuing on the topic of motherhood, I questioned participants about the expectations they had for themselves and expectations imposed externally. Devora was living alone in Calgary at the time of the interview. Her husband was committed to living in Israel while Devora preferred living in Calgary. Her two grown children were away at school and she was living alone. When I asked her to think back to her aspirations about what she would "make of herself" she replied:

> I grew up to be a professional and a mother. No. I'm sorry. A mother and a professional. Or a wife and a professional. So I was led to believe that unlike my mother's generation, I could – I know it sounds trite, but it's true. I could have it all. I wouldn't have to stay at home and take care of kids. I could do both. I could be both at home and outside the home.

Devora articulated the stories she expected, lived, and was living. She assumed that women in her generation could have it all – marriage, children, and career.

> That's how we grew up, my generation – the women. We were going to be wives, get married, have children, and be professionals. All of us went to university and that was taken for granted. My mother's generation . . . their education had either been broken, severed, many were refugees and many were holocaust survivors.

Devora was about my age and her description of her expectations sounded very similar to my own. I was quite surprised by the similarity between us as I had assumed that everything, including aspirations in life, would have been so very different in Israel. Even though I am aware that life in Israel is cosmopolitan, the images of kibbutzniks picking oranges and dancing Israeli dances was still lodged in my mind. This is an image of people putting the welfare of society before, or at least on par, with their own well-being.

Devora married at the age of twenty-two and she explained that she was "proud to be a wife." She described her life in Israel from the age of twenty-two to thirty in idyllic terms. "I was very much in love with a wonderful husband . . . and that was wonderful and I had friends and I was glowing." It was clear that she was pleased with what she was making of herself at that point in time. As she began referring to the political situation, she explained how, around age thirty, she became "frustrated" and "wanted out."

Devora and her husband moved to Canada temporarily hoping their lives would be better, but life turned out to be more difficult. First, leaving Israel indefinately was never part of the original plan. She told me that after spending some time in Canada, "all of a sudden those difficulties were insurmountable." Second, although she had expected more for herself, the only job she could get was teaching Hebrew. By the time she found employment she had two young children; she realized the adjustment to living in Canada was more difficult than she had anticipated. Part of the problem for Devora was that she did not understand Canadian social cues and could not enter the surrounding discourse.

> It took me years to learn the ground rules, those taken-for granted matters. To read in a deeper way what a woman meant when she said I'm not sure. When I said, "do you think we could get together? How about having a carpool or how about having a, you know, you take the kids one day and I'll take yours. 'Well I'll think about it. I'm not sure.' I thought that was – it meant just what was said but, in fact, it meant "No." So I was unnecessarily hurt too.

Devora was hurt by misunderstanding what Canadians see as a polite way of saying no. She and her husband felt like outsiders in Canada, and their friends and family viewed them as traitors for leaving Israel. They were not meeting anyone's expectations, including their own. I had insight into Devora's experience having experienced the pressure of other people's expectations.

Devora never considered not having children. It was assumed, given her family history. Her sense of discomfort with her Jewish identity was probably visible to her children. For an Israeli Jew there is also a pressure of, as Devora explained, "educating kids to be good Israeli citizens." How could she educate her children to be good Israeli citizens when she had difficulty balancing her own feelings about Israel? For her Israeli meant Jewish. It was difficult for me to understand her dilemma until I went to Israel. In Canada there is a separ-ation between being a Canadian and being a Jew; for many Jews living in Israel that separation does not exist.

The idea that women are attached to the home and family came through in most of the interviews. For both Diaspora Jews and Israeli Jews producing children signifies loyalty to the culture or nation. In some ways, this activity supports Western feminists criticism that considers the separation between private and public domains as oppressive to women. When I spoke with Orit, she had difficulty understanding Canadian women's attitudes towards family. When I asked her about Canadian Jewish women's attitudes she answered:

> There are many differences that I will point out in terms of fam-
> ily. Connections in the family are very different . . . we're
> amazed to hear about people that live far from their parents
> because kids here really lose the nest, go away from the nest
> really early. And they don't feel comfortable to be with their
> family again. That amazes me, maybe because I come from a
> family that really cared about each other. And although we live
> far, in terms of Israel . . .we still had such great connections, my
> father came to visit for three weeks. We had a great time. I wish
> he would stay for six months. Parents here come to visit for
> three days and they would complain, "I couldn't stand him," like
> it blows me away. No respect for their parents. Nothing. And
> they come and judge us.

Orit felt that Canadian women were judgmental of her, and she expressed this resentment by pointing out what she sees as a Canadian lack of character; "the way they behave to their parents, that really annoys me." She was also critical of what she interpreted as Canadian women being "self-centred."

> The reasons they would give for delaying having kids. Okay,
> since I came here I realized that being thirty and having two
> kids, that's a huge accomplishment in Canada. Because by they
> age of thirty they think, 'Maybe I should get married,' and they
> have one, two kids one after another.

Orit perceives that Canadian women have the luxury of taking their time about making major life decisions. According to Orit, in Israel women usually get married and have children at a younger age; this pattern is the normal way that life unfolds. Israeli Zionist discourse includes early marriage and child bearing. Orit admits that she now has reconsidered these expectations, and she sees how it may be a good thing to wait. She also explained that in Israel concepts of family were "limited." She now thinks it is important "to see that people think differently." A integral part of the collective narrative in Israel is that women have a traditional role in the family.

Most of the participants in this study would not define themselves as feminists. While with the women I interviewed, I was cautious about even mentioning the word "feminism" because I sensed that they connected the word to Western women who really could not understand Israeli women's lived reality. When speaking with Orit, the topic of the right age to have children came up. She mentioned that she overheard two women at work talking about not having children.

> That was really amazing for me. How can someone think of not having kids? And I said, 'Okay. Maybe they have all their high things – there are enough kids in the world.' There is misery and don't add to that, but for me, that's a basic thing. Even now that I have two, and I feel like maybe it will be too much to have a third child, that's a thought that would never have occurred to me if I had lived in Israel.

Orit was stunned that some Jewish women might consider not having children at all. Although she acknowledged the possibility that there are enough children in the world, she did not see this as a sufficient reason not to have children. Having children, for her, was "basic." Yet, she has also noticed a change in her thinking since coming to Canada. If she were living in Israel it would have been part of the expected plan to have a third child. Now that she lives in Canada, she is not as sure about what she used to consider as "basic."

Kaye/Kantrowitz's emphasizes issues regarding children and family for Jewish women in the Diaspora. However, Israeli women who come to live in Canada are confronted with a Diaspora discourse. From Orit's Israeli perspective, children and family should have a more prominent place for Canadian Jewish women. She may not yet have noticed that there is a different sort of emphasis on children and family in Canadian Jewish communities. Many Canadian Jewish families have moved to Calgary from other Canadian centres. In many cases they have left their families behind. The synagogues and Jewish Community Centre, as well as various social organizations, make an effort to provide an environment where Jewish families can come together with other Jewish families creating a family-like atmosphere. There seems to be a more external emphasis on the importance of family, possibly because it is disappearing at a more intimate level. The myth of the tightly-knit and loving Jewish family remains strong. Kaye/Kantrowitz points out that:

> Jewish families are probably as riddled with abuse and dysfunction as other families. Yet there is a myth about the close, happy Jewish family, that Jewish men don't drink or beat their wives or sexually abuse their daughters. These myths make the reality hard to bear for the individual suffering in a non-ideal family. The anguish felt by many Jewish women about revealing family secrets is exacerbated by a sense that Jewish families in particular need protection.[31]

She goes on to explain that reason Jewish families are in "particular need of protection" is the fear that people will find out that Jews are no "better than the goyim (non-Jews)."[32] Jews expect that they should have higher standards than the rest of society. Kaye/Kantrowitz claims "that by telling the truth we're validating anti-Semitism."[33] It is possible that Israeli Jewish women coming to Canada may be unaware of the particular kinds of loyalty issues that confront Diaspora women. What Israeli women perceive as a basic lack of values may in fact be part of another set of Jewish values. It seems that new Jewish identities need to emerge in order for Canadian and Israeli Jews to come to a better understanding of each other. Canadian Jewish women may have different expectations about themselves in terms of family and children, but this does not mean that the pressures about women's "reproduction performance" is necessarily less stressful.

There were not many remarks about dysfunctional families during the interviews. This supports Kaye/Kantrowitz's statement that the image of the Jewish family needs to be protected. Family problems were conspicuously missing in the interviews. However, just having met most of these women, I did not expect that they would tell me intimate details of their lives during a two hour interview. Most of the participants spoke about their Israeli childhoods in idyllic terms. They described their families as warm and loving, making me wish I had grown up in their homes. However, there were some exceptions. I asked Devora to describe her childhood and she answered that she would do it differently "if she had a choice." She continued:

> Yeah. I would like to have had a different childhood, but nevertheless it was horrible . . . I think I both enjoyed being a child, I was quite a reflective little person, but I also suffered a great deal. I come from a very difficult and violent family.

I was shocked that she said this, knowing she was being taped, because it really is very unusual for a Jewish person, Israeli or Diaspora, man or woman, to make disparaging remarks about her family unless she is in a therapy session or talking to an extremely close friend. Part of my discomfort was Devora's apparent lack of respect for the myth of the perfect, loving Jewish family. Even though many Jewish families are far from perfect (including my own), I felt threatened by her public statement of this private fact; Jews are somehow supposed to be better. I tried to change the topic by asking "when did you feel like your childhood ended?" Devora responded:

> I don't think it ever started. I was – there's an expression in Yiddish for it, an *altecop*, [old head]. I'm not sure what the equivalent in English would be. But you know when you run into a little girl and she's an old woman.

Although I wanted to hear more about her childhood, it felt dangerous and inappropriate, so I changed the tone of the interview to a lighter one. The interview might have unfolded differently had it not been for my own discomfort.

One of the topics Devora commented on was money. She wanted to know kind of car I drove, and she considered my Honda to be a luxury automobile. I sensed that she judged Canadian Jews as being overly concerned with material wealth. She did not want to see herself in the same mirror as Canadian Jews. There is a stereotype image that Jews are overly concerned with money, or that Jews are rich and they control the world. This factor contributes to making the topic of money difficult for many Jews to discuss. Jews in the Diaspora are exposed to this particular stereotype more than Jews in Israel, although there are other stereotypes to contend with in Israel. As Kaye/Kantrowitz explains, "to many non-Jews, Jews *are* money."[34] Thus the topic of money is to be avoided when interacting with non-Jews, because of their hyper-sensitivity to this Jewish stereotype. Kaye/Kantrowitz claims this stereotype creates more stress when considered in combination of the Jewish concept of charity

> The concept of charity deep in the Jewish tradition . . . is fundamentally different as the notion of poverty is fundamentally different – neither a blessed state (Catholicism) nor a sign of damnation (Calvinism), but an unfortunate reality to be ameliorated, anonymously, by those who have more.[35]

More often the anonymous part seems to be ignored in Jewish communities, so that a hierarchy often emerges based on who gives the most money. Thus the emphasis on money is perpetuated.

One of the participants, Naomi, brought up the topics of money and family as part of same the issue. Naomi is the woman who considered herself to be very European and more cultured than the average Israeli. She had met her Canadian husband in Israel. I asked her if there were areas of her life where she experienced conflict because of her move to Canada. Up until this point in the interview everything was on a positive plane. She was well-adjusted to Canada, her children were happy, she was involved with various Jewish organizations, and she was very successful in her job. She had obviously 'made something of herself.' Her response concerning conflict came as a bit of a surprise. It took her a while to begin to discuss the actual problem.

> My family. Family in the sense that because I'm the kind of person – I'm not trying to paint myself as an angel because there's not an angel walking on the face of this earth. I would paint myself as a relatively easy-going, non-confrontational sort. I've been called this all the time because I'm outspoken. But, I'm not a hard person to get along with. And my in-laws, because they're primitive, they're uneducated, view this engagement and marriage as I'm here to marry a rich boy and have an easy life. And I was told so by my mother-in law.

Naomi detailed the conflict-ridden relationship she had with her mother-law. By this point she was very animated:

> It was my mother-in-law who told me that I got married for money. Who has not been – I'm not going into detail because it has nothing to do with your work –who had told me awful things along the way. I mean, if your mother in-law told you that you married for money, you'd probably scratch her face out! I mean, not you, personally, but most people would.

It was very clear that she had not married into the perfect family and that money was a sensitive issue. My response was, "so, this is because you're Israeli that she would say that?" She continued:

> Yes! I was an outsider and she perceived me to be poor. Which I was in a sense. I mean I wasn't poor. My father was in research. We lived on a salary, you know. My in-laws are entrepreneurs. Very primitive, but very wealthy, had a lot of money. They thought, 'Oh here's the poor Israeli girl who came to use our money,' And that conflict, you know was underlying all along, and sort of still is.

Naomi was open about her hostility toward her mother-in-law. She was also angry with her father because he sided with Naomi's mother-in-law in family conflicts. This continues to cause problems for her, although she feels guilty about it. In her words, "it was getting to me because of the second generation guilt and my own personality and my father!" Her parents are Holocaust survivors and most of her relatives were killed in the death camps. She did not want to cause a family disturbance because survivors (her mother-in- law included) already had enough grief in their lives. However she pointed out that, after being accused of marrying for money, she has worked to be financially independent by running her own business. "I've always had something of my own and I still hold on to it, only because of this underlying conflict." When I suggested that she sounded like a feminist she responded:

> Yes. Very much so. Very much. I'm the independent sort. So what happens is, and I don't have to label myself . . . I am a feminist to the extent that I've always done my own thing because I'm a very independent person . . . Whoever tries to step on me, they won't really win because I'm too independent.

It was important for Naomi to establish that she could look after herself, and, although her performance as an independent woman was convincing, it was also clear that she had been wounded deeply by the accusation that she married for money.

Like Naomi, I felt wronged by the innuendos that suggested I married Ken because of money. Yet, there was gossip about money before I even arrived on the scene because Ken's brother and sister-in-law had been well-off financially; there were insinuations that Ken was after their money. In fact, they did leave substantial provisions for their children and the children's trust was carefully administered by both government and appointed trustees. Until the children came of age, we had to account for every penny spent. The money enabled the children to continue with extra lessons and schooling, but it was a difficult balancing act for us to live a modest lifestyle and to raise all our children with reasonable, non-extravagant values. The assumptions people made about our finances put a great strain on our relationship. I could understand why Naomi was so disturbed by other peoples opinions.

Naomi's ambivalence came through in her comments about being a good Jew. She had explained to me that she grew up in an Orthodox family and she viewed herself as traditional. She talked about her sister-in-law, who Naomi saw as limited in an Orthodox Jewish life. Talking about an Orthodox Jewish life Naomi explained:

> Very limited in some ways. I think that my sister-in-law, a professional, and she's ten years younger than me so she'd be forty-two with four children. Four girls. Four daughters, so there's five women in my brother's life. He's the only man in that family who was brought up in a very traditional setting with a mother of the fifties who never went to work. And never had her own cheque book, right? So my sister-in-law covers her head, I can show you a picture later. She was brought up in Montreal. She's Canadian as well. But I don't think that matters. She's a very religious woman. Looks down on my kids. They were not accepted very nicely in my brother's because they're not religious, you see. Anyway it would be an interesting thing to ask her, but I would say in that setting, she's entirely free to do everything. My brother cleans. She doesn't. She doesn't like to, and he's spotless. She has a cleaning lady and my brother. The girls do everything and she goes to work.

Naomi believes that her sister-in-law's judgements of Naomi's children implies a judgmental of Naomi. Naomi's complaint is that she and her family are being judged for not being Jewish enough. Yet, she also criticizes her sister-in-law's mothering skills, suggesting that her sister-in- law is filthy and a terrible housekeeper.

This representation contrasts Naomi's brother, who is spotless (which may be tied to the stereotype of the dirty Jew). Naomi also seems to imply that a good wife for her brother would be a woman like their mother "who never had a chequebook." The comment about her brother having five women in his life might be a disparaging remark implying that her sister-in-law did not produce a son. Although Naomi expressed that Orthodox women's lives are "limited in some way," she finishes her statement by calling attention to how her sister- in-law does what she likes under the cover of being Orthodox, or a good Jew.

Personal wealth has also been an issue that has come up often in my life in subtle and sometimes not so subtle ways. Awareness of the stereotypical connection between Jews and money is almost impossible to avoid. Knowing this, I am careful about how I present myself in the world. For example, I choose my clothing cautiously, especially when I am at the university. Because my family is in the fashion business, I have easy access to fashionable clothing at low costs. However, I am careful not to wear the latest fashion when I go to the university lest I be judged as a "rich Jew." I am careful not to dress in a flamboyant manner, lest I be judged a crass and vulgar Jew.

As a student I rarely invited other students to my home fearing that my house might be judged as too extravagant – too Jewish. I worried about how I dressed my children for school or for synagogue. I did not want to appear too extravagant or too stingy. This behavior has become a habit for me. I know that people make judgements, so it is not something I give much thought to anymore. However, it has recently come into my awareness again because my eighteen year old daughter has been dating a non-Jewish boy. She became exposed to many anti-Semitic remarks, which disturbed her deeply. When my daughter told her boyfriend that she would not tolerate anti-Semitic remarks he and his friends did not understand her concern. It is distressing when a person discovers that she is hated for being Jewish and is stereotyped as the rich and powerful Jew. Jews growing up in Israel would have less chance of confronting this particular money stereotype, at least with non-Jews, because they are surrounded by a Jewish population.

In the Jewish Diaspora one must consciously work at being Jewish, whereas in Israel all one has to do to be Jewish is to live there and of course, serve in the army. To be Jewish in Canada, the perform- ance is demanding and there are many expectations on the actor. Orit professed her love of Israel yet in the next breath, she hesitatingly explained her children – who will grow up not knowing their family in Israel – "can have better lives, better future. I can provide for them more." Then she backtracked, questioning the word "better" which she had used.

> What is it? Is it better that they're more secure? I can see them,
> like in school, they won't struggle as much as they would in
> Israel in terms of even the number of kids. Or the system, or
> other things. And even financial – it's much more.

Then she changed direction. She began to defend the education system in Israel. She said that her children would have it easier in Canada, because the education here is not as advanced as it is in Israel. Describing school in Calgary from a teacher's perspective, she explained:

> It's totally, it's really easier. A lot easier. But in terms of what
> they have here in terms of the class and the number of kids and
> it's easier to control what's happening in the class. And it's –
> although it seems easier, well the results show that in Israel
> they do progress well. But socially, I think, for teachers it's hard-
> er to teach in Israel.

It seems to me this backtrack was motivated by guilt about stating something negative regarding Israel, which would be disloyal. By insisting that life is more difficult in Israel, perhaps she was saying better and stronger Jews live there. Yet she had chosen to have a "better" life in Canada. She did not want to see herself mirrored back as a Canadian Jew. Was she berating herself for being weak? Perhaps she thought I was judging her. In any case, it was unclear as to whom or what was "better."

Perhaps with each look in the mirror comes a hope to see oneself as somehow better than the last time viewing. But if the mirror is a metaphor for judgement, then who is doing the judging, and why do we choose to listen to a particular judgement or opinion? We never really know what people see when they look into their private mirrors. For me, it has been important to learn that sometimes people look at each other to mirror back what they need or want to see.

I keep mindful of this idea so that I can avoid being hurt by the disappointment of others if they are using me as their mirror. Similarly, I have to monitor my own tendency of using others to reflect back what I want to see in myself. Unless we can find a way to work at establishing a more open dialogue about these unspoken issues, we will continue to feel alienated from each other as Jews. On a broader level it is important for people of all cultures to search for less distorted images of each other if we want to move forward towards a healthier society.

[1] Kearney, *On Stories.*
[2] Ricoeur, *Onself As Another*, 117.
[3] Kearney, 129.
[4] Kerby, *Narrative and the Self*, 38.
[5] Ibid. 24.
[6] Goffman, *Stigma*, 2.
[7] Kaye/Kantrowitz.
[8] Ibid., 7.
[9] Ibid.
[10] Ibid.
[11] Ibid.
[12] Ibid., 8.
[13] Ibid.
[14] Ibid., 8
[15] Ibid.
[16] Ibid., 9.
[17] Ibid.,9.
[17] Ibid.
[18] Siegal,
[20] Ibid., 41.
[21] Ibid.
[22] Ibid.
[23] Ibid.
[24] Ibid.,42.

[25] Ibid.
[26] Ibid.
[27] Ibid.
[28] Ibid.
[29] Ibid., 11.
[30] Ibid.
[31] Ibid.
[32] Ibid.
[33] Ibid.
[34] Ibid.
[35] Ibid.

Five

Difficult Times: Remaking the Self

The notion of 'making something of oneself' is a continual process throughout life. For instance, when students complete high school they have succeeded in making themselves high school graduates, but in our Western society being a high school graduate is usually not enough to be considered successful. Professor of Philosophy, David Carr, maintains that "the individual's concrete sense of self, which will presumably be different for each individual, is . . . essentially linked to the social past."[1] From Ochberg's view point, "the stories we tell about ourselves are shaped by our personalities and by the intersubjective codes of our communities."[2] Either way, 'making something of oneself' is inextricably connected to the social situation in which one lives. Although we choose and construct the stories we wish to tell, our stories are also constructed by society.

In order to project the self to the world a performance is involved. If we think of ourselves in the many different roles we play in everyday life then imagining this projection is easy. The roles we play in private are not necessarily the same roles we play in public. In the privacy of one's home one can be quiet and contemplative, whereas in an employment or social situation one is expected to me more outgoing. In both private and public spheres it is possible to play different roles as the situation demands. For instance, when I lived alone in Vancouver the roles I played were quite limited. They included the roles of daughter, music teacher, friend, and sister. The number of roles I played was determined by own goals and values within a particular social context. Erving Goffman, a social psychologist, explains that, "society establishes the means of categorizing persons and the compliment of attributes felt to be ordinary and natural for members of each of these categories."[3] There is a constant interplay between what society defines as normal and how we see ourselves in relation to that definition.

Only after I moved to Calgary did I begin to fully understand society's version of an acceptable role for a woman: a mother and wife. When I lived as a single woman I knew that the world was divided into singles and couples, but I did not really understand the social importance of having children. Suddenly, in my new life as wife and mother, I was a not only an acceptable person, but I was extraordinary! All I had to do I was follow the rules.

I found myself becoming a different person even before I made the actual move to Calgary. Many of my friends thought my decision was totally out of character for me, and they really could not understand why I would leave my wonderful, independent life in Vancouver to play what they probably saw as a mundane role in Calgary. Yet at the same time they thought I was doing a remarkable thing becoming a mother to two orphaned children. I have to admit that I enjoyed their approval. I started to read books about blended families and any other book I could find that might shed light on my new life. Unfortunately, there were no guide books I could find that were written specifically for a thirty-year-old, single Jewish woman moving away from her familiar and comfortable life to marry a man she barely knew and become the mother of his brother's orphaned children!

I moved to Calgary in July, 1982; after a short honeymoon in Arizona, Ken and I returned to Vancouver for the Jewish New Year, *Rosh Hashanna*. Sitting with my parents in the synagogue I had attended for years, the full impact of the changes in my life were not yet apparent to me. Although I am not a religious person, I had always attended synagogue with my family on the High Holy Days days. *Yom Kippur* – the day of atonement – is ten days after Rosh Hashanna. By that time we had returned to Calgary so Ken and I attended synagogue there. He was familiar with that particular synagogue because he had attended services everyday – morning and evening – for a year during the mourning period of his brother's death. Thus he knew the Rabbi and several of the regulars. I, of course, barely knew anyone. However, many of the congregants knew who I was and I could hear a swell of whispering "she's the one," when we walked in. After a while the buzz seemed to stop and I paid attention to the service. It was strange to look around and not see any familiar faces. That first year we were invited back to join the children's maternal relatives for the holiday meal. At this point the children were not yet living with us, and they did not attend the evening meal because it was very late in the day. Had they been there I am sure that many eyes would have been watching my interaction with them. The people were extremely warm and welcoming but I felt as though I were on display, and, in fact, I was. I remember feeling relieved that I had worn something appropriate and even more relieved when it was time to go home. Although my situation was completely different than the Israeli women I interviewed, we all faced a similar challenge of moving to a Jewish community which was unfamiliar. We were all facing a new beginning with unknown challenges ahead. Misinterpretation of social cues can result in what Goffman calls stigma:

> As he explains, The term stigma . . . refer[s] to an attribute that is deeply discrediting, but it should be seen that a language of

relationships, not attributes, is really needed. An attribute that stigmatizes one type of possessor can confirm the usualness of another, and therefore is neither creditable nor discreditable as a thing itself. For example, some jobs in America cause holders without the expected college education to conceal this fact; other jobs however can lead the few of their holders who have a higher education to keep this a secret, lest they be marked as failures and outsiders.[4]

This means that in one setting or culture a particular attribute can be seen as a positive symbol but in a different culture the same attribute may be viewed as negative. In the above case, stigma is not the education itself, but rather it is the value to which a particular society attaches to that education. Thus, contextual meaning can make moving from one culture to another confusing. Moreover, one does not need to move to a different country to experience a different value attached to a particular attribute. Within one community attitudes change from group to group. In a group of Orthodox Jews, people may be judged according to the extent to which they keep a *kosher* home. If for some reason a *non-kosher* item made its way into an Orthodox home, the observant Jews living there may feel shamed or discredited. In a group of less observant Jews keeping a kosher home may not be valued at all and the less observant family would not feel any discomfort should that fact become known. When I moved from being a single woman in Vancouver to being a married woman in Calgary I was not fully aware of the system of social rules in place. Extending the metaphor of the mirror, the members of different cultural groups – and even members of the same cultural group – do not look into the same mirror, despite Canada's official policy of multiculturalism. If members of various cultural groups do happen to see themselves in the same mirror, the image reflected back may not be acceptable to them. In other words, Canadians do not necessarily celebrate each other's cultural differences. Israeli Jews who try to mix in with the Canadian Jewish community are not always welcomed, and they may be surprised by the unexpected challenge of trying to fit in to a community that they expected to welcome them.

For me, one of my biggest obstacles was how much growing up I had to do; part of that process was to realize the social rules in place around me. In the past I had given this consideration little thought. In achieving most of my goals I had faced very self-centred challenges. For several years I competed in classical piano competitions and taught piano lessons to support myself, so I was familiar with long hours of dedicated practice and the ability to be patient with struggling students. However, this experience did not prepare me for the kind of diligence needed to be in a committed relationship where I was also responsible for children. I was also not prepared for the sense of loss I would experience. Not only had my physical surrounding changed, but it felt as though my Self was disappearing. In the new situation I no longer had a past to define myself. Luckily, I did not realize any of this until the middle of the actual experience – if I had I might not have made the same choices, which have enriched my life.

In my interviews with the Israeli women I noticed that they seemed much more prepared for real life experience. One of the interview participants, Ilanit, was very clear about her sense of loss when she left Israel. When I asked how her friends reacted to her decision, she responded, "it was hard on everybody, especially on me. On the person that leaves, it's really hard because you leave everybody behind. They leave just one person. I'm leaving everybody." Ilanit came to Canada to attend university and she noticed many differences in the university culture. She noticed a difference in maturity between herself and the Canadian students. As she explained:

> In [Israel] at the university you see grownups. And I'll tell you what I mean by that. In Israel everybody that goes to university, more or less, I would say 80% or 90% of them, after being in the army. Service. So you see, basically in university kids that are in the age of twenty to twenty-one starting university.

In contrast, when she came to university in Canada, she explained:

> I see kids seventeen and eighteen years old and I felt surrounded by kids, basically. They had freshman stuff that I thought was completely silly and I – there were many things that I saw that I really could not believe that I'm in a university. . . . University in Israel was a lot more serious than here. Also people are more mature after they finish the army.

The loss of culture that she was trying to explain was more than just about behavior in university students.

She felt that Canadians were just playing at life, whereas in Israel they did not have that luxury. There was a sense of pride that Israeli youth were stronger and more serious. The difference between the Canadian students and Israeli students was unmistakable for Ilanit. She expressed disbelief that university students could be so immature. In Israel one does army service at the age of eighteen, while Canadians of the same age are more concerned about drinking beer and 'finding themselves.' I tried to imagine myself in the army at age eighteen, or any of my children: the image was laughingly inconceivable. No wonder Canadians seemed very frivolous to her. She continued:

> Here I find people at the age of eighteen going on a trip to "find themselves." That's the new expression that I heard here. I never heard that kind of expression before. Look to find myself. So, some going to school. Some going to find themselves, or anything like that.

The message I heard was that serious people, with real concerns, do not have the time to waste on a journey to 'find themselves.' The implication was that Jews should know who they are. They have a history and a national home. After listening to Ilanit's comments I felt a bit awkward that I was interviewing her as part of the process of "finding myself." I started to realize what an easy and self-indulgent life I had in the past and that by living in Canada in my particular situation I had been given the luxury of being immature for an extended period. It was not until I faced the responsibilities in Calgary that I could see how easy my life had been.

Orit also discussed some of her difficulties adjusting to Canada. She realized that she moved to a place where the social customs were different than in Israel, and she was willing to make some compromises in order to fit in or avoid, what Ochberg refers to as, being "revealed as flawed."[6] However, Orit would rather be viewed in a negative light than compromise what she believed was right. "I'm not going to cover it with anything." A completely different environment provides an opportunity to reconsider what one is making of oneself.

> I really do see myself, or saw myself as a woman of principles, if something really matters to me, but here [Calgary], I am more flexible. If I'm told [at work], "Look, the Canadians . . . like this to be this way. Please." So sometimes I said, "Okay." I came to Canada. This is a different culture. Maybe in this thing I do need to make the adjustment, which is valid. But when something is really important to me and I make it a point that I don't care if it's in Canada, or where ever it is. This is something that I will not deal with differently than I am . . . because I'm saying the truth. I'm not going to cover it with anything.

Orit emphasized that she was not going to change her core values in order to fit into her new life. However, unlike Orit, I had never established my values firmly, so my transplant to Calgary caused me significant turmoil. I was not even sure what my values were.

Orit seemed to have a very strong sense of who she was and who she would continue to be. She possessed a definite identity. I was still searching for myself. Being aware of our own identity over time allows us to discover who we are. It allows us to see ourselves as individual agents rather than as products of social forces and language. The Israeli women I spoke with can continue to choose to have a connection to the self they left in Israel; whereas I no longer felt a connection to the self I left behind.

Judith Butler addresses some of the tensions that exist for women concerning connection to the self. One of the main points of contention between feminism and postmodernism is the issue of a subject with agency and the way in which this affects an "emancipatory politics."[7] As Morny Joy, a feminist scholar in religious studies, explains:

> It has now become something of a commonplace remark that just when it seemed women were discovering what it was to

have a self, to take responsibility for self-definition, to assume some form of autonomy, along came postmodernism and declared that there is no such thing as a self.[8]

Linda Nicholson, also a feminist writer and scholar, explains that Butler forces us, at the very least, to question the use of the authorial 'I' so that we do not "lose sight of how the subject itself is constituted by the very positions it claims to possess."[9] For Butler, the important issue is not the way we define the subject or agency, but rather, to ask "why it is we come to occupy and defend the territory we do, what it promises us, from what it promises to protect us?"[10] While Butler does not deny the possibility that subjects have agency, she envisions a limited form of agency whereby the individual exists in a social situation where one's ability to have autonomy is, in large part, socially circumscribed. She also suggests that "agency belongs to a way of thinking about persons as instrumental actors who confront an external political field."[11] That is to say, the ability to act in the world comes into being when the individual realizes that something is expected of her. If the individual person does not first recognize that she is expected to behave in a specific way then she cannot exercise any choice in the matter.

Butler's image of defending territory works particularly well for the topic at hand. Butler is referring to intellectual territory concerning feminism and agency; however, her thinking can be extended to many kinds of territory, including nationhood and Jewish identity. She insists that it is crucial that women continually question the discourses (including feminist discourse) that impact their lives. Butler's argument can be applied to other situations. The argument for human rights is ongoing in the State of Israel. Still, Butler acknowledges there may be times when it is strategic for some groups to lean on concept-ual foundations. This stance does not rule out negotiation, nor does this strategy dismiss the existence of a Self – at least a Self as it has meaning within a particular discourse. Butler uses the upper case for Self which I interpret as the 'public Self,' the Self that has agency in the world. This is different than the private inner self. It is important for me to consider Butler's arguments because she asks us to consider the ways in which the Self is understood within the context of discourses. In relation to the topic of Jewish identity, the foundations and the universals continue to be contested. Who is a Jew? Who is an Israeli? Who should live in Israel? And how do these questions bear on women and Canadians?

Following Butler's line of thinking, the conflict does not mean that we should stop trying to articulate meaning. Also, using Butler's idea of the subject as it exists within a given discourse, the Jewish subject can also be considered within a particular discourse. This makes it possible to consider the Jewish subject in various Israeli and

Diaspora discourses. By effecting an ongoing and provisional discourse creative ways of naming identity becomes possible.

Butler offers a compromise, explaining that:

When words engage actions or constitute themselves a kind of action, they do this not because they reflect the power of an individual's will or intention, but because they draw upon and re-engage conventions which have gained their power precisely through a *sedimented iterability*. The category of 'intention,' indeed, the notion of the 'doer' will have its place, but this place will no longer be 'behind' the deed as its enabling source.[12]

More simply, Butler does not deny that a subject can have "intention" and she does not get rid of the "doer," the one who performs actions. She proposes that the subject is not "fully" determined by discourse and the "agency" occurs when discourse is interrupted in some way. Once I am aware that I have a part in the discourse then I have the possibility of agency in trying to grasp what it is that I am a part of. For Butler, this coming to awareness can only take place with the "invocation" of discourse.[13] The subject must answer the invocation to attain agency. As Butler explains, "that this is a repeated process, an iterable procedure, is *precisely* the condition for agency within discourse."[14] Butler's ideas concerning the interruption of a discourse could apply to the participants' in my study. After living in Israel within a specific discourse, they had interrupted the discourse by leaving the "Promised Land." Leaving Israel is not part of the Zionist narrative. It is occasions like this where agency arises. However, the subject is still affected by the interrupted discourse and must strive for an understanding of another discourse to achieve the type of agency Butler discusses. In other words, the self is always connected to some discourse and the only agency possible is the degree of awareness of its embeddedness.

Tali was one of the participants who maintained a strong connection to Israel. She felt that Canadians might judge her as being "crazy" because of her Israeli ways.

Sometimes I feel that people feel I'm strange, for some reason. I don't know why. Because I like to do things my way or don't always like to do what everybody else does. That's why maybe I would fit more in Israel. Maybe that's why I'm not – because I was born there, or because I'm Jewish or anything. Maybe because it fits my personality more. So I find that all the people who want to go back, all the girls here that want to go back, have more or less the same personality like me. They need to see people; they need to see things; they need to talk.

Even for Tali, who spent some of her childhood in Calgary, she felt that a significant part of her identity was left behind in Israel while only small fragments of her self were alive in Calgary. Although she knew

Canadians in Calgary from before she returned to Israel, the friends with whom she felt most comfortable with in the present were Israelis.

In a way I reacted in a similar manner to Tali in my choice of friends. I also worried that the new people I met in Calgary would find me very strange. Even my Vancouver friends and family found me a bit strange, but they accepted me. I did not want to be unacceptable in my new home and I was very unsure of myself. I found that in Calgary I met many people who had moved from Winnipeg; I was drawn to these people even though I had not lived there since I was fifteen years old. I even ran into some of the same people I had grown up with in Winnipeg and found a certain comfort in their company. The connection to Winnipeg made me feel that I actually did have an identity before I lived in Calgary. During the early years in Calgary was difficult for me to visit my family and friends in Vancouver. After a trip to Vancouver I would always go through a grieving period when I returned to Calgary. I longed to be the person I used to when I lived in Vancouver. Somehow that woman was more dynamic and interesting than the woman I was becoming in Calgary. My past memories of Vancouver were quite distorted because, in reality, I was not particularly happy when I did live there. I was lonely much of the time and I found the rain oppressive. I often felt desperate in the winter in reaction to the constant downpour and grey skies. It took quite a while before I could even begin to recognize any of the positive attributes of Calgary, in part, because my memories of Vancouver were distorted by nostalgia.

After I moved to Calgary I had to remake myself in order to adjust to the new situation. I did not want my flaws to be revealed, especially now that there were children involved. I felt that I could no longer continue to play the role of the oddball living on the fringe as I did in Vancouver. This was an extremely difficult task for me. At one time I was a very shy person but because my small circle of friends in Vancouver accepted me I did not realize that I was still a very introverted person. I had managed to reach the age of thirty without ever having to speak to a large or even a medium sized group of people. I lived alone for many years and I saw piano students one at a time. I taught the same students for many years and so I was able to avoid speaking with strangers. In a social situation, such as a party, I would usually find one person with whom I thought I might feel comfortable and spoke to that person all evening. Although I could perform on the piano in front of crowds, I never had to speak to the audience or even look at them. It took me a very long time to conquer my fear of speaking in front of groups. Even after living in Calgary for several years, when I was asked to speak to a Jewish women's group about combining work and mothering, I answered "I would rather die." The women who asked thought I was joking, but I did turn down the request.

It is strange that I did not worry more about moving to a new city and I thought things would magically fall into place. Meeting new people was one of the most difficult aspects of the move. In large part, the strain was due to the fact that most of the new people I met, at least in the Jewish community, had definite expectations about me. According to Goffman, "social settings establish the categories of the persons likely to be encountered there."[15] He continues:

> The routines of social intercourse in established settings allow us to deal with anticipated others without special attention or thought. When a stranger comes into our presence, then, first appearances are likely to enable us to anticipate his category and attributes, his "social identity."[16]

I did not really understand or even consider what category of person I was to become. Nor did I give much thought to the fact that I was an "anticipated stranger." Over time I tried to settle in by reintroducing some familiar aspects to my life. Before the children moved in, I had built up a clientele of piano students and set up my studio at home. I also joined an association of music teachers. Teaching piano helped me remember who I was. Even so, I sometimes felt that I was living someone else's life.

During the six month period before the children moved in, while I was carpooling and taking Carie to some lessons, I got to know, very gradually, one of Carie's friends, Emily, who was very shy. This turned out to be a great gift. At least once a week I would have lunch at Emily's house before the ballet class. Emily's mother, Vivian, helped me immensely because she was easy-going and non-judgmental. As it turned out Vivian was also from Vancouver. I had never met her when I'd lived there, but we knew some of the same people. She was an artist and, by spending time with her, my own interest in painting became rekindled. As a young girl my dream had been to become an artist. I attended art school after high school and I loved the time I spent there. Unfortunately, it became clear to me that I would have a very difficult time supporting myself as a painter so I dropped out of art school and was accepted into the music department at university. My friendship with Vivian helped me rediscover part of myself that I had abandoned years before. At her house I did not feel that I was under constant scrutiny. To this day Carie and Emily are still close friends, and we think of Emily's parents, Vivian and Ben, as part of our family.

Loneliness aside, it was easier to live alone than to live in a household. Since I did not have to get along with anyone but myself I considered myself as an amiable person. It was a shock to realize how differently I felt when I lived alone compared to when I lived with other people. I had to learn how to compromise; moreover, I found that, with other people around me on a daily basis, I was not as nice a person as I was when I lived alone. I did not like this new person I was becoming. At first I had to get used to living with my husband. When

Carie and Daniel did finally move in with us, their nanny Linda, who had been with them when their parents were alive, came to live with us as well.

Linda knew much more about the children than I did, and she felt closer to them than I did. She was the perfect nanny. She cooked, cleaned, ironed, sewed, and knew every detail about the children's likes and dislikes. She knew how to calm them if they were upset. She dressed them and groomed them – Carie's hair was always perfectly braided. Most people, including Ken, would say how lucky I was to have Linda, and I knew how fortunate I was. I knew that the situation was also very difficult for her. Her first employers, Robin and Allen, died and then she had to adjust when she moved in with the children to the home of Robin's parents. Then she faced another unfamiliar situation when she moved in with us. I respected her and appreciated her. In fact, I was in awe of her and even a bit intimidated. I felt guilty that I had any negative feelings at all about Linda, but as much as she eased the whole transition for the children, eventually her presence in our home became an obstacle for all of us to bond as a family. Unfortunately it took me much too long to figure this out.

The first year was difficult for all of us. Belle and Al, the children's grandparents, felt a tremendous loss when the children moved in with us even though it was something toward which we had all worked. Neither of them was in good health and taking care of two young children was a huge strain on them. Shortly after the children moved in it was Carie's fifth birthday, April 16, 1983. Belle gave me a list of children and relatives for me to invite for a birthday party. Some of the children's parents chose to stay during the party rather than just drop their children off. For me the performance required to put on a child's birthday party was more difficult than any piano concert I had ever given. It felt like our family and our home was on display. I wanted everything to be perfect even though I was not sure what that would take. The last birthday for five year olds that I had attended was probably my younger brother's party more than twenty years earlier. My mother would have served party sandwiches. We ended up serving hot-dogs and potato chips and, of course, birthday cake. As I found out, five year olds really do not eat much at all. The smallest details still stand out in my mind. One mother phoned just before the party started to say that her son would not be attending. She apologized, saying that her son felt he was too old for this group. I remember feeling quite hurt especially after I had taken the trouble to carefully set each place with party hats and noise makers and had put together loot bags for each child.

Realizing that everything I did would become Carie's memories of her childhood, I felt tremendous pressure to make her memories good ones. We began our own family album with pictures of birthdays, holidays, and even everyday events. It somehow did not feel real unless we had photographs. Although I have no memory of buying a video camera, we must have had one because we have videos of each child's birthday. It was part of my own family tradition to document each occasion with movies and still pictures. My father had used a sixteen millimetre camera complete with bright lighting to record special occasions. He also took thousands of slides. As children, my brothers and I loved to watch the pictures of ourselves. Several years ago I had all the slides and films put on to video so I could continue to watch them. I hoped that my children would also treasure their memories. As it turned out they love to watch these old videos. They also made many of their own videos to document the play dramas they created. We have had endless hours of enjoyment watching their childhood creations.

During that first year I felt as though we were following a script. Nothing seemed to come naturally for me. I felt as though Linda's eyes were always were always on me, judging me. She was probably more concerned with her own problems, but, from my insecure point of view, I felt judged by most people. Ken was a member of s tennis club before I moved to Calgary so he changed his membership to a family member-ship. I had never learned to play tennis but the club also had a regular swimming pool as well as a children's shallow pool. I had been used to going to the beautiful beaches in Vancouver, but in Calgary the swimming pool was the new beach. It made the arid and dusty hot summer more bearable. One day at the pool I was sitting with the mother of one of Carie's school friends. As we baked ourselves in the sun, she decided to fill me in on her complete reproductive history, (although we really did not know each other very well). It seems that she had a great deal of trouble conceiving her child and she had to go through all manner of fertility treatments. After several attempts at in-vitro fertilization, she and her husband were able to have a child. At this point in time I was thirty-two years old. After hearing this story I wondered if I would ever be able to bear children. Up until that point it had not been a pressing issue because I already had two beautiful, healthy children, Carie and Daniel. But after that day I started thinking about the possibility of having another child. When I learned that perhaps this was something I might not be able to accomplish, I suddenly really wanted it and I became worried that perhaps it would not happen easily. That day I went home and discussed it with Ken. He was not in any hurry to enlarge our family at that early stage. I suggested that maybe we should stop using birth control because it could possibly take years for me to become pregnant. By the next month I was pregnant. That was July 1983.

Although I was happy to be pregnant, I really had not expected it to happen so quickly, but in my mind nine months seemed a long way off. I remember a comment that Linda made that felt like a stab in the back. She asked me how I could possibly manage to have a baby when

I could barely look after the two children I had. Until that point I had been able to delude myself into thinking I was doing a pretty good job as a mother but after that day I felt like a failure. I should have realized then that it was time for Linda to move on but I was still very dependent on her. I also knew that most people saw her as a saint and if I complained or fired her I thought I would be seen as in a negative light. However, I knew then that Linda was watching me and tried to be a better parent. I started taking Carie and Daniel with me whenever I went out, but this only served to alienate Linda more.

As my pregnancy progressed I went through a metamorphosis both physically and emotionally. I had always been a bit moody but while I was pregnant if someone even said the word "mother" to me I would begin to weep. And when I was not crying I was laughing. Everything seemed more intense. I had been a heavy smoker and I quit on learning that I was pregnant. I know this seems like the obvious thing to do in today's world but in 1983 a lot of people still smoked. I was such a heavy smoker that when it became clear that Ken and were first becoming serious about our relationship, I said to him, "I'm a smoker and I love smoking. I don't ever intend to quit, so if you can't accept that we'll have to stop seeing each other." He was not a smoker but stayed with me in spite of it. I was truly addicted. I knew I had to quit while I was pregnant but I fully intended to start again when the pregnancy was over. I lasted ten years without a cigarette, although went through a brief relapse around the time of Daniel's Bar Mitzvah. But the first time I quit was before nicotine patches or gum or any smoking cessation aids were readily available. To say I found quitting difficult would be an understatement. I would dream about smoking every night. But my taste buds came alive and eating became an extremely enjoyable experience for me.

While I was a smoker I was quite thin. At a little over five foot one I weighed about 105 pounds and I liked being thin. During my pregnancy I gained over fifty pounds! The strange thing was that it did not bother me. The world seems to love pregnant women. The extra hormones racing through my body somehow gave me the illusion that I was the most beautiful woman in the world; I believed most men were lusting after me and my new ever-growing voluptuous body. My mood was never better than when I was pregnant. Unfortunately I developed a condition called pre-eclampsia also known as toxaemia. My blood pressure went way up and my organs were not functioning properly so I had to be hospitalized. It was good thing that Linda was still there to manage things at home. I actually loved being in the hospital. It felt like a holiday. For three weeks before I gave birth I was on strict bed rest.

In addition to my high blood pressure the baby was breech so my doctor decided that a caesarean section would be the best choice. I was delighted with the idea because the whole idea of a baby coming out of my body seemed unnatural to me. I was terrified about going into labor. When it became too dangerous for me to remain pregnant I was taken into surgery and Sarah was born on March 23, 1984. I was in a daze of bliss (augmented by the injections of Demerol I was given for pain). I stayed in the hospital for at least another week. I remember when Carie and Daniel came to visit they suddenly looked like giants. In fact, the whole world looked different to me after I gave birth. I thought eventually everything would go back to normal until I realized after several months that "normal" would never be the same again. The next month was Carie's sixth birthday and now we had three children.

For the first couple of months I was on top of the world in spite of the pain I felt from the surgery. People came by to visit and they brought gifts for the baby as well as for Carie and Daniel. I was overwhelmed by how nice people were being to me, even people I barely knew. By about the third month Ken and I were almost psychotic from lack of sleep. Sarah had a difficult time learning how to sleep and I could not bear to hear her cry. When she cried, I cried too. In the months before the birth we had attended classes for pregnant couples and in one class the topic of postpartum depression was discussed. I really did not give it much thought at the time. But as I became more and more sleep-deprived I also spent more time crying. Still I did not realize I was depressed. Then about a month later I found myself crying in the shower one morning and thinking about how much I hated everyone except the baby. I wanted to escape. I remember thinking to myself. "Maybe this is what they mean by postpartum depression?" Later that day I fell apart. I remember the tearful call I made to Ken to come home. He must have been horrified when I told him that I needed to leave with Sarah. It really did seem like the only possible solution given the way I was feeling. We both recognized that indeed I had postpartum depression; we contacted a doctor.

During that difficult period, I did not trust anyone, even Ken. Perhaps that was what the Israeli women felt in moving to a new country. How does one know who can trusted? Later when I interviewed the Israeli women, I wondered if the loss they felt leaving their homes and families was similar to what I had experienced as postpartum depression. They were parted from all that was familiar to them in Israel. Some of them gave birth to babies in Canada. I was sorry I had not explored this topic further in my interviews. It is only in looking back that I can see a connection.

With the help of a doctor, Ken and I worked out a plan to reduce my depression. This is not to say that we all lived happily ever after. We had many challenging years ahead. The children and Linda were to move back to their grandparents' house over the summer. I was not very hopeful that this would help but at least it served to calm me down. I felt a great deal of shame about my lack of coping skills and I did not want anyone to know what was going on so I became very isolated except for a couple of very close friends. This occurred long before the advent of call-display, so I was afraid to answer the phone because I did not want to talk to anyone who would judge me as flawed. It was the first time I allowed Sarah out of my sight. Ken would take her to visit with Carie and Daniel. I felt too ashamed to face the children and even more so with Belle, Al, and Linda. I had failed everyone. Being on my own with Sarah during the day was difficult but I also realized during that period that it was definitely time for Linda to move out. I was so much more relaxed without feeling what I perceived as hostility from her. She was probably just as happy to get away from me and to have the children to herself.

During this time period when I was alone with Sarah and all my senses seemed to be heightened, I was able to more fully comprehend and feel the enormity of the tragedy of Robin and Allen's deaths. Giving birth to my own child added a dimension to my understanding that I had never before experienced. I found myself in mourning for Robin and Allen even though I had never met them. I realized the kind of love that Carie and Daniel were entitled to only after I gave birth to Sarah. I knew then that my life would never go back to any semblance of what it was before and that I was no longer the same person. I felt everything more deeply. I began to understand why people I barely knew were being so nice to me. These were people who had known Robin and Allen and who had already felt the huge impact of their deaths. I was only now beginning to come to awareness about the role I had undertaken. Through Sarah's birth I also became a real mother for Carie and Daniel.

At the end of the summer I was ready for the children to move back in and at that time Linda gave us her notice. I panicked at the thought of being without Linda and so we started the process of looking for a new nanny. Although part of me resisted being someone's boss, I did not have the confidence to handle everything on my own. I also wanted to begin teaching again by September. When the children did return I felt like I was getting a second chance.

Through an agency we found a British nanny who was living in England at the time. We started the process of bringing her to Canada. I was quite nervous about having another person in the house but when she did arrive she was experienced enough to put us all at ease. Carla had been trained as a nanny and she did not seem nervous about moving in with us. She was more comfortable with the children than she was with Ken and me. It was clear that she was experienced with babies as well. Sarah was about six months old when Carla arrived. I remember taking umbrage when Carla casually commented that Sarah was very strong-willed. How could she make such a comment about my baby? As it turned out, Carla was right. After a couple of months I trusted Carla enough that Ken and I went away for a short vacation. Up until that point Sarah had never slept for very long. By the time we came back, Carla had managed to get Sarah onto a regular schedule of sleeping and eating. My life really improved after that. I began teaching piano lessons again and Carla was able to manage the children even though I taught right through the dinner hour on some days. I did not feel threatened by Carla as I had with Linda. As time passed I realized how difficult it must have been for Linda. She managed to keep in touch with Carie and Daniel, and their grandparents, for several years. Although she did get married, she died tragically a few years later.

September is usually when the Jewish New Year begins. Because the Jewish calendar is lunar, the actual date changes from year to year, but autumn is always the time for new beginnings. Carie started first grade in September 1984 and Daniel started nursery school. At the time, we had decided to take them out of the Hebrew school. Due to my own insecurities, I was still uncomfortable around many people in the Jewish community, and I did not want to see these same people day after day. Most Jewish children in Calgary attend one of the Hebrew schools, so taking Carie and Daniel out of the Jewish system was frowned upon. At their new school a bus picked them up at our home and brought them home at the end of the day. I did not have to deal with any other parents. I still felt the need to hide from prying eyes.

We attended all the various concerts (including Christmas celebrations) and went to parent-teacher interviews just like the other parents. The new school was also a private school and it seemed that most of the families were very wealthy. After a couple of years I noticed that I was no more at ease with this group than I had been at the Jewish school. During those two years we had tried to fit in Jewish education for the children on weekends at the school connected with the Reform synagogue. Unfortunately classes were held on Sunday mornings and it interfered with our family time. In the end we decided to send Carie and Daniel back to a Jewish day school that was bilingual, Hebrew and English. Carie was now in the third grade so she was behind in her Hebrew skills but after a few months she was at the same level as the other students. We had made an effort to stay in touch with her Jewish friends while she attended the other school, so the transition was not difficult for her. Daniel was a very shy boy and everything in life seemed more difficult for him. The two-year break from the Hebrew school had given me the time to come into my own as a parent so that I did not have the same difficulties relating to other parents. I learned what the limitations were as far as relationships with other mothers. The focus was on the children's relationships with each other rather than on friendships with the parents. I had made other friends unrelated to the parents at the Hebrew school by then and my feelings were not as fragile.

Daniel's classes ended at 11:30 a.m. and Carie's classes ended at 3:30 p.m. So I made two trips a day to pick them up. As I became more relaxed with the whole situation I left Sarah at home with Carla which made everything easier. At pick-up time there were certain groups or pairs of mothers who kept to themselves. I watched them all very closely. I took note of what they wore and what they talked about and I made an effort to talk to those mothers who had children in the same classes as Carie and Daniel. I tried to fit in. There were many groups of Jews represented at the school. There was a group of women who were born in Calgary and had been life-long friends. There were also quite a few families who had moved to Calgary from various Canadian cities, a group of Jews who had emigrated from South Africa, another group who had emigrated from Israel, and then a small group from Russia or other places such as South America. I was not the only one facing new challenges. The various groups did not mix well. I noticed in particular that many of the original Calgarians pretty much ignored anyone new. I was the exception because everyone seemed to know that I was the Goldstein children's new mother and they seemed to be genuinely friendly. Later I realized that many were just curious or they felt the need to "help" me in the form of advice. I found myself drawn to the mothers who had moved the furthest distance from their homes. Although Vancouver was geographically close to Calgary, I felt that life as I had known it was very far away.

In this social situation – mothers waiting to collect their children from school – many people had something in common. There we were, mothers from all over the world, thrown together for a short time each day. All we really had in common was that we sent our children to the same Hebrew school. Although the women were friendly enough, I felt more like an observer than a part of any group. Over time I noticed that some of the groups shifted and different women would become friendly. Often the shifting seemed to be related to the children's choice of friends. There was one group that arrived perfectly 'made-up' every-day, dressed in very expensive clothing. Others were dressed in exercise attire making it clear they were either on their way or had just come from an exercise class. Some women were dressed in what I thought of as house clothes, such as jogging suits or jeans, and they usually wore no make-up. The Israeli women seemed to stick together, often speaking only in Hebrew. I really did not fit very well into any one group. I would always try to chat with someone for those un-comfortable few minutes and usually my choice was based on my children's choice of friends, which seemed to span all the groups. Sometimes women chose to come up to me so I was spared any decisionmaking. Some children were picked up by their nannies or even by cab. There seemed to be an unspoken consensus that those who had hired someone to pick up their children were somehow remiss as mothers.

Another pattern that I noticed was that the Israelis and Russians did not mix well with the Canadians. Again, I was the exception. I made a point of getting to know the women who seemed most out of place. This was probably the first spark that led to my later research. I found it especially interesting that the Canadian women were almost hostile toward the Israeli women. Many Jewish charities focus on sustaining Israel, but when it came to living with Israelis in Canada the good feelings seemed to erode. The presence of Israelis seemed to be threatening for Canadians. It was a cause for confusion. Here we were sending our children to Hebrew school and teaching them to be good Zionists but if Israelis wanted to share the easier lives we enjoyed in Canada, it was too much. We sent our children to a Hebrew school so that they would learn every detail about Israel and Jewish history, but the Israelis were not acceptable unless they stayed in Israel. I would never have gained an awareness of this unspoken attitude if I had not seen it myself.

My suspicions concerning feelings of hostility were later confirmed in my research. As researcher it was difficult, if not impossible, to remain neutral when a participant expressed negative feelings about Canadian Jews. Although I encouraged the participants not to hold back or spare my feelings, hearing their words was much more than simply recording them. I did not anticipate some of the feelings I experienced. When they expressed negative feelings about Canadian Jews, I found myself feeling responsible for their pain. I have noticed when reading the transcripts that there were several times when I changed the subject because of my own discomfort. Some participants expressed anger and even disgust towards Canadian Jews. Several women were unhappy with the way their children were treated at school, particularly at a Jewish school. They expected to be welcomed, at least by the Jewish community, but instead, in some cases, were treated like unwanted outsiders.

Raya, a research participant, commented, "in Calgary, you [are an] immigrant. There is nothing that can change it. A different mentality and different point of view." Then she spoke directly to me. "You think differently, probably. Act differently. I don't know. Maybe you see it in a different way than me because you were born here probably, right? In Canada." At this point in the conversation the only hint of anger was in her tone of voice. She became more animated when she discussed her son who had attended one of the Jewish schools.

> His social life ... was terrible and it's a very long story and probably won't be so interesting, but he had a terrible time in grade four. His grades went down. I couldn't even accept it because he was a very good 126 student. He's very smart but because of his social life and it was so hard on him. He couldn't get concentrated and focused on academics. It was very important for him to make friends and it was very important. He

didn't know just how to do it because each that he tried didn't work. And he was ready to please everybody by making himself feel bad.

She continued with this story for quite a while and it was clear that she was very upset about her son. She was told by the Israeli teachers (in Canada) that her son needed to change his attitude. It seems that the Canadian children were insulting her son and Raya told me that the feeling she got from the teachers was that "they wanted to protect the Canadian kids." She had hoped to hear something more supportive from the Israeli teachers. But instead they said, "you're right, but this is Canada. It's not Israel." At this point she threw her arms up as a gesture meaning what could she do? She had purposely enrolled her son in a Jewish school because she "wanted him to be involved with the Jewish community."

As she explained the situation further the problem became more obvious. Her voice got louder and louder as she told the story. Apparently her son was the "number one student in Hebrew" which was not surprising because he was born in Israel. Other children recognized that he could help them with their work in the Hebrew subjects. Before her son arrived, another (Canadian) boy had been more popular and was at the top of class academically. There were some days when the students in the class marked each other's test papers and on one occasion this particular Canadian boy marked Raya's son's paper. "He gave him zero out of 14!" In fact, all the answers were correct but the marker explained, "I don't understand your handwriting, so for me, it's zero." When her son spoke to the teacher about the low grade, the teacher, looking at the test, said, "I would say it's right but you see it's not Israel, it's Canada, and the handwriting has to be the way that Canadian children can understand it." Raya was appalled at the situation. Being a newcomer, she did not want to make trouble for her son, by complaining to the teacher. The situation worsened and Raya finally confronted the teacher at a parent-teacher interview. She suggested that in the future, the teacher should be the only one who grades the papers. Her son was ostracized by the other students. According to Raya, "every single recess he was looking for the corner where nobody will find him there. He was sitting in the corner and crying." The situation did not improve so she finally took her son out of the Jewish school and enrolled him in a public school. Raya's son was much happier in his new school. As she told her story, I was becoming more and more uncomfortable. I felt somehow responsible for her son's pain. Instead of staying on the same topic I moved on to a different topic, one that was more comfortable for me.

The interview with Raya might have gone very differently had I not changed the subject. My own emotions prevented me from sticking with a topic that was embarrassing for me. Although her tone of voice was no longer agitated, I felt that her anger was directed at me, as a

Jewish Canadian, and I thought that she had good reasons for being angry. Yet, we continued in a polite tone.

Around 1985 my children returned to Hebrew school. At that point I had not even thought about going back to university. It was enough for me just to get through each day. I drove the children to various lessons. Even Sarah attended a "Mom and Tot" swimming class. I was absolutely exhausted by the end of each day. Although our English nanny, Carla, knew how to drive, we made sure she had a few lessons to become accustomed to driving on the right side of the road. Once she became comfortable with driving, Carla would take the children to some of their lessons and even pick up Carie from school on the days that I taught piano. I knew this would open the floodgates of gossip about my mothering abilities, but it was important to me that I continue teaching piano.

By 1985 I was just getting used to my new life. I now thought of Calgary as my home and I did not pine as much for Vancouver. This does not mean that life was easy. Al, the children's grandfather died while I was still pregnant with Sarah. I had become close to him and we all felt a tremendous loss. Also, at some point during that time, Ken's construction company went bankrupt and the bank tried to seize the children's trust fund. I remember changing our telephone message to "I'm sorry we can't come to the phone right now. We're in debtor's prison." My sense of humor helped me get through some of the most difficult times. Ken took a series of different jobs and he was unable to spend as much time at home. We also moved to a different house. The house we were in was in a new district and was beautiful. It was an open style with cathedral ceilings and the latest appliances. However, the open style made it feel like we were all living in one big room which I found difficult with so many people in the household. At this point there were six of us, including Carla. My piano studio was on the main floor and although it had a separate entrance it was difficult for Carla to manage three children especially over the dinner hour. Also, because the house and the area was new, there were very few trees. I found the lack of foliage felt particularly barren after having lived in the lush rain forest of Vancouver. Rather than put money into landscaping, we decided that it would be better to move to an older area with mature trees. We also wanted an older style of house where rooms could be closed off and more privacy was possible. And so we began the search for another home. We also put our own house up for sale.

We looked at many homes before finding one that would work for us. I wanted my piano studio to be in the basement and I wanted that basement to be easily accessible to an outside entrance so that I would not have my students traipsing through the family space. This turned out to be the main difficulty in finding a house. Eventually we found a four-bedroom house that was within walking distance to the Hebrew school. The area was built in the 1960s, which, for Calgary, was considered old. The house was smaller than the one we were in and it was in need of renovation. It still had all the original fixtures as well as the original floor covering and draperies. It was decorated in very dark tones making it feel like a cave. But I could see that it had potential. Although this new house had less square footage than the house we were in, the space was much more usable. Most people thought we were crazy to move from a beautiful new house to an older and smaller house. I have to admit that I did suffer some buyer's remorse. I worried that we had made a big mistake. We had a month to do renovations before the buyers took possession of the house we sold. We basically just painted white over everything, including the wallpaper. We also replaced the light fixtures and installed a neutral color carpet throughout. Over the years we continued renovating room by room. On moving day Belle offered to look after the children. Carla was still with us so she also helped Belle with the children.

By August of 1985 we were in our new home. The children were able to walk to school and we were much closer to the city centre. The area we moved to had once been a Jewish area but most of the Jewish people had moved out to the newer districts. I was able to set up my new piano studio in the basement so I could begin teaching again by September. It was another new year and another new beginning.

I was generally more comfortable in our older new house. It was not as ostentatious as the previous one and having trees made a big difference to me. We were also closer to the city, cutting down on my sense of isolation. Shortly after we moved Ken and I made an official application to adopt Carie and Daniel. Up until that point we were only their legal guardians. It was a rather disconcerting process. We had to prove ourselves all over again. Social workers made home visits. At this point Carie was nine, Daniel was seven, and Sarah was almost two. When Carie and Daniel first moved in with us they called us Uncle Kenny and Aunty Melanie. After a while we had them drop the Uncle and Aunty titles. At that time it was not unusual for children to address their parents and their parents' friends on a first-name basis. I did not feel that I could ask them to call us mommy and daddy at the beginning. I still felt like an interloper and I wanted to spare the grandparents' feelings. Ken was at least a blood relative. But I was a total stranger and I knew it must have been painful for them every time they saw me in their daughter's role.

By the time Sarah was two, she was talking almost fluently. She had no idea that Carie and Daniel were not her natural siblings. Once Sarah began speaking and using the words "mama" and "dada" we felt that in was time to ease Carie and Daniel into referring to us as Mom and Dad. It took a bit of reminding, but they did not object. Several months later, the adoptions came through, which meant that even on their birth certificates we were named as the legal mother and father. Just as things were beginning to settle down into a routine of sorts I started thinking about having another baby. My tendency has always been to do everything in excess, never moderation. If I had not been that way, I would probably have never moved to Calgary in the first place. Ken was, and still is, more level-headed than I am. He was not keen to enlarge our family. But once I got the idea in my head about having another baby I could not let go of it. In my mind it was the perfect way to round out our family. Again, I became pregnant very quickly. Carla had been with us for about two years and she was ready to go back to England. She gave us a few months notice so we could find a replacement. No one could ever replace Carla though. The children loved her. It was very sad when she left, but she kept in touch with us for many years. She sent the children presents for every birthday. She even sent gifts for the baby she had never met.

Although I had pre-eclampsia with my first pregnancy, I was told that it usually only occurs in a first pregnancy. And even though I had a caesarean section with Sarah, women at that time were encouraged to try natural childbirth. There was a whole movement called "Vaginal Birth After Caesarean" (VBAC). Ken and I attended another set of pregnancy classes. I was a bit worried about postpartum depression but not enough to stop me from having another baby. As it turned out, we did not need to use what we learned in class. I became toxic again, this time even more severely and again I was hospitalized. This time I was so ill that that it was necessary for me to go under full anaesthetic rather than remaining conscious during the surgery. I actually preferred being unconscious. When I regained consciousness on December 13, 1986, Ken was holding our new baby daughter, Kylie. This time I was in a lot more pain because I had not been given an epidural injection. However, I recovered much more quickly, in part, because I did not experience the trauma of being cut open while being awake. Natural childbirth was not for me.

Our new nanny, Lorna, was Filipino although she had lived in Canada for a while. She was very good with babies but the older children intimidated her. I remember that I liked her but I do not remember much else about her. Sarah moved into Carie's bedroom which was the largest of the children's bedrooms. Kylie slept with us because I was too tired to get up and feed her. Sarah would also join us on many nights. I actually started teaching again after three months but I was always tired. This time the depression did not strike, at least not then. The reason my memories of that year are not particularly vivid was probably due to my constant tiredness. In fact, the whole decade of the 1980s is a bit hazy in my mind. We looked like a happy family in the photographs we have of that time but it is difficult for me to actually focus on who I was in those pictures.

Sarah started morning preschool classes at the Hebrew school in September of 1987. Daniel would have been in the second grade and Carie in the fourth grade. Sometime during Sarah's third year, we told

her the story of Carie and Daniel's parents. It became necessary at
that point because Carie and Daniel were often invited to the homes of
their maternal relatives and Sarah was not included. She was much
more upset about the death of Robin and Allen than she was about
being excluded from the invitations. Sarah cried for days about the
tragic story. Carie and Daniel were no longer visibly upset and they
were becoming accustomed to their lives in the present. The death of
their parents was ancient history to them. Daniel had no memory of
them at all. Luckily their grandmother Belle kept Robin and Allen's
memories alive. We had their baby books, which had been lovingly
kept by Robin, and Belle had pictures all over her house and told stories about their parents. Ken also had many pictures but the whole
topic was still much too painful for him to talk about.

    Ken was very angry about the way we were treated by some of
Carie and Daniel's maternal relatives. I thought it was rude that they
did not include Sarah and Kylie but part of me was glad that I did not
have to reciprocate. Things were already complicated enough for me.
But I felt it was important for Carie and Daniel to stay in touch with
their extended family. Over the years this situation was the cause of
much distress in our family. As Carie and Daniel grew older it became
awkward and embarrassing for them to leave their younger sisters
behind.

    We were by then a family of six. All of our photographs and
movies had images of four children with Ken and I as the parents. The
pictures and videos helped to "make" us into a real family. It was
almost as if I needed documented proof that this was really my life. It
was reinforced further because the children loved looking at all the
family images. On one level the new baby, Kylie, brought us all closer
together because she belonged to everyone in the family. On another
level life was more difficult because the family dynamics had changed
once again. Looking back I sometimes wonder how we managed to get
through those years. There was always something new happening.

    With each passing year we became more and more entrenched in
the Jewish community. Our names were inscribed in the *Calgary
Jewish Phone Book*. I had become more Jewish than I had ever been
before. Sending the children to the Hebrew school was a key
component of this new reality. The Hebrew school only celebrated
Jewish holidays. In our little world Christmas did not exist, since the
Jewish holidays follow the Hebrew Bible. The dates commemorated
sometimes go back over five thousand years. Some of the holidays
celebrate more recent events such as Israeli independence. Because
the children learned about all of these cultural and religious customs,
we all became more aware of anything related to Judaism. When I was
growing up I only attended Hebrew evening classes after my day at
public school and so it had a much more limited impact on my life. Now
our lives revolved around the Jewish calendar even though I was not

a religious person. All the children's school concerts were related to Jewish experiences. Because they spent half of the day learning Hebrew subjects, their Hebrew language skills far surpassed my own. Outside of school we still lived in a Christian world and followed the Christian calendar. The school did not recognize secular occasions such as Halloween or Valentine's Day but I allowed the children to take part in these non- Jewish festivities. Our closest friends, who were also our neighbors, were Catholic. Our children spent a lot of time going back and forth between the two houses. During the month of Christmas they spent time making gingerbread houses, shortbread cookies. and even decorating a tree at the neighbors' house. I saw these experiences as enriching.

I remember one day when Sarah was only three years old she started asking me questions about the Holy Trinity. She sat in the back in her car seat while I watched her in the rear-view mirror. I guess she had heard about the Trinity in the home of our Catholic friends. I tried to explain the Holy Trinity to her as best I could. Then following my explanation I said, "but Jewish people don't believe that Jesus is the Son of God." She responded, "yeah, well I do!" That was the end of that discussion. I really was not bothered at all. I thought it was actually quite funny that she would assert her opinion so strongly. In any case, overall, our lives were infused with mainly Jewish customs.

Eventually Kylie was old enough to attend Hebrew school, so at one point all four children were at the same school. I think my family in Vancouver was surprised that I had accepted so many Jewish customs. As I mentioned, I kept my distance from the Jewish community when I lived in Vancouver, so they were pleased to see that I had become more connected to a Jewish community and more importantly, that their grandchildren were being raised with Jewish traditions. On top of that Ken was fluent in Yiddish (a combination of German and Hebrew). My parents also spoke Yiddish but usually it was when they wanted to say something that they did not want my brothers and I to understand. Through Ken, I began to speak and understand Yiddish as well.

By the time Kylie was ready for the first grade, I was ready to go back to university. That was in 1992. I was tired of teaching piano lessons or at least the way that I was teaching. I started with non-credit evening courses at the university. During that time I went back to painting. Before I knew it, I had created a new career for myself. People were actually buying my paintings in galleries. Like most other areas of my life I did not understand the meaning of the word moderation. I continued to paint even while I worked at doing a degree at university. It really was not my intention to do a degree but I kept taking courses. Within two years I had completed a Bachelor Degree in Women's Studies. I then thought that I wanted to go to law school. I was still having a difficult time finding a comfortable place for myself.

After I was accepted by a law school I realized that it was not really what I wanted either. However, I did want to continue going to school. I ended up doing a Master's Degree in Women's Studies and then a Ph.D. in Education. I was also hired to teach at the university. Somewhere along the line the painting faded out of my life. I knew I would go back to it some day but something had to give way. It was not just the painting. My relationship with Ken was also suffering as I was always thinking about my schoolwork. I became impatient with the children as well. I found myself wondering why I had the need to push myself so hard. I had an unrelenting urge to make something "better" of myself. But I had lost sight of why I needed improving. Ochberg's description of the "effort that goes into maintaining a positive self image" was taking over my life. Although I was continually learning new things and changing for what I thought was growth and progress, at the same time I was constantly being "unmade" by each new situa-tion. Just as Ochberg claims, one must be constantly alert in order to avoid being "revealed as flawed."[17] It was during my years at graduate school that my interests turned to Jewish identity. I knew there was a link between my constant need to improve myself with my confusion concerning Jewish identity. Since that time I have been on a continuing journey exploring many aspects of memory and identity. I knew that it was time for me to look further into the impact of Zionism on my identity. I had tried to avoid confronting Jewish issues for many years because I had so many conflicting feelings. In the next chapter I will discuss some of the various narratives concerning Zionism.

[1] Carr, 115.
[2] Ochberg, 116.
[3] Goffman, 2.
[4] Ibid., 3.
[5] Ibid.
[6] Ochberg, 116.
[7] Nicholson, 4.
[8] Joy, 35.
[9] Nicholson, 5.
[10] Bulter, 127 (1995a).
[11] Ibid., 46.
[12] Ibid., 134.
[13] Ibid., 135.
[14] Ibid., 135.
[15] Goffman , 2.
[16] Ibid., 2.
[17] Ocheberg, 116.

Six

Conflicting Zionist Narratives in Israel
and the Diaspora

By kindergarten I realized Jews were considered to be different than other people. As I mentioned previously, my parents sent me to public school in the morning and Hebrew school in the afternoon. From the first grade through to the sixth grade, 1956 to 1962, I attended public school full days and Hebrew school in the evening. There was a distinct difference between the two. At public school, the Jewish children who attended Hebrew school seemed almost embarrassed about their afterschool learning activities. The non-Jewish children found the Hebrew writing very strange. Once in a while someone would blurt out a Hebrew word by mistake in public school class and it was always humiliating because it drew attention to our strangeness. We knew we were different; multiculturalism was not even a word yet.

Hebrew school felt more like home than public school. The curriculum consisted of Hebrew language, Jewish history, and Zionism. We wrote to Israeli pen pals as part of nurturing a connection to the people there. Israel, as a new country, needed the support of world Jewry on both a spiritual and financial level, so from an early age we were taught to give money to Israel unquestioningly. In addition to Hebrew school, many of us belonged to Jewish youth groups well into our adolescent years and in the summers we attended Zionist summer camps where we were immersed in a combination of religious and Israeli forms of Judaism. Many of us formed life-long bonds made with the children we met at summer camp. At one summer camp I attended, Camp Herzl, in Wisconsin, we sang three national anthems everyday – those of the United States, Canada, and Israel. There was even a plot of land that we ploughed in an effort to simulate life on a kibbutz. Our connection to Israel and Judaism developed easily while we were singing Israeli songs and enjoying the summer heat.

Being immersed in a Zionist culture at Hebrew school, summer camp, and various Jewish youth groups had a profound effect on me; I became a Zionist without really knowing it. Even though I drifted away from Judaism for a while in my twenties, I married a Jewish man and sent my four children to Hebrew school. I was not sure I was making the right decision for my children, but I did it anyway. I consider myself to be part of the Jewish community in Calgary although I am not particularly active in community events. It was through my children that I was introduced to Israeli women immigrants. Our children would have swimming lessons together at the Jewish Community Centre, so we would often chat while watching the lessons. Our children also attended Hebrew school together. I noticed that the Canadian Jews and Israeli Jews did not mix very well. Over the years I became more and more interested in the differences and connections between us. Later I would learn much more both in my research interviews and on my trips to Israel.

It is only after hearing people's stories that they can be transmitted. Before that happens the stories are untold. They are silent. Like Ricoeur, Guy Widdershoven, also a philosopher, claims that "life has a pre-narrative structure which is changed into a narrative structure by the plot and story told about it."[1] This does not mean that some lives have no meaning, but rather that "life has an implicit meaning, which is made explicit in stories."[2] Along with Ricoeur, Widdershoven asserts that "in the process of emplotment the relatively unclear preunderstanding of daily life is changed into a more lucid literary configuration. Thus the stories told about life change it and give it a more specific form."[3] In other words, one's life is always connected to history and culture or "pre-understanding."[4] Even though the narrated story might be different than the actual past, the telling of one's story is what makes it human. I argue that Zionist narratives prefigure individuals' lives and emplot stories in a particular way. Zionism is one of several narratives intertwined with gender and Jewish identity. While I was interviewing participants in my research and their stories unfolded, my understanding of the people and their stories influenced my life as well as theirs. By telling their stories about a specific time in their lives they presented themselves in a certain manner. The interaction between the interviewer and the participants also becomes part of the story within a particular context.

The collective narrative of Zionism and Jewish identity is a story that is told in many ways. This chapter will look at some of these combinations and the ways in which people and stories become enmeshed. The philosopher, Husserl, suggests that "present and past function together in the perception of time somewhat as do foreground and background in spatial perception."[5] As in a painting, the perception of depth is only possible if an object is seen against a background, or horizon. That is, in order to see the object it must stand out from the background. In this analogy, the present is the object. The present can only be interpreted as the present if it exists within a past history. The "consciousness of the present" can only exist with reference to a background. In Ricoeur's terms, the horizon of the past corresponds to prefiguring. Configuring and refiguring of lives can only unfold in the present with an awareness of "emplotment." I will focus on different versions of the Zionist *mythos* in an effort to make connections between people and their horizons.

Visiting Israel was a must for people in my parents' generation. They wanted to feel that they were an important part of the Zionist narrative. They wanted to see the results of their financial support. My parents went on several trips to Israel. They were disappointed that I was not particularly enthusiastic when they wanted me to look at their photographs from their trips. To me, Israel seemed so far away and unimportant at the time. At the time, the war in Vietnam was in the news and I met many American draft-dodgers in Canada. Their narratives seemed to be much more exciting than anything happening in Israel. Later my feelings changed drastically.

Much later, when I had children of my own, sending them to a Jewish Zionist school was a difficult decision for me. I felt they would only see a narrow version of the world. In Calgary, however, very few Jews attended the public schools. I did not want my children to be the only Jews in the class. In addition, I was not willing to put much effort into teaching them Jewish customs so sending them to a Jewish school relieved me of that task. I had conflicting feelings about my own connection to the Jewish community. I did not want to be defined by the community. I wanted to define myself. Eventually I gave up on that idea when I finally realized I had no control over what other people say or think. When I returned to university in 1993, at the age of forty-two, I struggled with my Jewish identity in almost every paper I wrote. I studied the history of the Holocaust with a morbid fascination. In 1995 I signed onto "March of the Living" which was a tour of the concentration camps that was to culminate in a visit to Israel. My husband had no interest in joining me. As it turned out, not enough people signed up for this particular tour – not everyone's dream vacation – so I ended up taking a different tour that visited Jewish historical sights in Turkey, Israel, and Jordan. This was my gift to myself for completing my undergraduate degree.

In some ways I looked at my trip as a test. Many of my friends had spent several years in Israel and some had moved there permanently. I wanted to find out if my sense of Jewish identity would be affected by going to Israel. The trip did make a difference. The tour originated in Vancouver and was part of a Canadian Jewish fundraising mission that raised money for Israel, and we were treated like royalty. Each day was filled from early morning to late at night with various tours and meetings with diplomats. The fundraising aspect was not my own goal, but it was one of the only tours available in the time period allotted. The tour company wanted to make up for the cancelled tour so they offered me a chance to go on the mission tour. I was required to make a substantial donation to Israel in order to take part. The donation was approximately what the price of the other trip would have been. I was interested to see if I could resist the seduction of Israel that I had heard about from so many people. When the plane landed in Tel Aviv, some people cried tears of joy. When we disembarked, the Israelis who met us held out their arms and greeted us warmly with the words "welcome home." It was difficult to resist. The visit to Israel did have an impact on my Jewish identity. I felt welcome and this was something I had never experienced in Canada in the same way. I stayed on after the tour to spend more time in Israel. When I returned home I wanted to move to Israel but eventually that feeling wore off. The reality was that Israel was a very difficult place to live. The intensity of being in Israel was stimulating, but I was happy to be home in a less stimulating environment. However, the trip changed me. I finally understood the sense of yearning that I had learned about all my life, and I had a glimpse of the harsh realities for those who live there. This was my first visit to Israel.

Faydra Shapiro, a Religious Studies professor at Wilfred Laurier University in Waterloo, Canada, has written several articles on "Israeli Experience" programs and the construction of Jewish identities.[6] She has interviewed young North American, Jews who have taken part in an Israeli Experience program. Specifically she focuses on "*Livnot U'Lehianot*" (to build and be built) – a three month, work-study program designated for Jewish young people in their twenties who have had a weak Jewish background and little Jewish education. It is a well-established program that has been teaching about Israel for more than twenty years. This program, and others like it, seek to instil Jewish, Zionist values in Diaspora youth, and the trip that I took, sponsored by the Jewish Federation, works toward similar ends with adults. For me the experience succeeded in reinforcing my connection to Israel. During my stay in Israel I consciously tried to resist the pull of the history, the culture and the people. But it was irresistible. Everything and everyone felt so alive – so full of energy. It was 1995, and although there is always some form of political unrest in Israel, the violence was not at a peak while I was there. Often we would pass places and the guide would tell us that someone was killed in that spot last week or last month, but I did not fear any imminent danger.

The following descriptions of Zionism only touch the surface of a huge body of literature on this complex topic. The narratives I was exposed to in my youth are a compilation of several versions of Zionism. There are many Zionist narratives and these accounts have changed over time. Zionism existed long before the state of Israel was established in 1948. There were conflicting definitions then, and the connection between Zionism and Jewish identity is still contested. With statehood a new set of narratives emerged and different versions continue to develop as conflicts remain unresolved. The narratives I grew up with were those that were articulated just after the events of the Holocaust and Israeli independence. I am only beginning to understand the ways in which my own identity has been shaped or "emplotted" by Zionism.

Zionist Narratives

Zionism is a topic that is difficult to discuss briefly. Toward that end I will divide Zionist narratives into two specific types. The descriptions that follow provide a very basic sense of the variety of Zionist narratives. The first category sees Israel as a "historical peculiarity" in history. In this category Zionism is referred to as "an aberration," "a case like no others," and "a paragon of nationalist success."[7] The other way of looking at Israel and Zionism suggests that "even if Israel does exhibit some atypical qualities – and it does – this does not justify its exclusion as a case."[8] This point of view places Israel within world history as well as looking at Zionism in the context of world history. My goal here is not to argue for one category or another. Rather, the purpose is to illustrate the complexity of the situation.

Arthur Hertzberg, the historian, leans toward the unique-state narrative, but he also acknowledges other possibilities. He argues that "Zionism exists, and it has had important consequences, but historical theory does not really know what to do with it."[9] He explains that the solution for many historians is to place Zionism "within the milieu of European nationalism in the nineteenth century" which accomplishes its acknowledgment of Zionism "for the sake of completeness."[10] For Hertzberg, Zionism cannot be fit into history in a seamless manner. He attributes this difficulty to the fact that "Zionism cannot be typed, and therefore cannot be easily explained."[11] One of the important differences he points out is that Zionism was different from other "nineteenth century nationalisms." While other types of nationalism "based their struggle for political sovereignty on an already existing national land or language," usually both, Zionism proposed to acquire both of these usual preconditions of national identity by the *elan* of its nationalist will.[12] There was neither an existing national language nor an agreed-upon parcel of land, so the Zionist movement depended on an ideological impetus.

As Hertzberg explains, many historians simplify the task by assigning Zionism "as belonging only to the more parochial stage of the inner history of the Jewish community."[13] That is, some scholars view Zionism as a very narrow slice of Jewish history. However, Hertzberg points out, "for Jewish historians Zionism is . . . one of the pre-eminent facts – for most, it is the crucial issue – of Jewish life in the modern age, and therefore it engages their complete attention."[14] He contends that historians are still debating "how to place it in some larger frame" and he acknowledges that making sense of Zionist discourse is complicated.[15] He makes the point that the "crucial problem of modern Zionist ideology" is "the tension between the inherited messianic concept and the radically new meaning that Zionism, at its most modern was proposing to give it."[16] Although he published this idea in 1959, the tension has not abated. He explains the many versions of Zionism, which often conflict with one another. Hertzberg says that Zionism is:

> The heir of the messianic impulse and emotions of the Jewish tradition, but it is much more than that; it is the most radical attempt in Jewish history to break out of the parochial moulds of Jewish life in order to become part of the general history of man in the modern world.[17]

The attempt, on the part of Zionism, to enter the world scene has always met with difficulties. Hertzberg contends that up until the Jewish Emancipation (1789-1791), during the Enlightenment Era, "the Jew saw himself as part of a holy community, a divine priesthood and the elected of God, in an attitude of waiting for the Messiah."[18] However with Emancipation came the need for a new perspective "in order to make Jewish existence analogous to the categories by which western man has been defining himself."[19] For this reason, he sees modern Zionism as "unprecedented" in the history of the Jews. The infusion of reason and nationalism contributed to the difference in attitude.

Michael Barnett, who sees Israel and Zionism as belonging to world history, claims that "social science and international communities continue to deny Israel historical normalcy because of the belief of Israeli particularism."[20] The very creation, maintenance, and understanding of the Jewish state is viewed as different than other cases.

> Outside history, if part of Zionism was about attempting to give Jews the Jews a new conceptual status, to categorize them so that they would become less strange, then the modern project of comparative social science has helped to reproduce their status as outside history. [21]

Barnett does not put all the responsibility for Israel's 'outside of history' status as "solely a product of imposed isolation by the dominant community."[22] He asserts that "scholars of Israel have also contributed to the sense of Israel's otherness and peculiarity in various ways." [23] Yehezkel Dror, an Israeli scholar, speculates that Israel may benefit from its sense of uniqueness. He prefaces his comments with "the view of Israel as unique does not represent a value judgment, for being unique in and of itself does not necessarily have any sense of moral or any other sense of superiority." [24] He also makes it clear that Israel is not the only unique state. Dror claims that policy planning in Israel benefits from the notion of a unique state. As he explains:

> To lose that sense of uniqueness may propel decline because of external and internal attrition processes, diminished high-energy levels that are needed for long-range survival in the

Middle East, and added decay processes that are very dangerous to Israel's geo-strategic situation.[25]
Although he acknowledges that for Israel to see itself as unique may
require "some degree of self-deception," the future survival of the state
depends on this attitude.[26]

I was heir to the special case version of Zionism. This made sense
when I was growing up because I had not seen any reference to the
Jews or Zionism in textbooks that were used throughout public
elementary school and junior high school. To me this signalled that
Jewish history was somehow in a different category than other
history. The notion of Zionism as a special case in history seemed to fit.
Growing up as a Jew in a non-Jewish society, I felt invisible. The only
time I heard about Jewish history, Israel, and Zionism was in my after-
school Hebrew classes. It felt like a secret. The exceptionality of
Zionism also served to make many Jews feel special, which was
important after the devastation of the Holocaust.

On the other hand there are scholars that try to connect Zionism
to world history. Smith traces the beginnings of modern Zionism to
some of the events happening in both Western and Eastern Europe:

> The future of East European Jewry was decided by the partition
> of Poland that occurred in three stages in 1772, 1793, and 1795.
> Portions of the country went to Russia, Prussia, and Austria. As
> a result, Russian Jewry, heretofore a small community, expand-
> ed significantly and created, in Russian eyes a question they
> had to deal with in a decisive manner. Their response was both
> harsh and contradictory. They attacked Jews for their
> separatism but usually imposed laws forbidding their right to
> participate freely in Russian society unless they converted. In
> 1790 and 1791 they passed laws creating the Pale of Settlement.
> These decrees stipulated that Jews could not live in the major
> Russian cities of the interior.[27]

As Smith also explains the enforced living situation for East European
Jews during the nineteenth century "ensured the continuation of
strong religious and communal bonds."[28] In Western Europe at this
time, Jews were exposed to Enlightenment ideas and their "attachment to tradition was loosening."[29] Smith contends:

> Modern Zionism found its roots among Russian Jews who had
> already broken with communal life in the Pale, many of whom
> had hoped briefly for the opportunity to assimilate into Russian
> society. The bases of these aspirations lay in the modernist
> movement among Russian Jewry called the haskala which arose
> in the 1850s.[30]

Haskala is the Hebrew word for enlightenment and those who accepted the new enlightenment were called *Maskilim*.[31] The members of
this movement were impressed with the "Western European literary
models and the idea of legal equality with the non-Jews that was
occurring there."[32]

Smith continues this account explaining that during this time Tsar Alexander II reigned in Russia and many of the restrictive laws against Jews were relaxed. For instance, Jewish students were permitted to attend the university. However, Alexander II was assassinated in 1881 and the regime of Alexander III was "hostile to modernization and Jewish integration."[33] Smith describes this hostile environment:

> The first series of attacks, or *pogroms*, erupted in 1881 and lasted until 1884. They consisted of assaults on Jewish quarters accompanied by rapes, looting, and some killing . . . . The impact of these pogroms lasts to the present day. They signified to many Jews that Russia would never grant them legal emancipation. The result was the beginning of a vast emigration movement which between 1900 and 1914 saw 1.5 million Jews leave Russia.[34]

My grandparents were part of this wave of migration. I grew up with visions of the pogroms that Smith describes. The lasting impact was a legacy of fear.

Zionist ideas came up in many parts of Europe. It was clear that Jews were not wanted as citizens of any country. Jewish scholars Barbara Swirski and Marilyn P. Safir contend that "the idea of a Jewish state was originally formulated in 1862 in Germany, in a book entitled *Rome and Jerusalem*, written by Moses Hess, a colleague of Karl Marx."[35] They go on to explain that "it was further developed by Leon Pinsker, a Russian Jew, in *Autoemancipation*," published in 1882. Pinsker argued that "the Jews were despised because they had no home of their own" and he concluded "that Jews would be respected only if they acquired a territorial base."[36] Although Pinsker appealed to the Jews of Western Europe, his ideas were also of interest to Eastern Jews. Smolenskin and Lilienblum, two Eastern European Orthodox Jews pursued the idea of a Jewish homeland locating it in Palestine which was at that time part of the Ottoman Empire. As Swirski and Safir continue":

> The idea of Zionism took on concrete political form with the convention of the first Zionist congress in Basel in 1897, by Theodore Herzl. This idea was based on three assumptions: that Jewish identity was essentially national, that assimilation was impossible, and that the liberal world would aid the Jewish people in their efforts at national restoration.[37]

Jews arrived in Palestine in three main waves. The first wave (1882-1903) were Zionists from Eastern Europe who established farming communities. "The second (1904-1914) and third (1919-1923) waves of immigration consisted primarily of socialist Zionists from Russia and Poland."[38] These groups were inspired by the Russian revolution of 1905.

> These men and women created social forms which later became the hallmark of Israel: the kibbutzim and moshavim – the

cooperative farming communities; the Histadrut – National Federation of Hebrew Labor Unions; the Shomer, Haganah and Palmach – prestate military organizations; and the Representative Assembly – the predecessor of the Israeli legislature. These were all Jewish institutions; that is they were created by Jews and for Jews.[39]

Swirski and Safir further explain that "the Zionist movement understood the word "Jewish" not merely as a religious or even national, but also as an ethnic one."[40] Quoting Tzartsur, a Palestinian educator describing the dilemma of Israeli Arabs, Swirski and Safir point out that "in a Jewish Zionist state (as in every other state), the citizen must accept the basic ideology of the state, in order to receive his due, get ahead and realize his civil rights."[41] Zionist ideology continues to be a problem for Arabs in Israel. It is also problematic for many Jews in Israel and in the Diaspora.

The above accounts represent only a small part of the literature on Zionism. My point is to show the lack of consensus concerning the beginnings of Zionism. However, all of these accounts stress the need for Jews to have a national home.

Jewish Diaspora Identity

When Israeli Jews move to Canada, the sense of having their unique status of residence in Israel no longer applies. They arrive in a country where there are different narratives about Jews and Zionism than the ones to which they were accustomed in Israel and which made them a part of Israel. The only Israelis I met in my childhood were those who taught at the Hebrew school I attended. Thinking back to how the classrooms were managed, it is quite likely that they were not trained as teachers. However, they were fluent in Hebrew and we attended Hebrew school in order to learn the language. As I recall, these teachers had little or no fluency in English. They only spoke to us in Hebrew. We knew that they could not understand us if we teased them in English, which meant that we did not treat always them with respect. Only later in life did I consider how difficult their lives must have been. They left the warmth and their sense of belonging in Israel to face the brutal Winnipeg winters. They probably had very little money and were dependent on their earnings from teaching Hebrew. And to make matters worse, they were not treated with respect by the children they taught. Coming to Winnipeg, the Israeli teachers found themselves in the Jewish Diaspora with a very unfamiliar pre-existing narrative.

Morton Weinfeld, a Canadian scholar and specialist in Canadian Jewry, describes the connection between Canadian Jewish identity and Israel in his book *Like Everyone Else . . . But Different* illustrating the extent to which loyalty to Israel permeates Diaspora Jewish communi-

ties. He argues that the Jewish Diaspora is very much different than
other diasporas.

> For many Canadian Jews, Israel is an indispensable element of
> their identity. For some this results from Zionist ideology. For
> others, it flows from a reaction to the Holocaust or admiration of
> Israel's achievements or simply because it is a place where
> many Jews live. Emotions range from blind love to critical sup-
> port, with the exception of fringe anti-Zionists among left-
> wingers and the ultra-orthodox.[42]

He compares the Jewish attachment to the land as similar to
"Hutterite colonies in the West, First Nations reserves and territories,
and the Quebecois attachment to Quebec."[43] However, he qualifies this
comparison by explaining that "none of these examples fully captures
the role of Israel, as state and as territory, in defining Canadian
Jewish identity." Canadian Jewish identity rivals and at times
combines with a connection to Israel that is religious, ethnic, and
cultural.[44]

Weinfeld also discusses what he refers to as Israel's symbolic
connection to Canadian Jews. Again he emphasizes the importance of
Israel to Canadian Jews.

> Israel has both a symbolic and real meaning for Canadian Jews.
> Accordingly, Israel is a holy land – the Holy Land – promised by
> God to the Jewish people. It is not by coincidence that one of key
> moments of the Passover Seder is the call 'Next Year in
> Jerusalem!' . . . The theme of exile, or galut, is also at the core of
> traditional Judaic thought.[45]

Weinfeld's above description of Canadian Jewish identity is also part
of the Jewish Canadian narrative to which I was exposed in my youth.
In this particular narrative, Weinfeld assumes that all Canadian Jews
are Zionists and that all Jews dream of living in Israel at some point
in the future. Weinfeld describes this vision:

> In the second half of the twentieth century, Israel assumed
> mythic, quasi-religious proportions for other reasons. The
> Israeli experiment has been and remains, a source of pride for
> most Jews. In the aftermath of the Holocaust, the success of
> Israel, whether in pioneering, farming, fighting, immigrant
> absorption, or basic economic development, has helped reshape
> the general image of bookish, nerdy Jews. Despite these suc-
> cesses, most Jews still worry about Israel's security and welfare,
> which in turn strengthens the identification. A terrorist bomb in
> Jerusalem is like a bomb on their street.[46]

He contends that Jews feel more "bereaved" when Israelis are killed in
terrorist attacks than when innocent victims in other countries are
killed. At the same time he asserts that the attachment to Israel does
not negate the attachment to Canada. He depicts a universal Jewish
attachment to Israel. I would argue that this is a huge generalization.
He does however, qualify his statements by explaining that "many

Jews . . . worry about the quality of Israeli democracy or Israeli Jewishness and all these worries reinforce the tie to Israel."[47] In other words, whether Jews in the Diaspora have positive or negative opinions and feelings about Israeli politics, they are still emotionally engaged with Israel on some level. However, for many Jews in the Diaspora, the fusion of Judaism with Zionism is problematic. There are also many Jews who choose to detach themselves completely from Judaism and Zionism. There are several areas of conflict concerning Jewish identity in the Diaspora and in Israel and especially the challenges that arise when Israelis leave Israel. It cannot be assumed that all Jewish communities in the Diaspora are homogenous. Each community in each country develops differently depending on such variables as differing host communities, population of the community, countries of origin, and the list goes on.

Canadian scholars, David Taras and Morton Weinfeld point out some of the differences between Canadian Jewry and American Jewry. They explain that "each community has been shaped by and has had to adapt to the forces, rhythms, and patterns of nations which have had substantially different attitudes towards ethnic and religious minorities."[48] Canada, with its official multicultural policies, offers more encouragement "to some degree" for ethnic and religious minorities to "maintain their traditional cultures."[49] According to Taras and Weinfeld, there is "fervent patriotism and a fulsome sense of national mission and destiny" in the United States, and "minorities must convert to American political beliefs."[50] However, the encouragement of cultural minorities "to some degree" is impossible to measure.

The author Rhea Tregebov writes that while growing up in Winnipeg in the 1950s and 1960s, she "experienced a sense of dislocation" and an "absence of roots."[51] Her story resonates with my own.

> The ties with Europe were abruptly cut with my grandparents' immigration near the beginning of the century and their lack of interest in telling stories about the 'bad old days.' Of course any remaining connection was then further eradicated by the Holocaust, into which much of my remaining family vanished.[52]

Although Tregebov felt isolated as a Jew in Canada, she also adds that living in a strong Jewish community in the north end of Winnipeg, in some ways made up for her "sense of being cut off from family history."[53] In contrast however, she explains that "in mainstream society . . . as a Jew, [she] felt invisible."[54] She attributes this, in part, to "the reluctance of the larger society to recognize our minority status by virtue of our so-called invisibility as a minority."[55] She maintains that Jews have long been accustomed to this type of treatment. For Tregebov, there is much more involved. "The invisibility of being Jewish was a product of looking out into the available cultural paradigms and seeing next to nothing that reflected [her] own experience."[56] Even three generations later her Canadian born son asks "where do I come from, Mom?"[57] Tregebov explains her difficulty in answering her child's question "from a sense of not belonging *here*."[58]

Like Tregebov, I remember feeling a sense of dislocation as a child. The first fifteen years of my life were spent in Winnipeg. Weinfeld, in his discussion about Jewish immigration to Canada, explains that "Winnipeg deserves special mention in any discussion of the early Jewish community."[59] He is referring to the time period of 1896 and later when there was a "change in Canadian immigration policy" under Prime Minister Wilfred Laurier which created "more opportunities . . . for Jewish migrants to the West."[60] After Montreal and Toronto, "Winnipeg emerged . . . as the third centre for Canadian Jewry."[61] It was during this time period that my grandparents came to Canada from Russia and Poland. Weinfeld describes the early community:

> Jews there, of Russian origin, were more rooted in Yiddish culture, more progressive in outlook and politics, and more integrated into mainstream social and political life than in Montreal and Toronto . . . . According to Abraham Arnold, Historian of Western Canadian Jewry, there is indeed a 'mystique of western Jewry,' and Winnipeg acquired a reputation as a new Yerushalayim [Jerusalem]. [62]

Jewish culture was and is still very strong in Winnipeg. This community in a large part of my background and I carry it with me. Even though I left Winnipeg thirty-nine years ago, I have maintained friendships with my childhood friends, which in some cases go back as far as nursery school. Perhaps it is the sense of dislocation that contributes to the tenacity of these friendships.

It was my parents who told me about the persecution of Jews that my grandparents experienced in Russia and Poland. I really do not remember my grandparents ever discussing this with me. My father's parents came from Poland and his father died in Canada when my father was only seven years old, leaving my grandmother alone with four children. My father, who died in October of 2003, was an excellent story-teller and described his childhood to me so many times and, in such detail, that his stories feel like an earlier chapter of my own life. His mother never learned to speak English, so all her stories came through my father. Every Sunday when my father took my two younger brothers and myself to visit my grandmother in the north end of Winnipeg, she and my father spoke only in Yiddish. I particularly remember the photographs she had on her walls and in her china cabinet. The ones from the "old country" had a very different look than more recent pictures. They were very dark, sometimes in sepia, and very serious. No one smiled in the photographs. The hardships of life were etched on my grandmother's face both in the photographs and in real life. I knew there had been great suffering just by looking at her. I knew she loved us and wanted a better life for us than her own children had experienced, but at the same time I felt a sense of shame that our lives were so easy by comparison.

Having lived in three Canadian cities I recognize differences between the Jewish communities. To the south, in the United States, Jewish communities are also distinct. Taras and Weinfeld explain that although there are many differences between the American and the Canadian Jewish communities there are also many similarities. "The two communities have been profoundly transformed by the monumental events of contemporary Jewish history: the Holocaust, the emergence of the state of Israel, and the wars and dramatic events of the Middle East conflict."[63] These events have resulted in "a strong identification with Israel" which "has reshaped Jewish life in North America and given North American Jews a new political agenda: advocacy on behalf of Israel."[64] Thus the emigration of Jews from Israel leaves North American Jews in a puzzling position.

Focusing on some of the differences between the attitudes of Canadian and American Jews, Taras and Weinfeld explain:

> They [Canadians] speak more Yiddish or Hebrew, provide their children with more years of Jewish education, are far more likely to identify with religious Orthodoxy and much less likely to identify with Reform, practise a greater number of religious rituals, have lower rates of intermarriage, contribute more generously on a per capita basis to Jewish and Israeli charities, and are more likely to have visited Israel and to express a concern for Israel's welfare.[65]

This chapter by Taras and Weinfeld comparing Canadian and American Jews is written with the aim of examining attitudes towards the state of Israel. It does not however, discuss attitudes towards Israelis who leave Israel.

In "An Overview of the Canadian Jewish Community," Brodbar-Nemzer, Cohen, Reitzes, Shahar, and Tobin point out that "the gaps between Canadian and American Jews are even more striking" in terms of how close they feel to Israel.[66]

> When asked how close they feel to Israel, 42 per cent of Canadian Jews answer in the strongest possible terms ('very close'), roughly double the number of American Jews (22 per cent) who answer in like fashion. Consistent with their higher rates of previous travel to Israel, almost twice as many Canadian as American Jews say they intend to travel to visit Israel within the next three years (44 per cent versus 24 per cent). A large gap also separates the rates at which Canadian and American Jews regard themselves as Zionists (42 per cent versus 25 per cent). Consistent with Zionist ideology, almost as many (35 per cent) feel they can 'live a fuller Jewish life in Israel than in Canada.' (Only about 10 per cent of American Jews have similar views about life in Israel and the United States).[67]

Describing the differences between Canadian and American Jews, they go on to explain that "most indicative of the deep and widespread commitment to Israel among Canadian Jews is that over a fifth (21 per cent) say 'they have seriously considered living in Israel,' as compared with 13 per cent of American Jews."[68] This extensive study of similarities and differences between Canadian and American Jews shows that "not only are Canadian Jews more attached to Israel" but "they also seem to know more about Israel."[69] Continuing this comparison they point out:

> American Jews enjoy a reputation for avid and passionate support for Israel. If so, then the attachment and concern of Canadian Jews must be seen as more avid and more passionate. When compared with American Jews, Canadian Jews were more in touch with Israel and Israelis, more knowledgeable, more involved, more pro- Israel, and more Zionist in many senses of the term.[70]

What is interesting, in addition to the differences between Canadian and American Jews, is the fact that these authors seem to view the differences as some sort of a contest and, Canadians seem to be the winners. Having a strong connection to Israel is viewed in a very positive light by these particular authors.

Brodbar-Nemzer and colleagues also explain that although Canadian and American Jews are different in many ways, they "seem to share many of the same instincts toward the major social divisions within Israel."[71] One of the social divisions being referred to here is the controversy over "who is a Jew?" This question concerns both Israelis and Jews in the Diaspora. As mentioned previously, Israel's Law of Return is still disputed.

The following quotation taken from an interview I conducted with Dafna, a professional Israeli Jewish woman who travels back and forth between Israeli and Canada, begins to explain the many levels of the collective Jewish narrative. She claims that for her, Jewish identity is not a personal issue.

> There are a lot of major cases where the whole history of Israel is involved with the question, "Who is a Jew?" But this has nothing to do with the everyday life of the majority of my generation, and even the generation before me – as I said, I'm fifty-seven so it's not recent – it's not only young people. I mean there is a whole generation which grew up in Israel who were born to people who came in the thirties, even before, even the 'twenties. The question was never a personal question to them – it's part of the political issues which involves life in the country but it's not a personal question at all.

Here, Dafna comments on the complexity of Jewish identity. She prefers to describe Israeli Jewish identity as a political issue rather than a personal issue. As she explains, this question of identity is connected to "the whole history of Israel." I mentioned to her that I found it interesting that one can be Israeli and not be Jewish. She replied, "Of course you can. First of all there are Arab Israelis who are not Jewish." Then I asked her what it would say on that person's passport and she responded, "it will say an Arab, but with an Israeli citizenship." When I asked what her passport said, she explained that the nationality is "Jew." She could tell that I wanted to hear more about this, so she continued. Dafna maintains that the question "who is a Jew?" is a political issue, which does not intrude on everyday life (at least for her own generation and the generation before her). She does not see the issue of Jewish identity in Israel as a "personal question." Rather, "it's part of the political issues which involves life in the country but it's not a personal issue at all."

Yaron Ezrahi, an Israeli writer, discusses his Jewish identity in more personal terms. Describing the difficulty of situating himself within the epic of Jewish history he explains:

> To be born in Tel Aviv in 1940 and turn eight about four weeks before the Declaration of Israel's Independence was to grow up in the shadow of monumental history, to be dwarfed by a narrative stretching between catastrophe and redemption.[72]

Dafna and Ezrahi would have grown up during approximately the same time period in Israel. Although my own background involves a completely different set of circumstances, I still experienced the ambiguity and confusion concerning Jewish identity growing up as a Jew in Canada. The emphasis on particular Jewish narratives is different in the Diaspora than in Israel; however, those raised as Jews learn that they are definitely attached to an enduring saga. I was born in 1951 only three years after Israel's Independence, and only a short time after the end of Word War II and the horrors of the Holocaust. Like Ezrahi, I also felt diminished by the monumental history of the Jews, both the recent past and the history of ancient times. In the context of over five thousand years of history my own life seemed rather insignificant.

Contexts change over time and furthermore, people may forget or be unaware of the context in which they live. It is easier to forget or be unaware if one simply accepts particular narratives without question. There are many varieties of Zionism that appear in different historical contexts. Alvesson and Sköldberg remind us that knowledge is always "historically conditioned."[73] It is the contingent nature of situating oneself in a narrative that renders the "truth" always open to interpretation. The question of truth or fiction is not as important as the need to tell the story.

Even for those Jews who do situate their identities within some part of a collective Jewish narrative there are multiple circumstances and factors that influence individual self-perception. Among the women I interviewed there were a variety of narratives shaped, in part, by differing situations. For instance some of the women are the children of Holocaust survivors who found refuge in Israel after World War II. Some are the descendants of the very early settlers in Palestine in the 1800s. Others have lived in several countries and some have sought refuge in Israel from countries such as Russia, Iran, and Africa.

The horizon, for Jews living in Israel is very different than for those in the Diaspora. Some of the women I spoke with came from families that had lived in Palestine before it became Israel. Understandably, their attachment to the land is very different than mine, since I grew up in Canada. Dafna, who has not made a final decision about moving to Canada, came from a family that had lived in Israel since the early days. When we were discussing the recent pro-liferation of anti-Israel news coverage, she commented:

> It is upsetting, but it's something that you cannot – as an Israeli I can say it's upsetting and I don't agree with it. I mean, there might be a very, let's say, basic problem, the fact that Israel has settlements in the West Bank. That's true and it's a basic problem that should be resolved. On the other hand, the whole issue of the Palestinians becoming a very extreme society which fights through terrorist methods is a very – it is a horrible thing that actually brings it to no – it prevents any road of going to a political solution. I mean, the terrorist attacks are really the ones now that prevent any way of talking between the two sides. But the fact that you have a world opinion which is pro-Palestinian. What can you do about it? I mean there isn't much you can do about it.

Dafna is painfully aware of the problems in Israel, but her commitment to the country is strong. She made no attempt to sugar-coat the difficulties of living in Israel. I was struck by Dafna's sense of certainty about her identity. She said she "would be very glad . . . to go back to the '67 borders." By telling me she was in favor of going back to the 1967 borders, Dafna was letting me know that she could be considered as taking a more liberal stance on the issue, because it would mean the return of some land to the Palestinians. She also discussed a flexible opinion on the settlements which are Jewish communities set up on land that the Palestinians see as their own. "But," she said, "this has nothing to do with the fact that there is an extreme society which is educating their children toward a murderous society. I can't say any other word about it." Throughout the interview it was clear that Dafna felt she belonged in Israel no matter what the political situation was. I envied her strong sense of belonging, but it was clear the situation frustrated her.

It was Dafna's passion about her life in the present that I envied. In North America it is easier to let one day slide into the next without really being present in one's life. As cliché as it is, I have recently noticed that somehow my children grew up, and I am a grandmother!

The time seems to have just disappeared without my awareness. I felt that Dafna and the other Israeli women I spoke with would not experience this loss of time because they described the moments of their lives with such clarity. I felt that something was missing in my life when I listened to their emotion-laden stories. What I experience is more like an absence of feeling. I do not notice this emptiness every-day, but it happens when I am confronted by Israelis or by Diaspora Jews with passionate opinions about Israel. I feel as though I should have passionate ideas. I wonder if my feelings have been dulled by living in a place where everyday life is easier (and perhaps taken for granted).

Some of the participants, who decided to make a permanent move to Canada, still identify themselves as Israelis. When I asked Tali, who had lived in Canada for a short time as a child, whether she considered herself to be Canadian or Israeli, or maybe a combination of both, she answered, "Israeli. I always felt at home in Israel. I always felt best when I was there. I don't know why. That's how I felt." In comparing myself to Tali I have to admit that I do not feel strongly about being a Canadian. That is not to say that I do not appreciate my life here, but rather, I do not feel connected in the same way that Tali describes her link to Israel. If anything, I feel more connection to Israel than to Canada.

My own confusion about Zionism is only one of the pieces in my fractured identity. There are many Zionist narratives in both the Diaspora and in Israel. Aviva Cantor claims that "the Israeli and American Jewish establishments have colluded to keep the majority of Jews in both countries ignorant of one another's real lives."[74] Although Canadian scholars Taras and Weinfeld contend that there are many differences between the Canadian and American Jewish communities Cantor's statement is applicable to both North American Jewish communities.[75] As she further explains:

> The masses of Jews whose support the Zionist movement won in the post-World War II period did not believe America was an Exile. They were concerned only with the practical goal of the attainment of a Jewish State, viewing it as a place of refuge where other Jews – those who were persecuted – would set-tle . . . . For them America was the Promised Land, not Israel.[76]

Thus we have at least two conflicting narratives: Israel is the Promised Land and North America is the Promised Land. As a child growing up in the post-World War II period, I believed both of these narratives. The incongruity of these ideas left me feeling incomplete and confused as a Jew. It felt like a centering part of me was missing. Throughout my life I was warned that Jews are still persecuted in Canada and everywhere else for that matter. Would it not make more sense to move to Israel where Jews would not be persecuted? Where is the Promised Land? Feeling insecure about my Jewish identity was and is a reason for my constant underlying anxiety. There are many questions that I still do not even know how to formulate.

[1] Widdershoven, 5.
[2] Ibid.
[3] Ibid.
[4] Ibid.
[5] Carr, 21
[6] Menkis and Ravvin, 489.
[7] Kook, 196.
[8] Barnett,8.
[9] Hertzberg, 15
[10] Ibid.
[11] Ibid.
[12] Ibid.
[13] Ibid.
[14] Ibid.
[15] Ibid.
[16] Ibid., 17.
[17] Ibid., 20.
[18] Ibid., 21.
[19] Ibid.
[20] Barnett, 16.
[21] Ibid., 17.
[22] Ibid. 13.
[23] Ibid.
[24] Dror, 247.
[25] Ibid., 257.
[26] Ibid.
[27] Smith, 27.
[28] Ibid.
[29] Smith, 27.
[30] Ibid., 28.
[31] Blumberg, 28.
[32] Ibid.
[33] Ibid.
[34] Ibid.
[35] Swirski and Safir,7.
[36] Ibid., 7.
[37] Hertzberg as cited in Swirski and Safir, 8.
[38] Ibid.
[39] Ibid.
[40] Ibid.
[41] Ibid., 9.
[42] Weinfeld, 32.
[43] Ibid.

[44] Ibid., 33.
[45] Ibid.
[46] Ibid., 34.
[47] Ibid.
[48] Taras and Weindfeld, 293.
[49] Ibid.
[50] Ibid.
[51] Trebegov, 292.
[52] Ibid.
[53] Ibid.
[54] Ibid.
[55] Ibid.
[56] Ibid.
[57] Ibid.
[58] Ibid.
[59] Weinfeld, 84.
[60] Ibid.
[61] Ibid.
[62] Ibid.
[63] Taras and Weinfeld, 293.
[64] Ibid., 273.
[65] Ibid., 295.
[66] Brodbar-Nemzer et al, 49.
[67] Ibid., 49.
[68] Ibid.
[69] Ibid.
[70] Ibid.
[71] Ibid.
[72] Ezrahi.
[73] Alvesson and Skolberg, 62.
[74] Cantor, 286.
[75] Taras and Weinfeld
[76] Cantor, 283.

Seven

Gendered Zionism, Individualism, and Collective Narratives

In Judaism there are definite rules for every aspect of one's life. There are rules that instruct how to be a good Jew. There are rules that instruct how to be a Jewish man and a Jewish woman. There is no reason to have questions or gaping holes in one's identity according to Jewish law. There are answers for everything. Yet throughout my life I have been unable or unwilling to simply acquiesce to what is considered to be acceptable. Along with issues of Jewish identity I have also persistently questioned my role as a woman in society. When I interviewed Israeli women I found that very often they view their roles in different ways than Jewish women in North America. They may not have had doubts about roles while living in Israel but moving to Canada placed them in a situation where the rules by which they lived no longer worked. Similarly, the rules were not working for me.

My own story did not follow the rule book. Yes, I got married and had children, but I did not really fit the role I had chosen. My life also did not follow the plot I had imagined for myself and I found it very difficult to reconcile my imagined life with the one I was living. Imagined promises had been broken. I was no longer a happy child dancing Israeli dances in a protected Diaspora Jewish environment. I had trouble even identifying myself as Jewish. One of the disappointments I experienced was my sense of inadequacy in the attempt to be an autonomous person. I came of age during the second wave of feminism and my goals were in large part shaped by the drive to be independent. I did not want to rely on a man. I did not want the same life as my mother. Although I had attempted to be financially self-sufficient, I found that combining work with raising children an impossible task. It did not stop me from trying, but looking back I wish that I could have loosened the reins on my own need to feel self-sufficient. Looking back I realize that I needed to be more flexible, but at the time I did not even understand the meaning of the word. My life did not work out as I had expected, and I felt a connection with Israeli women who had left Israel because their lives also had worked out differently than expected. Jewish identity was also part of refiguring the plot of their lives.

Knowing that feminist ideas are viewed differently in other parts of the world, I was careful about my choice of words when I interviewed the Israeli women for my study. Although I have no problem calling myself a feminist, many women, both Canadian and Israeli, avoid the feminist label. When I ask the students I teach at university if they identify themselves as feminists, many of them are extremely hesitant, including students enrolled in Women's Studies classes. The word feminist seems to have many negative connotations. My students have suggested such words as, "man-hater," "angry," "butch," "ugly," and "self-centred," just to name a few. Since these are some of the images they connect with being a feminist it is understandable that they distance themselves from the label. For Israel women there are added negative connotations.

Swirski and Safir, Israeli scholars, explain that although it is common knowledge that Israel is a Jewish state, "what is less well known is how Israel's definition as 'Jewish' affects the lives of its female citizens."[1] As they explain:

> Living in the Jewish state of Israel involves not only the domination of a particular national and ethnic group, but also that of a particular brand of Judaism, namely Orthodoxy. . . . The movement developed in Western Europe at the beginning of the19th century, in opposition to attempts to introduce into Jewish society changes similar to those occurring in the larger society. . . . In Israel, this reaction is expressed in, among other things, clear separation of the sexes within the religious educational systems and in daily activities: in manner of dress (women wear long-sleeved blouses or dresses, thick stockings, long skirts and wigs), in rejection of radio and television, and in reading only books and newspapers approved by religious leaders.[2]

From this description, life in Israel sounds very different for women than it is in Canada. The everyday lived experience for most Jewish Israeli women is not quite so constrained even though the laws of the country have a religious basis. Dafna, one of the participants in my research, has lived for extended periods in Canada and in Israel. She commented on the everyday reality of living in Israel. Although her comments were not directed to women's lives in particular, she does raise some important points about looking at difference. As she explains, "it would be ridiculous to say that it's the same [in both] countries. It is not. I mean, one is a Middle Eastern country with all the characteristics of the Middle East – with the smells and sights and thinking of the east." She stressed the point that Calgary is a North American, western culture, whereas Israel is a Middle Eastern culture. However, she also explains that even with the extreme differences in culture, when it comes to personal relationships with family and friends, there is not a "major distinction." In other words, on the surface the culture is very different but she claims that she is able to live with the same freedom in Canada as in Israel.

Dafna's middle class status in both countries may be part of the reason she makes no distinctions. Yet, some women's experiences are different. Rahel R. Wasserfall, a Jewish feminist writer, points out:

> It is extremely difficult to untangle Judaism, Feminism and Ethnicity in Israel; those are in fact interactive and linked to each other in more than one way. In regard to Judaism, intense struggles over the meanings of Jewishness leave little room for any other particular category of identification, especially gender.[3]

She argues that "issues pertaining to the definitions of Jewishness may have undermined a commonality based on shared gender."[4] In her article she offers a feminist viewpoint on the complexities of identifying with other women based on being Jewish. In other words, Jewish feminists, especially in Israel, may find it difficult to find common ground with other women because of the political divisions between Jews. She is referring to the conflicts between Ashkenazi Jews and Sephardi Jews. It is not surprising then, that Jewish feminists living in completely different countries would feel a sense of discord.

Galia Golan, a founding member of the Israel Women's Network, explains, in an interview with Kaye/Kantrowitz and Klepfisz, that the Israeli public is particularly resistant to feminism.

> The first reason for resistance to feminism is the myth that has existed in Israel since before the founding of the state: a belief that there wasn't really a problem, that because the country was built on egalitarian, socialist ideology, women were equal.[5]

She points out that there really never was equality. The War of Independence "fortified" the myth of equality because "women did take part." Perhaps this is one of the reasons that Dafna could not articulate differences in the way women may be treated differently in North America than in Israel. She also explains that there were ideals of equality but these ideals were "never realized."[6] I have always thought of women in Israel as stronger and more independent than I am. To me, that meant that they were better feminists. However, that is not necessarily how they see themselves.

The second reason Golan attributes to Israeli resistance to feminism "is the security situation."[7] Because of the constant warfare in Israel there is:

> The feeling that whether there was equality or not, everyone has to pull together and put particularistic demands or grievances to the side, be they women's issues or other issues. As a result, Israel is a very macho society, because of the need for, and therefore the glorification of the army.[8]

Regine Waintrater echoes this idea in an article entitled "Living in a State of Siege." She explains that "war . . . imposes something close to self-censorship on women; they do not feel they have the right to complain, or they do so with a great deal of guilt."[9] Golan also points out that the "nationwide taboo" affects the way women behave among themselves. "Women compete for courage and adulation."[10] The intensity of living in a state of siege complicates all relationships for Israelis. I find this reality impossible to understand since I have grown up in Canada, a peaceful country. Although I have an awareness of anti-Semitism that can never be the same as actually living day to day in a state of siege.

Going back to Golan's discussion of feminism in Israel, she points out that the third reason for public resistance is "the fact that we don't have separation of church and state and the religious establishment has a great deal of power [in Israel]."[11] She continues:

> There are plenty of religious feminists who argue that Judaism does not have to be chauvinistic or anti-feminist, nor does it have to create a situation for inequality. But the more conservative side of orthodoxy dominates here and that side certainly dictates inequality for women and an anti-feminist approach.[12]

Included in this religious domination is that "all family law," including marriage and divorce, is "exclusively in the hands of the religious courts, and "women not being able to be judges or witnesses in the religious courts."[13] Women are discriminated against in ways that are very particular to Israel. These were also points Dafna did not mention. In every day living there are systems of thinking that are taken-for-granted. Having grown up in a country that separates church and state, at least in theory, my assumptions about how life is "supposed" to be is different from those who have grown up in Israel.

Laurence J. Silberstein, an Israeli writer, labels himself as a "post-zionist," using lowercase letters when he refers to zionism and postzionism. In his words, "one of the effects of a feminist critique of zionism and Israeli culture has been to problematize the dominant notions of Israeli identity."[14] He discusses some of the feminist writings he sees as being applicable to the discourse on Zionist/Israeli identity. For instance, he refers to the work of Delilah Amir, in a study that "calls into question such taken-for-granted terms as 'Israeli,' 'Israelis,' 'Jew,' and 'Sabra'" because "these terms have the effect of concealing the ethnic, gender, religious, age and class differences within Israeli society."[15] In other words, those terms make inequalities less obvious. Referring back to my interview with Dafna, it is possible that she did not notice any differences because of the effort to conceal them in Israeli society.

What is accepted as collective memory can be also viewed as the outcome of a power struggle.[16] Israeli Jewish collective memory has been shaped for the purpose of creating a "New Hebrew," much different than the image of the weak Jew in the ghetto or in concentration camps. Silberstein contends that "conventional studies of zionism (and postzionism), particularly those written by Israelis, tend to ignore or minimize power relations."[17] In his discussion of Mazpen, a radical Israeli socialist group, he comments on women's oppression:

> As they see it, the condition of women in Israel is a product of secular zionist parties' ongoing support for religious parties. To acquire this support, secular zionist parties are willing to compromise on a number of issues relating to women, such as abortion, marriage, and divorce laws.[18]

Mazpen argues that "the inequality of women in the Israeli economy is a direct product of the zionist program" and that "the status of women in Israel [can] not be significantly changed without changing the zionist framework."[19] However, the women interviewed in my research did not refer to a sense of disempowerment. They see feminism as a Western phenomenon and not relevant to their own lives. The Zionist narratives may be strong enough that women in Israel are unaware of the extent to which they have been disempowered or they simply do not experience the Western feminist definition of disempowerment.

If, as Judith Butler describes, gender is a construction and a performance, then gender is not performed in the same way in different cultures. Although Butler is specifically referring to the idea of gender as a performance, she also speculates the theory of perform-ativity may also apply to the matter of race (and I would include ethnicity), Butler maintains that "no single account of construction will do," meaning that one cannot separate race from gender, and "that these categories always work as background for one another."[20] What I might see as a feminist issue in Canada may not even be seen as a feminist issue in the context of Israeli society. In Israel what is expected and authorized as appropriate female Jewish behavior is different than in the Diaspora.

Summarizing her theory of performativity, Butler emphasizes two main ideas. The first is that "the performativity of gender" is dependent on the "anticipation" of what society expects. The second is that performativity is not a singular act, but a repetition and a ritual, which achieves its effects through its naturalization in the context of a body, understood, in part, as a culturally sustained temporal duration.[21] In other words, what society defines as gender is substituted for the individual's concept of her self. This leads to the idea that there are as many expectations as there are cultures. It is possible to extend this process to the societal production of what it means to be Jewish. Butler makes it clear that "performativity is not a singular act."[22] Rather the expectations become more rigid through repetition. The participants in my research have been exposed to a certain set of expectations in Israel, but when they come to Canada, it is quite likely that they will encounter a different set of expectations about being Jewish and about being a woman. In this way it becomes more obvious that collective narratives have a constitutive effect on those involved.

Silberstein contends that part of the conventional Zionist collective narrative was to masculanize Jews. He cites Michael Gluzman who writes in *Theory and Criticism,* "Gluzman speaks of Herzl's Zionist discourse as being 'to a large extent, a discourse of masculinity, more precisely, of the yearning for masculinity.'"[23] Gluzman, who is from the Hebrew Literature program at Ben Gurion University, writes that a key theme in Herzl's utopian novel, *Altneuland,* is "'the effort to 'cure' the emotional illness of the melancholy and effeminate Jewish male.'"[24] Quoting Gluzman further, Siberstein writes, "this striving of gender polarization has the effect of marginalizing women. In *Altneuland,* 'Zionism is represented as a male idea, while the woman is the one who assists the male in realizing his dreams.'"[25] Herzl, as encoded in *Altneuland* through the masculinity of the Jewish male, promotes an ideology of gender polarization, as ideology that motivates the male to deepen as far as possible the differences between him and the woman.[26]

Although it is well known that women must spend two years in the Israeli army, their service does not include combat. Ezrahi, an Israeli author, describes his feelings when his first child, a girl, was born in 1969.

> I was relieved to learn it was a girl and not a boy. Israeli parents have learned the hard way that girls are safer, more permanent, more reliable presences than boys. One does not feel anxious about a girl's life, watching with apprehension as she approaches the age of eighteen.[27]

When he and his wife attended the ceremonies at the end of their daughter's military training, they found it "almost as cheerful as a graduation ceremony."[28] He describes the ceremonies concluding his son's training as "much grimmer."[29] Combat is a male domain and according to Ezrahi, in a battle situation "his comrades typically cry to him, 'be a man! Do not act like a woman.'"[30] Ezrahi quotes Debbie Weissman in her "Woman's Diary of the Yom Kippur War 1973":

> 'Can a person who hasn't even been in battle say anything meaningful about war? Can a woman.' . . . If a woman cannot say anything meaningful about war, can a woman say anything at all in Israel, a country whose short history can be seen as one prolonged war with only a few interruptions? The voice of history as the narrative of battles, as epic, is of course, not a female voice.[31]

Ezrahi argues that women have a specific role to play in "history as epic." He points out that "women are the mothers of all those boys who fight the wars or the wives or lovers of those men who march onto the battlefield."[32] Furthermore, he explains that "women are the putative reasons we call our army our 'defense forces.'"[33] It is the women who need to be protected.

> Conventionally, the woman is the very symbol of the home over
> which the battle is waged. She is meant to represent vulnerable,
> precious inner spaces of life and family, of intimacy and love –
> the very things that soldiers fight to defend and hope to return
> to.[34]

Even though it is mandatory for women to spend two years in the
army, they are not perceived as the warriors. They are still part of the
private domain even though many Israeli women consider themselves
to be equal because of their participation in the military. Mark Tessler
and Ina Warriner comment on the notion of mutual forces. They
maintain that "Israel has an overriding preoccupation with security"
and that this "reflects . . . the specific history of the Jewish people," as
well as "the particular conditions of the country's present-day situation."[35] They suggest that this combination of circumstances "fosters a
perception among many Jewish Israelis that feminist goals and
perspectives are in conflict with the national interest."[36]

They also imply that in unstable political situations "women's
participation in military or parliamentary activities" seems to hold out
the promise of "a partnership in the community's political struggle."[37]
However, these authors contend that, in this kind of situation, it is
more likely that the "male approach to international conflict" will
dominate.[38] In other words, women may have a sense that the country
is built on mutual interests when the reality is that women are
invited to take part in a male dominated activity. It is possible that for
many women the sense of Israeli equality is based, in part, on the
version that Tessler and Warriner put forward. When I suggested to
Orit, one of the Israeli women in my study, that many Western
feminists think that women in Israel are less liberated than in North
America, she answered:

> They have a problem with themselves. I think it's the same as
> here. Feminists are feminists. They will fight because they need
> to fight for something. The fact of sexual harassment, whatever,
> will exist always because we are different. We are women. If you
> want to use it for something, they will use it. I don't buy that.

Although Orit works full-time and made a point of telling me that her
name was on her mortgage along with her husband's name, wanted no
association with feminism.

Earlier in the interview with Orit, I asked her if she had
considered going back to Israel. She responded:

> It will be difficult to come back for sure. I already talked about
> it to my husband so I think he plans to – first he planned to
> come with me and return after two weeks and I'm staying there.
> I think now he wants to come after and make sure we come on
> the plane, to come back with us.

I must have looked a bit puzzled because she continued:

I said, 'I don't know if I'll come. I had my job waiting for me!' It will definitely be hard, but I know why we're here and how long we need to stay, for sure. So I'll have to make that sacrifice again. We're women. We have to sacrifice.

In coming to Canada or returning to Israeli, Orit felt it was up to the woman to make the sacrifices. I'm not sure if the situation is any better for Canadian women, but at least the topic is up for public discussion.

Orit agreed that there are problems with the Jewish religion as far as women and equality are concerned. At this point the discussion was about the difficulty for married women to obtain a divorce in Israel. Other than that, Orit gave me the impression that Israeli women are much better off. Although I know from what I read that gender equality is problematic in Israel, I got the sense from many of the women I spoke with that they were very sure of themselves. They seemed to exude confidence in what they said and in the tone of their voices. It is difficult to really know how much, if any, of the Western feminist discourse can be applied to women in Israel.

Ricoeur's idea of narrative identity views people as characters in a story as opposed to being separate from their experiences. Rather, "the narrative constructs the identity of the character, what can be called his or her narrative identity, in constructing that of the story told. It is the identity of the story that makes the identity of the character.[39] In this way the narrative and the self become inseparable in the telling of the experiences in the story, which are embedded in discourse. Like Ricoeur, Ochberg suggests that people do not just tell stories about themselves and their experiences "after the fact," rather, "they live out their lives in storied forms." [41, 40] In other words, individuals not only construct the story of who they are, but they are also constructed by the stories. Looking at narrative in this way changes the way in which we interpret the connection between stories and lives. Different questions are raised. First, rather than ask "how do people talk about their lives?" this paradigm asks "how do people perform their lives in storied form?" Second, rather than ask "how are the devices of life storytelling like those of literary narration?" it asks, "how does performing a life accomplish the same work as performing a story?"[42] Ochberg also explains that this way of viewing narratives, the "question emphasizes the consequences rather than the technique of living one's life in a storied form."[43] This way of looking at narratives recognizes that people's lives are in progress. The focus on action also recognizes that individuals have agency and it investigates what the individual is trying to accomplish in her life, rather than only emphasizing what makes an individual act a certain way. The participants in this study have made a major life choice by immigrating to a new country. Some choices are influenced by societal, cultural, and political factors, but the decision to begin a new life in a different country suggests that the women in this study are agents who have "affected the way they fashion themselves."[44] The individual actor always makes an entrance in the middle of an existing and ongoing story. For instance, in the west when a baby girl is born, her bassinet in the hospital is automatically labelled in pink. This is only the very beginning of a prewritten story of clear expectations. In configuring the personal narrative, the individual consciously or unconsciously finds a way to incorporate her connection into the collective prefigured identity. Because of the ambiguity of expectations, many Jews find the process of fitting in a difficult journey.

In previous chapters I have looked at some of conflicting expectations for Jews. The expectations for men and women are also different and are affected by external factors such as culture and history.

Israeli Zionism and Individualism

The pursuit of autonomy through wealth has a different history in Israel than in North America. The attitude towards personal wealth in the founding myths of Israel was ambiguous. A more prevalent ideology valorized the worker. Zeev Sternhell, an Israel scholar, contends that the focus on the worker in Israel's early years deflected attention from the "absence of far-reaching social change" and "of any real aspiration to equality."[45] He asserts that to counter this deficiency "great attention was paid to fostering the laborer's sense of cultural superiority – that is to myths and symbols."[46] Sternhell claims that:

> The labor movement's nationalist ideology set up the manual worker as an ideal to follow, but there was no intention to institute a policy that would change the laborer's standard of living. . . . The supposed cultural superiority of the labourer served as a kind of compensation for his low standard of living.[47]

As Sternhell explains the "ideology of worker's cultural superiority had far-reaching consequences."[48] His theory exposes the ambiguity of attitudes toward personal wealth.

> If the aristocrats in this land of immigration were laborers and not the educated middle classes living in relative comfort or the private farmers of the coastal plain north of Tel Aviv or the landlords in Jerusalem, then from a cultural or national point of view there was no need to seek change.[49]

Sternhell poses a question that challenges the ideology of the "New Hebrew." The consequences of the attachment to this ideology can still be seen today. The state was to always come first – nationalist socialism. If one remains attached to this notion, it is difficult to reconcile the desire to improve one's life by seeking personal wealth.

Sternhell asserts that:

> The doctrine of the worker's cultural superiority provided an excellent basis for building up the political strength of the labor

movement... If it was not the well-paid managers of the Histadrut [a sector of the labor movement in power before Israel was a state with Ben-Gurion as its leader] industrial sector but the construction workers who were the cream of society, the fulfillment of the Zionist dream, and the model for the new Jew growing up on the sands of Tel Aviv, how could one offer the worker's children possibilities of advancement that would lead them astray from physical labor, the true path to the reformation of man, self-realization, and the building of the land?[51]

Sternhell points out the problems with this system of belief. His suggestion provides some clues to the difficulties Israelis face when they migrate to a country where personal gain is openly encouraged.

The fact that the struggle against the bourgeoisie was cultural and not social paved the way for the labor movement's successful strategy for the conquest of power. The struggle in the cultural sphere was accompanied by the usual socioeconomic struggle over wages and work conditions, but the economic battle was waged with great caution; it did not represent a danger to the real status of the propertied class, and it did not attempt to close the widening social gaps.[52]

These disparities still exist today but the ideology has worn thin for those on the bottom rung of the societal ladder. This is one of the reasons that people leave Israel and come to Canada or the United States. They want to better their lives, partly through access to personal wealth.

The ideology of the worker is still in place in that those who stay and work in Israel consider themselves to be loyal citizens. They are improving the economy of the whole country. However, in comparison to Western democracies Israelis have conflicting feelings about pursuing personal wealth. According to Sternhell the reasons for the con-fusion concerning personal wealth and national loyalty go back to pre-state politics and attitudes.

Leaders of the labor movement never had any real objection to private wealth or to social and economic differences. However, they had two demands: on one hand, they expected preference to be given to public capital, that is Histadrut enterprises, from agriculture to industry to banking; on the other hand they firmly insisted that private capital be used to fulfill its task of developing the country and absorbing immigrants.[53]

The focus on settlement and building the country, rather than instituting sweeping social changes, according to Sternhell "greatly facilitated its [pre-state Israel's] relations with the middle classes."[54] In addition, the emphasis on settlement and developing the country "made it economically dependent on the Jewish middle classes of the Diaspora, which provided the money."[55] Sternhell continues:

[Within Palestine] settlement served as a common denominator for the salaried workers of the Histadrut and the middle and

upper-middle classes. Both sides were united in their national
aims, and both presented a common front against the Arab
threat and against the possibility of a blow to the national
interests by the mandatory government.[56]

These issues deflected attention from the need to "devote itself to the
problem of inequality in the cities."[57] The discrepancy among classes
was not the image that the new Hebrews wanted. A more positive
image was the "spirit of sacrifice and the pioneering fervor of the
conquerors of the wilderness, the builders of the roads, and the drain-
ers of the marshes."[58] These were the symbols of pre-state Israel in the
1920s and 1930s and to some extent these are the still the symbols
with which Jews in the Diaspora are familiar.

In Canada, I grew up with the narrative that speaks of Israelis
as "weaponbearing farmers" as the "symbol of the land's conquest"
which required "the economic and moral assistance of the entire
people."[59] These are still the narratives taught to Jewish children in
the Diaspora. For Jewish young adults in the Diaspora, going to Israel
and working on a kibbutz is still a rite of passage. In the Diaspora it is
seen an act leading to autonomy, because the young people leave home
to help build the land of Israel. At the same time it is an act of
communal altruism in the support of the State of Israel and helps to
unify the Jewish Diaspora. Sternhell explains:

> From the beginning, the kibbutz had a special place in the
> Zionist ethos. Agricultural collectives fired the imagination of
> millions of Jews throughout the Diaspora and were a source of
> pride for the Tel Aviv bourgeoisie. . . . This wonderful vanguard,
> which also realized itself in the dream of an egalitarian society,
> was the labor movement's supreme weapon. In its name
> budgets were provided by the Zionist Organization, and in its
> name national funds were collected for the Histadrut's
> enterprises. Agricultural collectives were exhibited with great
> pride to all visitors from abroad, and all of them. Jews and non-
> Jews, socialists and members of the European nobility, were
> thrilled and excited at the sight of the egalitarian utopia coming
> to life in the land of the Bible.[60]

Sternhell further explains that "the egalitarian ideology did not really
succeed in the society as a whole; neither did the kibbutz form of
settlement succeed in imposing its values on the Histadrut society." [61]
The image of Israel I learned about in school is very similar to Faydra
Shapiro's description. She describes the way in which Israel is
presented to North American youth groups. She points out that the
"construction of Israel is highly selective, idealistic and deeply
romantic."[62] This vision promotes the land of Israel as the best place
for Jews to live.[63]

Diasporism

Many Jews in the Diaspora see their relationship with Israel as one of support. It is an obligation which is different than charity. Jews in the Diaspora have created lives for themselves for several generations. Kaye/Kantrowitz explains:

> Although the State of Israel does exist as a homeland for Jews, current politics make *aliyah* (immigration to Israel) anything but a simple choice for many progressive Jews. They remain instead in the diaspora, committed to their respective communities.[64]

She refers to herself as "a secular Jewish feminist committed to the complexities of life in the diaspora" – "Diasporism" to use her term.[65] She explains that, although she is not completely happy with this label, she uses the term in the same way that Zionism, describes a commitment to Jewish nationalism. Her neologism describes a commitment to Jewish life in the Diaspora. She explains that she has invented this word because although "the majority of Jews continue to live outside the Jewish state, there is no name for the ideology of the political choice to do so."[66] This is her attempt to address the derogatory connotation of Diaspora Jews "as pitifully struck in *golus, galut, exile.*"[67] As Kaye/Kantrowitz explains, "Diaspora means dispersion; its premise, we were once a gathered people in the land of Israel, and now we are scattered, an inherently negative condition."[68] She proposes a more favorable opinion of the Diaspora raising some contentious issues:

> What would it mean to conceive of diaspora as the centre of a circle that includes but does not privilege Israel? . . . Diasporism means embracing [a] minority status, which leaves us with some serious questions: Can we embrace the diaspora without accepting oppression? Does minority inevitably mean oppressed? Do we choose to be marginal? Do we choose to transform the meaning of centre and margins? Is this possible?[69]

Kaye/Kantrowitz then goes on to outline what she would like to see as the "Tenets of Diasporism."[70] At the core of her idea of Diasporism is the need to recognize that Jewish identity is "not the bloodline" but is only "culture, history, memory."[71] There is no essentialism in Kaye/Kantrowitz's vision. What is unworkable in this vision is the expectation that Jews can stop identifying with "a victim-privilege of Jewishness."[72] It requires that Jews in the Diaspora separate themselves from the edict "never forget." But how does one forget the victims of anti-Semitism, especially the Holocaust? I recognize that seeing oneself as a victim can be non-productive in moving forward. However, I am not sure that it is possible to remember the past and forget the victimization. A more reasonable goal might focus on past victimization in a way that is more productive. How can we avoid being victims and victimizing others?

As I have mentioned in previous chapters, Zionism was an important component of my education at Hebrew school. Looking back on my Jewish education, when it came to the topic of Zionism, my classmates and I were exposed to many historical accounts. There were many combinations of the narratives described in Chapter Six. For me, the overriding message that came through was that Zionism was the hope for the future of world Jewry and that by having the State of Israel no one could ever send Jews to the gas chambers again. My formal Jewish education and that of many of my peers ended after we became Bar and Bat Mitzvah (coming of age ceremony) at the age of thirteen. The instruction we received about Zionism was not particularly sophisticated or analytical because, in part, it was aimed at young people, and it was intended to be pro-Zionist. In my Jewish c ommunity in Winnipeg, there was really no question that good Jews were also Zionists. As I grew older and began to have questions about Zionism, I realized that in the Jewish community, anything that challenged Zionist ideology was seen as seditious. So I was careful never to bring up these questions. I am still careful. Even as I write this book I am careful. I have become accustomed to living a cautious life. This painstaking guardedness contributes to my ambiguous self.

[1] Swirski and Safir, 7.
[2] Ibid., 7.
[3] Wassserfall, 155.
[4] Ibid.
[5] Golan, 249.
[6] Ibid.
[7] Golan cited in Kaye/ Kantrowitz and Klepfisz, 1986, 250.
[8] Ibid.
[9] Waintrater, 118
[10] Ibid., 119
[11] Golan, 250.
[12] Ibid.
[13] Ibid.
[14] Siberstrein, 192.
[15] Ibid.
[16] Foucault, 1980.
[17] Silberstein, 6.
[18] Ibid., 87.
[19] Ibid.
[20] Butler, 1999, xvi.
[21] Ibid., xv.
[22] Ibid., xv.
[23] Silberstein, 198.
[24] Ibid., 199.

[25] Ibid., 158.

[26] Ibid., 199.

[27] Ezrahi, 247.

[28] Ibid., 247.

[29] Ibid.

[30] Ibid., 242.

[31] Ibid., 235.

[32] Ibid.

[33] Ibid.

[34] Ibid.

[35] Tessler and Warriner, 90.

[36] Ibid.

[37] Ibid., 88.

[38] Ibid.

[39] Ricoeur, 1992, 147-148.

[40] Ochberg, 116.

[41] Ibid.

[42] Ibid., 118.

[43] Ibid.

[44] Ibid., 143.

[45] Sternhell, 88.

[46] Ibid.

[47] Ibid.

[48] Ibid.

[49] Ibid.

[50] Ibid., 194.

[51] Ibid.

[52] Ibid.

[53] Ibid.

[54] Ibid., 40.

[55] Ibid.

[56] Ibid.

[57] Ibid.

[58] Ibid.

[59] Ibid.

[60] Ibid., 40-41.

[61] Ibid., 41.

[62] Shapiro, 236.

[63] Ibid., 238.

[64] Kaye/Kantrowitz, 241.

[65] Ibid.

[66] Ibid., 242.

[67] Ibid.

[68] Ibid., 245.

[69] Ibid., 244.

[70] Ibid., 247.

[71] Ibid.

[72] Ibid., 250.

Eight

Inherited Identity

Just as Jews in the Diaspora share various versions of a collective memory, Jews in Israel live with a different 'official' story, which often conflicts with their lived experience. Yael Zerubavel, in her book *Recovered Roots*, discusses what she refers to as "the dynamics of collective remembering" in Israel.[1] She defines collective memory as the ways in which "members of society interpret [historical] events, how the meaning of the past is constructed, and how it is modified over time."[2] In this way collective memory provides "an overall sense of the group's development by offering a system of periodization that imposes a certain order on the past."[3] Past events are thus connected with the present and the group reconstructs its own history from a current ideological stance and by "drawing upon selective criteria, collective memory divides the past into major stages, reducing complex historical events to basic plot structures."[4] Jewish collective memory provides the plot structures of the *mythos* of a long and complex history. Describing the Zionist narrative in Israel, Silberstein comments that:

> Conventional studies of Zionism (and postzionism), particularly those written by Israelis, tend to neglect or minimize power relations. Focusing on individual motives and actions, these studies tend to obscure the multiple ways in which power is imbricated in and actualized through zionist practice. A clear indication of the limitations of this approach is its neglect or minimizing effects of Zionism on groups such as Palestinians, diaspora Jews, Jews of Middle Eastern origin, women, and nonzionist Jewish religious groups.[5]

The Zionist reconstruction of Jewish history and collective memory is a "binary model" that "portrays Antiquity as a positive period, contrasted with a highly negative image of Exile."[6] It is not unusual then, that Israelis coming to Canada would already have a negative view of Canadian Jews in exile. As Zerubavel explains, "since the main criterion for this classification is the bond between the Jewish people and their land, the period of Exile is essentially characterized as a lack."[7] She also points out that, "Zionist collective memory . . . constructs Exile as a long, dark period of suffering and persecution" and that "Jewish life in exile constituted a recurrent history of oppression, punctuated by periodic pogroms and expulsions of fragile existence imbued with fear and humiliation."[8] Zerubavel argues that "the period of Exile . . . represents a 'hole' between the two national periods" with "an acute lack of positive characteristics attributed to it."[9] This image of Exile is important to construct a new national identity. "This highly negative portrayal of Exile was regarded as a crucial counter model for the construction of a Hebrew national iden-tity and therefore raised as central themes in the education of the New Hebrew youth."[10] Zerubavel cites Michael Ish-Shalom in *"Anu Hotrim le-Atid"* (We strive for the future) in *Metsada* (Masada): "Anything that relates to exile, or anything that smells of Exile, should be out of reach of this youth. . . . Exile was portrayed as 'pollution' or 'disease' that might undermine the development of the New Hebrew Man."[11] Although the women I interviewed were born long after this collective memory was constructed, the division between exile and nationhood would have been an integral part of their education and identity.

When I began my interviews with Israeli women I believed that one of the reasons Israelis would leave Israel is so that their children would not have serve in the army. I could not imagine having to actually fight myself, or worse, having to send my own children off to war, so I, mistakenly, thought that Israelis would feel the same way.

Orit had been living in Calgary for about a year when I interviewed her. I did not directly ask her opinion concerning exile and nationhood; however, some of the doubts she expressed about moving to Canada echo Zerubavel's ideas. Orit said, "there are many Israelis who went outside for a year or two, three, to work outside. Although it was perfectly good in many, many, many terms and areas, they decided they wanted their children to grow up in Israel." When I asked her about the army she continued:

> It frightens me, and many people when they hear that I want to go back they say, 'Oh, you want your children to be in the army?' I don't want them to be in the army. I've been in the army. I want them to see there is an army. I want them to be there because they have to! Someone has to do the work.

I thought her next sentence might be, "it certainly won't be you who does the work," exposing my own sense of guilt over what I perceived she was describing as the cowardly, soft life in the Diaspora. She was getting quite worked up at this point. She asked:

> Why is it okay for my friend's son to go and not for my son? As much as I love my son, I would die if he would die. It's a terrible thing when I think of all the parents that lost their kids and husbands and everything. When I read the news on the Internet every day, I cry with everyone and I remember my mother crying for every soldier that got wounded, or whatever. But that's the Israeli reality and as hard as it is, we are, in a way masochists. Do you have this word in English?

At this point in the conversation she was no longer seemed Canadian. She went on:

> People tell me, "you feel very secure here and your kids are well treated and everything is well and you want to go back? Why would you want to do that to yourself? Why do you want a hard life?" I don't know why. I am Israeli. I was brought up that way. We live with this. . . . I felt more secure when I was with my people although I can go on a bus and explode. I don't know how to explain some of the things. But I lived there. That's the reality we're faced with and we're used to. And if we won't be there, who will be? I really feel like I betrayed my country, in a sense. What am I doing here?

From Orit's emotional comments concerning her ambivalence about living in the Diaspora, she is not only angry with Diaspora Jews who do not understand what living in Israel is like.

I asked her if other Israelis made her feel this way, or if her feeling originated internally. This question diffused some of the tension, and she went on in a more subdued tone:

> No. Many people would really encourage you to go because now we talk about concepts and big things but when you live the daily life and you have the hardships and it's hard, you want to better your life. You want to change. You want to do something, and you feel, even, the responsibility. You need to do something to move ahead.

It seemed as though she was reminding herself why she had left Israel, and she continued to talk about the everyday hardships of living there. As part of her inherited identity, Orit is proud of the strength that Israelis must have in order to endure the life there, but, at the same time, she wants to have a better life for herself and her family. She was struggling with contradictory feelings. It was painful to watch and listen to her self-doubt. Not only could I see the conflict she was experiencing, but I also felt a sense of guilt that I had not endured the same hardships of Israelis.

Like Diaspora Jews, Israeli Jews have many issues concerning Jewish identity. Many of the differences I perceived were related to the different collective narratives attached to the Jews. At some point in each interview I asked the women about their lives in Israel before coming to Canada. Their stories told of the narratives into which they had been born – the pre-existing plots.

Efrat, was very clear that she plans to remain in Calgary permanently. At first when I called she said that she was very busy and she would have to call me back. I assumed this was her way of saying she was not interested, but my assumption was wrong. Many of the Israeli women I spoke with complained about the inconsistent behavior of the Calgary Jewish community. They made it clear that if an Israeli person says she will do something, she will follow through. They found that Canadian sometimes say, "we'll get together" as a meaningless, polite gesture. In fact, I was surprised when she did call back a few weeks later to book an appointment on a Sunday, her day off from work with her family. This response led me to believe that she must have something she wanted to talk about. The fact that I was surprised that she contacted me as promised illustrates a difference in expectations concerning social interactions.

I began by gathering some information about her background. Efrat was fifty-three and she was born in Israel. Both her parents were also born in Israel, which is unusual, because Israel did not become an Independent state until 1948. Efrat's family was one of the earlier Jewish settlers before World War I. Her husband was also born is Israel, although his parents came from Lithuania. She has three grown children who were all born is Israel. Her husband came to Calgary in 1990, and the rest of the family followed in 1991, and 1992. Her oldest daughter was still in the army when they moved to Canada. They decided to come to Canada because of her husband's health. They had one friend who had immigrated to Canada several years earlier so they decided to give Canada a try. Their friends were not judgmental about their departure from Israel and they have kept in touch with their Israeli friends. She explained that their parents were very sad when they left, but that no one judged them. She mentioned that her husband's health may have made leaving easier. She also explained that she feels that she is Israeli more than Jewish, even though she is now a Canadian citizen. When I asked her about being connected to the Calgary Jewish community she explained:

> I'm more Israeli than Jewish. I'm not – I feel like I'm not part of the community, you know? And even with my daughter, she has lots of friends but the parents never got . . . We can call them. I can talk to them but there was never a connection over the telephone, you know?

She was very hesitant to say anything derogatory about Canadian Jews, but it was clear that some of her encounters were less than satisfying. She was struggling to explain that it was difficult to become friendly with the Canadian Jewish parents. The relationship only existed over the telephone. She also noticed that her daughter's friends' parents have a different standard of living and she thought that her daughter noticed that she was different than other parents.

> She has friends that on their sixteenth birthday they got a present: a car in the garage. I'm sorry. I wouldn't do it. I'm sorry. Or, they're going for vacation. They have vacations all over the year, I mean all over the world. We don't have the time. It's not the money.

Judging from her beautiful home in a prestigious neighborhood, it was clear that money was not an issue. The tone of her voice told me that she disapproved of the way some Canadian Jews live. When she said,

"I'm sorry," it was not an apology of any kind. This was her way of expressing her disbelief about what goes on in other families, and showing that her Israeli values were important to her.

As I mentioned earlier, my interview with Leora was quite different from the others. She interrogated me before she would agree to meet with me. Unlike the other women, Leora chose to be interviewed in a public place, the Jewish Community Centre. We began by eating lunch in the community centre restaurant. I did not turn on the tape recorder because it was much too noisy. She also seemed to need this time to warm up to the idea of being interviewed. After lunch we found a somewhat quieter spot to conduct the interview, but it was not at all private. People were constantly walking by and they all seemed to know her. She took control of the interview beginning with "My experiences are very unique. First of all my background is very different from your so-called average Israeli." She assumed that I would have a preconceived notion of the average Israeli. I knew by her assertiveness that I was going to have to follow her lead and improvise more than I had in other interviews. I found it quite challenging. When I asked why her background was different she replied, "My family, from my mother's side I'm eighth generation *sabra*" (literal meaning is 'prickly pear' and refers to those born in Israel). Cautiously I commented, "That's a long time." She continued:

> It is a lot. It is a very established family in Israel and they own a lot of land in the Galilee. And on my father's side, my father was an illegal immigrant. He escaped the Holocaust from Czechoslovakia. He was at a med school at the time and he was almost the only one from his family who managed to survive because when Hitler came to Czechoslovakia a few Jewish students managed to get some money and escape. So, I — from my father's side, I'm kind of a child of a survivor and I hardly have family.

She gave me a great deal of information. It was clear that she takes pride in the fact that she comes from a family that has been in Israel before it was even a state. Leora also identified herself as the child of a survivor. Both of these statements explain her connection to the Jewish collective narrative. She then went on to talk about the rest of her family. "I mean, I never knew my aunts and uncles. And on my mother's side, on the other hand, I have so many aunts and uncles and we are so established, and we are so part of Israel." Again she was emphasizing her connection to the collective story – the establishment of Israel. She continued without my asking a question:

> And for my parents, for my mother, especially the idea that I'm leaving Israel and going after my husband. I mean, it was something that she had to get used to. For many years it was a bit difficult for her. I decided to leave everything behind and come and live in a new foreign country. She couldn't understand it.

> They couldn't understand it because my sister and brother are
> so – we are such a closely knitted family.

Leora seemed to be trying to diminish how difficult her leaving was for
her family; she acknowledged her mother's sadness, but she also made
it clear that she experienced difficulty, stressing that she left "everything behind." Leora was beginning her own personal narrative apart
from the epic collective narrative.

Ezrahi argues that Israelis have an underdeveloped sense of self
and that one contributing reasons is that the Israeli national narratives tell the story of a collective and this leaves no space for the
individual narrative. He uses the example of the Israeli calendar to
illustrate the notion of collective time.

> By welding into the annual ceremonial schedule of memorial
> days, holidays, and festivals events of a few thousand years ago
> (the destruction of the Temple, the Exodus for Egypt) and events
> of more recent epic Jewish history (the Holocaust, the creation
> of the state of Israel) the Israeli calendar fuses historical and
> religious time.[13]

With the main focus of society on the collective history and future, the
individual seems insignificant. Ezrahi contends that the "radical
appropriation of time" for collective narratives of history "dwarfs and
marginalizes autobiographical time and renders what has been cast as
public time resistant to its use as a resource of the Israeli self."[14]
Individual identity for Israelis only exists within the national narrative. Following this line of thinking, it does not seem strange that
Leora identifies herself by describing her place in the epic narrative.
Nor does it seem unusual that her family was disturbed by her willing-
ness to change the story.

I asked Leora to reflect on some of the choices she made with her
three grown children. I questioned her about how growing up in Israel
was different than growing up in Canada. Her children all grew up in
Canada, whereas her sister's children grew up in Israel.

> So certain things – a lot of things in Israel, you know, you have
> – like, you don't have the struggle of Jewish school, not Jewish
> education. I mean a lot of things are kind of dictated, you know
> your past, you know what everybody is doing and you send your
> children to the same school that you went, like my sister. Her
> children are all going through the same system and carrying the
> same values. And here we had to start out with a lot of things
> that they are quite foreign to my sister or to my mother, for
> example. And their children are more or less about the same age
> as my children so they grew up completely different because of
> all the different experiences.

Leora echoes what Ezrahi says about education in Israel. The
education system helps to transmit the collective narrative and this in
turn contributes to "emplot" individual lives. Ezrahi refers to Ruth
Firer's examination of history used in the Israeli school system during

the first few decades of Israel's existence in *The Agents of Zionist Education* (1985). Ezrahi is in agreement with Firer's description as it pertains to his own education. Leora, who was fifty at the time of the interview, would have had a similar school experience. Ezrahi points out that Firer's study "indicates the overwhelming influence of collectivist, Zionist notions of Jewish history."[15]

> Their principle theme is the hatred of Gentiles for the Jews as the primary force shaping Jewish history throughout the ages. Only following the Six-Day War does Firer discern a move toward a more pluralistic and interpretive approach to Jewish (as well as world) history, an approach that reflects a greater balance between ethnocentric and cosmopolitan views of the past.[16]

When Leora says "we know our history," I interpreted it as a proud statement about her identity. She was also very clear that religion is part of her identity. Leora would have been in her twenties during the 1967 Six Day War so it is likely that she was influenced by some of the earlier collectivist themes during the time she grew up. If the foundation of one's identity is dependent on a collective narrative, it becomes even more important to remember and integrate that history in a new narrative when starting life in a different country.

Orit describes herself as non-religious even though her grandfather was "a big rabbi" in Iraq, where her family originated. When I asked if she was religious she replied, "no, but I'm more traditional." When I explored this further she explained:

> It means that in Israel, if you're not religious, you're a secular Jew. Then you would not make a point of going to the synagogue. You don't make any blessing, or whatever and you live your life like a normal person in Israel. You go shopping on Shabbat (the Sabbath), you do whatever, but still, you celebrate the holidays. If you're more traditional you do have a Shabbat dinner and you light the candles, and you do the holidays according to what you're supposed to do.

The impression I got from Orit was that she did not follow the religious rules and she did not have a problem with that. She then went on to describe her Jewish life in Calgary. "So now we had to come [up] with our own version. We have to go more to the synagogue and everything, because in Canada you have to make a point of being Jewish to show the kids and everything." In Canada, she and her family have become more observant than they were in Israel. She continued when I asked her if it is different being a Jew in Israel compared with Canada. In Israel, she did not have to make an effort to be a Jew. The state took care of that with the collective narrative. Living in Canada, she has to make a personal choice about how to be a Jew and how to teach her children to be Jewish. As she reinvents her life, configuration is in process. Orit's new narrative is part of her children's inherited identity.

In Israel, Orit did not have to negotiate her way through Christian traditions. She is very much aware that she lives in a Christian country now. She expressed this by talking about her young son when he saw *Hannukah* decorations at the Jewish Community Centre.

> Especially when my son walks into the Jewish Centre and sees all the decorations and said, 'Oh they're having Christmas here!' Because he got confused with Hannuka and everything.' . . . 'Can we decorate our house?' I said, 'No. This is for Christmas. We're Jewish. We're celebrating Hannukah. And in Hannukah we're not going to put any lights outside of our house and every-thing.' And then he walks in and sees decorations in the Jewish Centre and he says, 'Oh they're celebrating Christmas!' When he was three-and-a half. Now he knows. Still he would ask our neighbors, Where are you going for the *seder* (Passover meal)? And he doesn't understand why they don't understand what he's talking about.

Focusing on the way the holiday cycle influences Israelis, Zerubavel explains that "analysis of the ways in which historical events give rise to national myths highlights the intersection of ideological, political, literary, and educational interests in the creation of a national tradition."[17] She argues that a "selective version of history . . . re-inforces cognitive structures shaped by the master commemorative narrative."[18] Although Orit does not articulate it in so many words, she is talking about creating a new personal narrative for her family while she is still under the influence of the Israeli master narrative.

Orit's experience with Christmas symbols highlights Ezrahi's ideas about "state-controlled space."[19] The encounter with Christmas would never have occurred in Israel.

> For Jews, the lines in modern Israel between self and commun-ity or between individual and community do not divide between Jewish and non-Jewish spheres of life: in contrast with Jews in the Diaspora, the issues of private and public spaces appears in modern Israel as a domestic issues, a problem within a form of life directed and shaped by Jews, not a problem in the relations between Jews who leave their community and Jews who stay behind.[20]

After living in Israel, it is not surprising that Orit's son would expect his neighbors to be like him – Jewish. The question about the Passover *seder* would be normal in the Israeli context. As Ezrahi further explains, "for Jews, Israel is the first modern state in which the lines separating private and public spaces do not correspond to the socio-political separation of Jews and non-Jews."[21] In Israel Jews are allowed to be Jewish in public, whereas in the Diaspora, Jews are more likely to express their Jewishness in the private sphere. In Israel almost every aspect of life is part of the collective narrative.

Meshi, age twenty-nine, left most of her family in Israel. Her father was from Italy and her mother from Romania. Her husband's family came to Israel from Poland. Meshi, her husband and her two children were all born in Israel. At the time of the interview she had been in Canada for only a year. When I first contacted her, she did not really think she would have anything of value to contribute. I assured her that I was interested in her story. She agreed to talk to me at her home, but it had to be in the evening, once her children were in bed. I knew she was giving up valuable free time of her own, so I felt quite privileged. When I asked her why she came to Canada, she responded:

> We came for a lot of reasons. I don't know, a few reasons – to try something else, to check it out, the quiet, finance – all kinds of reasons. But the main reason was we're still young, so we're still going to do it, because if we were bigger we wouldn't do it.

I pushed a bit more by asking whether they had been considering this for a long time. Her response surprised me:

> I don't know if we were thinking, but it wasn't a problem leaving. The family, yes. The country, no, although I love it and whatever. It's my country. I always felt like I'm visiting here. But it wasn't a problem. I'm not Zionist. It's like, I want to see a different life – not such stress intense and worried.

She said that family and friends were shocked when she decided to leave Israel. Her friends wished her good luck, but with her family it was more difficult and it continues to be difficult. Her mother came with her to Canada for the first two months to help with the transition.

Meshi made a point of telling me she was not a Zionist but her description of herself said otherwise. She expressed her desire to see a different way of life, but she was also clear that she loves her country, Israel, and that she feels like a visitor in Canada. Meshi made it clear that she is a secular Jew. "I'm very secular. I've got nothing to do with religion." She went on to explain that she did not participate in Judaism or learn about religion until she came to Canada. She explained that the exposure to religion her children are getting in Canada would not have happened in Israel.

> So the first time they see something about religion, it's here. We didn't have it in Israel. We learn the Bible, but not the religion. We go to the main holidays like *Rosh Hashanna* (Jewish New Year) to the synagogue because of the grandfather. . . . But the first time they get religion, they're getting it here. They don't get it in Israel.

When I spoke with Meshi two years later, she made it clear that the choice to have religion existed in Israel, but it was her choice to be secular. Meshi claims she is not religious and she is not a Zionist, yet now that she lives in Canada she is more observant of Jewish customs.

Although Meshi is clear that she is making the choice to include religion in her life, for some Jews the choice is not as simple. Silberstein argues that many Jews all over the world are confused about Jewish identity. As he explains:

> In the pre-state era and in the early decades of Israel's brief life, Zionism provided the dominant language through which Israelis made sense of and rendered meaningful their collective history and identity. . . . For the generations growing to maturity in the period after the establishment of the state, everyday realities increasingly revealed Zionism's inadequacies. Unable to affirm the certainties that grounded previous generation's sense of Israeli history and identity, many Israelis have felt a growing skepticism concerning the historical narratives produced by Zionism.[22]

Meshi's comments revealed that one can be Israeli and at the same time not be a Zionist.

All of the women interviewed mentioned at some point that they knew where they came from. In other words, they knew their family histories as they fit into the Zionist discourse. They were very familiar with the Bible, if not from a religious standpoint, then as historical record. Silberstein contends "we talk and think by means of discursive systems."[23] Jews raised in Israel where Zionism permeates all knowledge cannot avoid being shaped by Zionist discourse. For some Israelis, the only way to find an alternative discourse is to leave Israel.

Meshi's experience with the Jewish holiday cycle is different in Canada than it was in Israel. In Israel the holiday cycle is part of the secular national narrative. In Canada, the celebration of Jewish holidays is confined to religious spaces (synagogue, Hebrew school) or private spaces. Zerubavel argues the Jewish holiday cycle in Israel "functions as *myth plot structures*, moulding the past into certain types of historic texts."[24] The celebration of holidays in Israel is an integral part of the ideology of the society. As she asserts:

> The holiday cycle determines which aspects of the past become more central to collective memory and which are consigned to oblivion: which events are commemorated as highly significant and which are lumped together in a single commemoration, or ignored.[25]

He also points out the ways in which the holiday cycle "has a marker role in shaping our basic views of the past."[26] This is particularly important for children. Orit was quite emotional when she remarked about her son's confusion with *Hannuka* decorations and Christmas decorations. Although confusion about holiday decorations might seem trivial, it is one example of the success of the collective states' myth plot structures:

> Children who are still considered too young for the formal study of history are introduced to the past through holiday

commemorations. Learning about the holidays often occupies an important place in early childhood curriculum. The early intro-duction to the reconstruction of the past through holiday commemorations and their annual repetition therefore have a decisive impact on shaping our primary images of the past.[27]

Zerubavel also contends that the Zionist collective memory tried to connect "antiquity and the modern National Revival."[28] This is not to say that new mythical structures were invented, but rather they were presented in a way to place more positive emphasis on the myth of the "'few against the many,' and subsumed Exile under the plot structure of persecution leading to victimization and death."[29] Explaining further, she contends that the narrative "shifted from the traditional religious framework of attributing historical developments to divine help and punishment to a secular national framework that emphasizes socio-political explanations."[30] The image of the New Hebrew was that of a strong and free individual. Zerubavel argues "preserving the structure of the traditional Jewish cycle, the Zionist Jews sought to counter what they considered to be an exilic overemphasis on the religious dimension of historical holidays, by reviving their national-political significance."[31]

By presenting history in this way "human rather than divine agents take the lead in commemorative accounts of the holidays."[32] This promotes the image of a Jew with agency, rather than a weak Jew who is led to the slaughter. Zerubavel then explains how this works for specific holidays.

> In Hannuka, for example, the Maccabees' success in liberation of their people from foreign oppressors has become the focal point of the celebration, rather than the divine miracle of the flask of oil and the renewal at the Temple. Passover brings forth the paradigm of liberation and national revival, led by Moses and Aaron. And in Purim, the celebration of collective salvation underscores Mordechai's and Esther's resourcefulness in obstructing Haman's vicious plan.[33]

The image of the strong Hebrew, undeterred by enemies is part of the Zionist view. Many Israelis would rather separate themselves from the perception of Jews as "oppressed, submissive, weak, and fearful people who passively accept their fate, hoping to be saved either by God or Gentiles' help."[34] Some of the women interviewed however, did not hesitate to share their exilic pasts with me. Perhaps they felt comfortable knowing that I am also in exile.

Leora was very proud of her Israeli identity. Before moving to Calgary she lived in Quebec. In Israel, students learn English at school, but in Quebec she had to deal with French. She continued discussing language.

> Some Israelis – my husband has a best friend that came with him to Israel. And then he met an Israeli girl and they got

married three months after us. They came back to Montreal and they lived near us and we were very good friends. She was Israeli, my husband knew her for years. Then she decided that she wants to speak English. Her husband knew Hebrew, like my husband. She decided that for her it's more important to kind of, she said, assimilate herself within the Canadian society. So she spoke English to her husband. And she is still speaking English to her children. And this was a conscious decision. And many times she used to tell me, 'You know, you still have this accent,' because during the years she kind of manufactured her own accent which is between both. You can never imitate – you can never speak like Canadians because there is always a point where people feel that you're not a native. Like if somebody speaks Hebrew, it doesn't matter how good. Language proficiency – you always get to a point when you know that he's not a native. He didn't grow up in Israel.

Zerubavel addresses the importance of the Hebrew language to the collective narrative. Yiddish was frowned upon in the new nation. It was considered to be a "hybrid" product of the "rupture from the ancestral land, Zion."[35] According to Zerubavel, "the vision of the modern National revival . . . centered upon three main elements: the Hebrew man, the Land of Israel, and the Hebrew language."[36] She writes:

> Zionist collective memory cast Hebrew as the language of the ancient Israelites who lived in the Land of Israel, which fell out of active daily use during Exile. Hebrew, accordingly, remained the Jewish sacred tongue of prayers and religious studies while other languages took its place in everyday life. As the Jews lost their unified territorial base in Zion, so they lost Hebrew as their unified national language. National revival thus required a return to Hebrew as a means of reconnecting with the hidden national spirit.[37]

Zerubavel points out that one of the several inconsistencies in this narrative is that "Aramaic competed with Hebrew as the language spoken by Jews during the later part of Antiquity."[38] She also argues that "the concept of the 'revival of the Hebrew language' is not accurate, nor is the celebration of the 'rebirth' of modern Hebrew in conjunction with Eliezer Ben-Yehuda's immigration to Palestine in 1881."[39] She contends that:

> The emergence of Hebrew as the primary and official language of the Yishuv [pre-Israel state in Palestine] was ultimately seen as a critical link to the ancient past, as constructed in Zionist memory. For this reason too, the eastern European settlers wished to adapt the Sephardi Hebrew pronunciation which they believed, follows the ancient Hebrew accent.[40]

In this way Hebrew was transformed from a "primarily sacred and literary language to a secular language of everyday use and the official language of the revived Hebrew nation."[41] The new language was a synthesis of both Sephardi and Ashkenazi Hebrew. With the New Hebrew man, the Land, and the Hebrew language, the construction of the collective memory was completed.

In discussing the constitutive nature of language, Schrag points out that "when we speak, we speak a language, and thus we always speak from a language."[42] Schrag claims that we exist within a discourse and that it is within this discourse "that the self is called into being, and it is called into being as the who that is speaking and listening, writing and reading, discursing in a variety of situations and modalities of discourse."[43] He asserts that this version of the self is "implicated in its discourse as a who at the crossroads of speech and language understands itself as a self that has already spoken, is now speaking, and has the power yet to speak, suspended across the temporal dimensions of past present and future."[44] The connection to language becomes more important for those who are not confident of calling themselves into being through language. Because I speak English and have always lived in an English-speaking country, the connection between language and the self is not as obvious as it is for those who must learn a new language. For all of the participants English is a second or third language. Devora's spoken English skills were excellent. She had spent some of her formative years in England. I asked her "at what point in your life did you consider yourself fluent in English?" Her answer surprised me:

> Never. I'm still not and never will be. I'm a non-native speaker and that is always there. Whatever I say, whenever I talk about anything, even if I for a minute forget myself. I hardly ever forget that this is not my first language. A bit of intonation I need to think what the next word might be. Verb conjugation. Preposition. It never, ever goes away. Never. So in that sense of fluency, never.

If she had not told me about her language insecurities, I would never have suspected that it was an issue for her. This is a difficult issue for many immigrants for whom English is not their first language. Although I have travelled extensively outside of Canada, I have never experienced the ongoing everyday frustration that links language and identity. Her language skills seemed to erode some of her confidence in the expectation that she would accomplish all her goals.

The self to whom Schrag refers appears to have a sense of continuity, or at least the perception of continuity over time. As he further explains:

> The self lives through a multiplicity of changing profiles and a plurality of language games in which it holds court, but not without some sense of self-identity – some sense of the same self being present to itself in its remembered past, its engaged present, and its projected future.[45]

This description echoes Ochberg's notion of "making something of one-self." Schrag recognizes the agency involved in "crafting a self" but he also factors in the components of discourse. He stresses that even discriminatory stereotypes that are part of every discourse are included in the way individuals see themselves. In other words, whether or not they have any truth, stereotypes of Jews must be considered in the examination of the making of Jewish self.

A Minority Community Within a Minority Community

As mentioned earlier, there are often negative feelings towards those Israelis who emigrate. In Israel, Jews in the Diaspora are considered to be in Exile.

> The highly negative perception of Exile often turned from *sheililat hagalut* (the repudiation of the state of living in exile) to *shelilat ha-gola* (the condemnation of the people who live in exile), the product of its demeaning and regressive lifestyle.[46]

According to Zerubavel, Israelis are taught from childhood to see themselves as the "New Hebrews," an improvement over the Jews in the Diaspora. Israelis who then decide to live in the Diaspora are likely to have negative feelings about themselves and about the Jews already living in the Diaspora. The Jews in the Diaspora are also aware that these feelings exist. With these layers of unresolved resentment it is difficult for both Canadian and Israeli Jews to make sense of their identities and their relationship to each other. The contradictions continue.

Naomi did not seem to have the same kind of connection to narrative of the "New Hebrew" that some of the other participants expressed. Naomi's family originated in Poland. She has very few remaining relatives because much of her family perished in the Holocaust. She referred to herself as "a second generation Holocaust survivor." Describing her origins she explained:

> I was born in Poland in September of '48, just after the war, and just to point out, my mother had to grab me out of the hospital, although she was haemorrhaging and I was tiny. I was two and one-half kilos, because she was afraid that those Catholic nuns would choke me to death. So she signed her life away, and my life away, and my father and the doctor looked after us and we left for Israel soon after. We left Poland in December when I was three months old. We spent about two months in France in some sort of camp, you know? And then we went to Israel by boat.

This explanation came about five minutes into the interview. She spoke very quickly, trying to squeeze in each moment of her history. At the very beginning of the interview she explained that she met her Canadian husband in Israel and they married in Israel. They moved to Canada because he had a job waiting for him. She told me that she had never visited Canada before moving here, implying that it was not a problem for since she had been a student in England.

> I also had lived in, what we call in Israel, an Anglo-Saxon kind of environment where people speak English. I was a student in England, once before undergrad, and once while I was already in graduate school. So I kind of knew that I could mix in an English-speaking society.

It was important to her that I knew she was different from other Israelis. When I asked if she had ever considered going back to Israel, she said:

> No. Not really. And I didn't have much of a desire necessarily, to go back to Israel because – I don't know, I was brought up – it's a very interesting thing. I never really pursued this myself. But I was brought up European, very much European, I grew up among Europeans, you know, Czechs, Yugoslavs, Polish people. Most of them are very educated – my father was a very edu-cated man. So, what happened was, that when I went to England at age eighteen, I felt quite at home in England. And I really missed England. Had it not been for the Six-Day War, I probably would have stayed in England as a student. I probably would have never left England. It's a very interesting thing.

Naomi wanted me to know that she was European and that this made her distinct from other different Israelis. I interpreted her comment as meaning that she also thought herself to as better than, and not just distinct from, other Isrealis. In contrast however, Zerubavel emphasizes that it was extremely important to the early Zionists, that they separate themselves from European Jews.

> The use of the adjective *ivri* (Hebrew) to reinforce the tie with the ancient past and to dissociate from the concept *yehudi* (Jewish) had appeared prior to the emergence of Zionism as a political ideology. But for the Zionists it was particularly appeal-ing as a way of marking the symbolic discontinuity between the period of Exile and the modern National Revival.[47]

She argues that the New Hebrew was to be seen as better than the "passive, submissive image of the exilic Jew ... the New Hebrew is seen as active, self-reliant, and proud. . . . It was only with the Holocaust that the Zionist commemorative narrative was able to draw a clear boundary indicating the end of exile."[48] She also points out:

> The fate of European Jewry sealed that period of misery and persecution and affirmed that the future belonged to the Zionist national revival in Palestine. It is not surprising, therefore, that the national Hebrew educational discourse emphasized this view of the Holocaust, implying a critique of the Holocaust victims for failing to understand that historical lesson in time and to join the Zionist effort.[49]

Many Jews in the Diaspora define themselves in relation to the Holocaust, whether or not there are survivors in their families.

Survivors are treated with reverence in the Diaspora. They are considered to be the bravest of the brave. In Israel, the bravest are the "New
Hebrews," the soldiers who fight for the survival of the nation. Sander
Gilman discusses the Holocaust and Jewish identity. The Holocaust
has been the most momentous force to shape modern Jewish identity.

> Its force was felt not only among those Jews who directly
> experience it but among all individuals who could even remote-
> ly perceive themselves as Jews. The translation of what had
> become abstract patterns of anti-Semitism into a program for
> action based on the Western stereotype of the Jew meant that
> all 'Jews' could be at risk. Neither the high cultural attainments
> of the society in which one lived nor the acculturation or even
> assimilation of the Jew into that society precluded the possibil-
> ity of individuals being identified as Jews. The treatment of a
> segment of society as Jews (whether Jewish or not) caused all
> those who had even the remotest sense of identification with the
> Jews to restructure their sense of self.[50]

Although none of my own family perished in the Holocaust, I was profoundly affected by its aftermath and constantly reminded of the way
Jews are treated by the dominant society. Strangely, this reminds me
of a childhood friend who lived across the street from me in Winnipeg.

I remember this friend because she reminds me how long the
Holocaust has been a conscious part of my life. Mia was a victim of the
early 1950s polio epidemic in Winnipeg. We played together almost
everyday, but it was usually at her house because she was always
recovering from one of her many surgeries. One leg or arm would be in
a cast or she would be in a wheelchair or on crutches. Her health was
never an issue in our friendship. We just accepted the situation as it
was. The reason that Mia comes to mind is that I remember her dancing doll. It was similar to a life-sized Raggedy Anne doll, very floppy,
but without all the hair. There were elastics attached to the doll's
hands and feet which were meant to be attached to the child's hands
and feet, thus allowing the child to dance with the doll. We must have
been about six years old. Of course Mia could never dance with the
doll, so I considered the doll to mine (it just happened to live at Mia's
house).

Around this time I was attending Hebrew school in one of the elementary grades. One day, we were all marched into the auditorium to
watch a film. We all sat cross-legged on the floor looking up at the
screen. The film was documentary footage taken in one of the concentration camps. A bulldozer was shovelling hundreds of emaciated life-
less bodies into a huge ditch. It was difficult to believe they were real
people. They looked more like the dancing doll, all floppy. After that I
did not play with the dancing doll again. I am still haunted by that
vision. Even for Jews who never set foot in Europe, the Holocaust was
a reality. I do not mean to compare myself to Holocaust victims or to

diminish their suffering in any way, rather, the point I emphasize is that, as a Jew, it is almost was impossible not be affected in some way by the Holocaust.

Naomi behaved more like a Diaspora Jew than an Israeli Jew as far as identifying with European Jews and Holocaust victims. In this respect she did not really fit Zerubavel's description of the Israeli Zionist mode. Naomi was quite resolute in her choice. When I asked how her family and friends felt about her living in Canada, she responded:

> They don't feel good at all about it. Most of my family is very right wing. There's this business where I was attacked by one of my cousins who said, 'You're still bringing up your kids in the Diaspora!' And I said, 'Yes I am. And because you're a principal in a school, why don't you let me speak to those girls and tell them what life is like for a Jew in the Diaspora, especially in a small community? It's not all rosy, but this is where I chose to be, and don't knock me for it.'

Throughout the rest of the interview it became clear that it had taken her many years to reconcile her feelings about her life in Calgary. Like Naomi, I too continue to struggle with choices I have made.

[1] Zerubavel, 3.
[2] Ibid.
[3] Ibid., 8.
[4] Ibid. 8.
[5] Silberstein,6.
[6] Zerubavel, 17.
[7] Ibid., 18.
[8] Ibid.
[9] Ibid., 19.
[10] Ibid., 20.
[11] Ibid.
[12] Ibid.
[13] Ezrahi, 60.
[14] Ibid.
[15] Ibid., 99.
[16] Ibid.
[17] Zerubavel, 216.
[18] Ibid.
[19] Ezrahi, 139.
[20] Ibid.
[21] Ibid., 140.
[22] Silberstein, 5.
[23] Ibid., 6.
[24] Zerubavel, 216.

[25] Ibid.

[26] Ibid., 217.

[27] Ibid.

[28] Ibid.

[29] Ibid.

[30] Ibid.

[31] Ibid.

[32] Ibid.

[33] Ibid.

[34] Ibid., 19.

[35] Ibid., 28.

[36] Ibid.

[37] Ibid., 29.

[38] Ibid.,30.

[39] Ibid.

[40] Ibid., 31.

[41] Ibid.

[42] Schrag, 17.

[43] Ibid.

[44] Ibid.

[45] Ibid.

[46] Zerubavel, 19.

[47] Ibid.,26.

[48] Ibid., 14.

[49] Ibid., 34.

[50] Gilman, 319.

Nine

Negotiating Boundaries

Since 9/11, I have become even more aware of the boundaries that separate people. We put boundaries around ourselves to keep strangers out and there are also boundaries built that serve to leave out certain people

There are many Jews who do not necessarily have a stereotypical Jewish appearance. This provides them with an invisible boundary. I mentioned earlier that in my own family my youngest daughter is a redhead with green eyes and very white skin. My father also did not fit the stereotype with his light colored hair and blue eyes. When non-Jews draw attention to the fact that a person "doesn't look Jewish" it is probably meant as a compliment. It means that the Jew who does not fit the stereotype can more easily cross social boundaries. During the Holocaust a non-Jewish appearance was sometimes enough to save a child's life. Some Jewish parents would leave their children to be raised with Catholic families in an effort to save their lives.[1] Historian, Laurence Rees, recounts:

> Of all the many terrible incidents from the history of the Nazi extermination of the Jews, the story of the murder of the Jewish children sent from France is one of the most profoundly affecting. At the heart of the story, of course, is the shocking image of the separation from their parents. But it is not just the horrific idea of children being ripped from their mother's arms at camps like Beaunela- Rolande that is so upsetting. It is rather that some parents, like the mothers who told their sons to run away during the initial round-up, had to act against instinct and abandon their own children so that they might survive. The emotional trauma involved in such action must have been devastating.[2]

For me, even reading about the separation of children from parents is emotionally devastating. In my mind it is an instinctual response to construct boundaries in order to avoid such atrocities. This is not to say that I think building boundaries, visible or invisible is good, but rather, it provides some insight into why this perceived need for protective boundaries comes about.

Most non-Jewish people do not "consider that the woman who looks . . . like a 'normal white woman' has experienced in her own life or through her parents experience serious alienation and even danger from being Jewish."[3] Some would consider this to be Jewish paranoia and this is often portrayed in Hollywood films as humorous. Woody Allen comes to mind as a master of combining paranoia with humor. In the movie, *Zelig* the main character does not really have an identity of his own. He takes on the personalities of those around him. He is a chameleon. The Jewish message in this film is about the fear of being recognized as Jewish. Zelig manages to blend in to any situation. The attempt to be invisible is the humorous point. Gilman comments on the fictional character Zelig in Allen's film.

> The film chronicles the life of an individual who assumes the identity and physiognomy of anyone with whom he is confronted. Allen sets this film in the 1920s, before the Holocaust, and presents the adventures of a 'madman,' as he is seen by the world, which treats his ability as a psychopathology. Among his various transformations, Leonard Zelig becomes, at one point in the film, an Orthodox Jew with a beard and accent, and later, a follower of Hitler on his way to seizing power in Germany.[4]

In the film, which is presented like a documentary, there are various experts who comment on the Zelig case "from a mock-scholarly point of view."[5] According to Gilman, Allen is satirizing the "specifically 'Jewish' qualities ascribed to the selfhating Jew."[6] Gilman includes Allen among the many Jewish writers who perpetuate the stereotype of the self-hating Jew. Zelig represents the self-hating Jew as a madman. His self-hatred is presented as a sickness that can be cured.

I was extremely uncomfortable watching *Zelig* because I recognized myself as the disappearing Jew. I thought I had developed the ability to blend with others around me and I was quite surprised when I found out that I did not blend as well as I thought. What is more surprising is that it took me such a long time to realize that I am perceived as visibly different. I assumed that if I said nothing about being Jewish that no one would know. Often this was the case. It was not until I was in my late twenties that I had what are considered an "exotic" appearance. People would often ask me where I was born, assuming it was not in North America. When I would answer, "Canada," I assumed that was the end of the discussion and any further speculation. Usually the topic does not even arise. In the early eighties many people were relocating to Calgary due to the oil boom. Asking someone his or her origins was no longer a strange question because so many people were new to the city. In the Jewish community questions were never asked, but when I ventured outside the Jewish Community it was not unusual for people to ask me if I was Lebanese or perhaps Italian. It became clear to me that somehow I did not quite fit the "Canadian" look. I did not feel forthcoming about announcing that I am Jewish. I believed that being Jewish was a religion and that it was nobody's business. I was also afraid.

The fact is that many Jews, including myself, "were taught that the world is dangerous because the world is dangerous."[7] Many Jews prefer to keep their fear hidden because being seen as paranoid is not acceptable in our society. I often make fun of my own paranoia. For example, if I am given the worst table at a restaurant, I joke that it is because they saw a Jewish name on the reservation list. Or in a hotel, if I am given what I consider to be a substandard room, I will complain to my husband "they know we're Jewish." In fact he does not even begin to unpack in a hotel because I have asked for a different room so many times. I say it in a humorous way, as though I am kidding. The truth is that I do think people treat me differently if they think I am Jewish.

The "New Hebrew" of Israel challenged the notion of the self-deprecating and insecure stereotype of the Diaspora Jew. The establishment of the State of Israel "projected a new militant image of the Jew as warrior."[8] Naomi presents herself as a warrior. No one will ever "step" on her because she is so "independent." Each participant, in her own way, presented herself as a conqueror. They each had many difficulties to overcome and they let me know that they were proud of themselves as strong women (even though they would not call themselves feminists).

I noticed in the interviews that some Israelis actually feel sorry for Canadian Jews. Some Canadians are pitied because they have not grown out the *shtetl* mentality. I would describe the term *shtetl* as a Yiddish word for Jewish ghettos in Eastern Europe. Mark Zborowski and Elizabeth Herzog wrote *Life is with People: The Culture of the Shtetl* as a way of trying to preserve the culture of the *shtetl*. In the introduction to the 1995 edition of this book, Kirshenblatt-Gimblett explains:

> *Life Is with People* in indebted to a strong Yiddish literary tradition not only for its tone and style, but also for its preoccupation with the shtetl as the locus of Jewishness. Champions of the Haskala (Jewish Enlightenment) . . . hoped to reform Jewish life by exposing the foibles of Jewish provincialism, which they considered an impediment to the integration of Jews into the larger society.[9]

She further explains that Zborowski "stated that the shtetl could be of any size, since it was not a place but a state of mind."[10] For the Jews in Israel, the *shtetl* mentality is seen in a negative light. The image of the "New Hebrew" was an attempt to destroy the stereotype of the narrow-minded religious Jew. Many of the Jews in Canada, including my ancestors, retained a *shtetl* mentality when they came to Canada to escape the pogroms. Because of their (justified) fear of the Gentile they act in unsophisticated ways and they are pitied because they are stuck somewhere in the twilight zone of the bitter past. Naomi described her in-laws as "primitive" and "uneducated." This would also describe the *shtetl* mentality. Although many Jews distance themselves from the image of the *shtetl*, there are also some who try to keep this culture alive.

One often remembers the experience of fear in a negative way. I was surprised that Devora described the period when her husband was in the army from 1976-1980 as a "good time" in her life. As she explained, "I keep saying it was a good time because I was able to – I'm translating from the Hebrew – dance in different weddings simultaneously." I understood this to mean that she was more carefree and flexible at that point in her life. She could do well anywhere. Five years later, Devora and her family returned to Israel. She explained that it was a time that was "a lot more uncomfortable." While they had been away, they had missed the war with Lebanon in 1982. Referring to Israeli soldiers she continued:

> That was terrible. That was the first time that Israeli soldiers said no to the government. Said, 'We're not going in there. We shouldn't be there.' That had never happened before. It was always, 'We are together and we're fighting against the enemy.' All these sayings, I don't want to say clichés, because they are very important, have been with me ever since I was born. A father who was a refugee and a person who had lost his family and so on and so forth. So this notion of sticking together and take care of ourselves because nobody else will, our history showed me that was true. These were not just platitudes, and maybe a country that's only forty years old or so, is too young to get rid of a history of two thousand years of persecution. Not just perceived. Persecution.

Devora seemed to be defending her perception of being persecuted, as though she had to convince me.

For Devora, whose grandparents and many other relatives perished in the Holocaust, there is always an underlying theme of persecution for every aspect of her life: "War. Extermination. Cossacks. Decrees. From the Book of Esther to Hitler. From Haman [the villain] to Hitler. And I'm not just mouthing it. It took me years to understand that. That it's true. It is so and it was so." These feelings permeate Devora's life to the extent that she has been unable to find an emotionally comfortable place to be. She has moved back and forth between Israel and Canada several times and is not happy in either place. She brought up the story of Noah's Ark to describe her state of mind:

> I kept having the feeling of, if you remember, when the waters subside, Noah sends a dove out to find if there's land. And the dove, I can't quote verbatim, finds no rest for its foot. And that's how I started feeling. Like that dove. No rest for its foot. Wherever I went there was discomfort.

The sense of uneasiness and restlessness she describes sounds like alienation. She could not find any place that was comfortable for herself. Even the discourse of the new "warrior Jew" of Israel did not diminish the horrific remnants of her history.

Kaye/Kantrowitz explains that "any minority culture which has encountered the force of . . . assimilation has lost much of itself."[11] And I have heard this complaint from members of other minority groups. They lose their language, culture, and history. As Kaye/Kantrowitz laments:

> Some Jews have lost more than others, and often we feel ashamed of this loss. Many of us have one Jewish parent, or received no religious education, or have a partner who is not Jewish. From a relatively homogeneous culture not so many generations back we have developed a tremendous range of experience and relationships to Jewishness but without a corresponding sense that this range is valid, acceptable. Jews tend to be judged by other Jews as not Jewish enough; this projection includes our own self-judgement, and makes us either undermine our sense of self or turn from the Jewish community, in an effort to avoid this undermining.[12]

I have at one time or another attempted to use all the "strategies" to which Kaye/Kantrowitz refers. As protective devices the strategies sometimes work for a while but usually self-judgement leads to self-doubt, not only for oneself but also for one's children.

Dafna, who had lived in Canada at various times in her life, explained that it was natural for her to feel like a "foreigner" in Canada. She tried to make light of her feeling of being "foreign." She really did not want to say that there was anything about Canada that she really did not like. She insisted that it was especially her own problem as opposed to being treated differently by Canadians.

> It's more my problem. It's my problem. Because like I said, I don't think a cashier in a store would treat me differently than they treat the next person after me. Mainly because in Canada there are so many foreigners and so many different accents. There's so many accents, anyway, so it's more my own feeling of being a foreigner. I don't like that particularly. But – it does come out, especially in my own feelings in terms of language. But you have to understand that I read fluently, for example, so it doesn't matter to me.

She stressed that language was mainly a problem for her professionally. As she explained, "I don't feel that I am as profound in English as I am in Hebrew and that I'm as sophisticated in the way that I relate to issues as I do in Hebrew and that's my own difficulty." The message I was getting from Dafna was that she felt better about herself in the Hebrew language and that the language had an impact on Dafna's perception of herself. However, she was giving me mixed messages. She was very cautious in not wanting to complain about anything either in Israel or in Canada. She said that she did not want to give me the impression that her life was more difficult in one country than the other. As she put it, "if I say, it would be an invention. I really don't find it very different." It was important for her to let me know that for her, life was good in either country. Perhaps this signalled to her that she had made a success of her life.

Dafna made it clear from the beginning of the interview that she was different than the other women in my study. In her words, "I think our lives are a bit different – I don't know. Maybe I'm imagining, but I don't think it falls into the pattern of Israelis coming." Throughout the interview with Dafna, she was adamant that living in Canada was not really that much different for her than living in Israel. In either location she would have a middle-class life. As I explained, Dafna has not made the decision to live in Canada yet, although she has spent several years living in Canada earlier in her life. She downplayed what she insisted were only minor problems of adjustment. When I asked her what adjustment was the most difficult, she replied:

> First I think adjustments are hard. Even if you are – since my twenties, I used to come to North America. Um, it always takes a time of adjustment, I mean, even going to the store. It starts with everyday life. I mean, you have to get used to the differences . . . Even in Israel. I mean we have to adjust, and it takes some time and it puts you into pressure.

By explaining that "even in Israel" she had to make adjustments she was minimizing any difficulty that she had experienced. I did not ask her what kind of adjustments she made in Israel; she might have been referring to moving back to Israel after having lived in Canada for a while, or she might have been talking about adjustments to the increased violence in Israel over the last two years. We had been discussing the violence earlier, but she insisted that fighting was a reality in Israel that did not disrupt her life. I pushed her on this topic because I could not imagine living with an ongoing war. It seemed to be more of a problem for me than it was for Dafna. She conceded that there were some disruptions. For instance "I could say to you to try not to go to shopping centres and so, but I mean that's what happens to many, many people and I'm sure everyone who walks into a shopping mall is aware of that." It seemed as though she was protecting Israel by saying nothing negative. I wondered if this was her way of convincing herself that moving to Canada would be a mistake. However, it is possible she does not see the fighting in Israel as an impediment of her everyday life.

She told me that at work they joke about the threat of a particularly tall building falling on them if they were attacked by a plane flying into it. The joke is that they speculate about which direction the building will fall. I found it difficult to see any humor in the joke she described and I think she became aware of how strange she must have sounded to me because she then continued in a more serious tone.

> Not to minimalize the burden upon a society which faces terrorism. . . . It would be very stupid even to say that – so it's

there. I would say it's like a big cloud which sits on you and to
some people it probably also has an affect on their everyday life
and it's also when talking about in terms of a society, you say
that society should not agree to such a way of life. It should not
agree to go on through life, the threat of terrorism, because it's
something that's really awful when you see it.

It seemed as though she was saying this for my benefit. Maybe she
thought I needed to hear this, because (to be honest) I did want to hear
it. But then I do not live in a situation where having a sense of humor
about violence is probably a survival mechanism. Dafna must have
noticed my disbelief because she continued without any more
prompting:

So, all in all if you ask me about – Israeli society is a very hard
life today. People would be very conscious about it. Just the fact
that you see the tragedies on television all the time, which you
don't see here. I mean, and there are lots of young people who
are getting killed. So just imagining it, and you do go through it,
it does go through your mind. I mean it probably does leave an
affect on you. It would be silly to say that it doesn't. But when
you come to operationalize it, in a way, then you see that a lot of
it is you say it's horrible, you say it's awful, but all in all, you
continue to lead your own life.

Dafna was beginning to see how she has split from herself. As she
described the reality of living under siege, she could sense my
distressed reaction to her seemingly light-hearted manner. In her
world, one self lives an uneventful everyday life and the other self lives
in a country under siege and fear of violence.

How is it possible to feel good about one's Jewish identity with all
of these obstacles? I have been struggling with this question for many
years. Like a family, a Jewish community can be constraining. If personal issues about Jewish identity have not been addressed, then it is
difficult to take part in a Jewish community and one's own life. Meshi
talked about her struggle in feeling like she was part of her new life:

You don't know the people you meet, but they're not your friends
at the beginning, you know, you have to make friends. Start all
over again. And all of a sudden, I have time. I never had time
before. This is the first time in my life, since the army. Since
twenty years old, I'm not working.

In Israel Meshi worked full time in a job she enjoyed. She felt that the
free time she had in Canada meant she was not involved in her own
life. When I asked her what she does with her time, she described a
typical day filled with various chores – driving children to and from
school, and to after-school lessons. Each day ends the same way: Meshi
makes dinner, bathes the children, helps them with their homework,
and puts them to bed. She told me that this is the first time in her life
that she has had time to read a book. The description of Meshi's day
sounds like a day in the life of many stay-at-home mothers . However,

if she had been in a similar situation in Israel, at least she would have had a connection to her own community and a support network of friends and family. She might not have experienced the same degree of alienation.

In Meshi's opinion there are distinct boundaries between the Jews in Israel:

> What you have to be afraid of in Israel in the next few years is the Israelis themselves because the Jewish is going to kill themselves because we are so much divided between the religious and not religious. It's so much of – the not religious don't do a lot of things. That's why Rabin was murdered. Live and let live, you know? But religious, no. They want to put their opinion on you, and that's it. So, it's hard. I don't want anything to do with them. I respect them. I won't bother them in their places, but I want to be left alone.

From Meshi's perspective there are divisive boundaries between religious and secular Jews in Israel. She blames religious Jews for Yitzhak Rabin's death. She explained bitterly that the religious Jews are trying to control everyone. Meshi would like to see stronger boundaries between Ultra-Orthodox and secular Jews in Israel. For Meshi, having blurred boundaries is not favorable for the Jews in Israel. She would prefer more separation between the communities.

Living in Community

Devora lived in Toronto before settling in Calgary. She felt ill equipped to fit in with Canadian society. When she and her husband first moved to Canada they had two young children. When I inquired about whether she had a social circle, she replied:

> Not initially. It took time to build that. I had two young kids. They couldn't go anywhere. I was with them all the time. After a few months I thought I was going out of my mind. It was horrible! And I remember my father calling and saying, 'but surely there is other mothers in the same situation.' Perhaps there were. It's not that I didn't try. I still tried to engage people in conversation, but it just didn't work out.

She had learned how to live in Israel with its particular myths, but in Canada, the rules were no longer the same. Her perception of her self was no longer of a woman who was successful in making friends. She explained, "It took me years to learn the ground rules – those taken-for-granted matters." She had difficulty reading the social cues between people. She went on to explain that she came up against "walls that [she] didn't know how to penetrate." She was unable to make Canadian friends until she moved to Calgary. This was not because Calgary was a particularly friendly city, but rather, she was beginning to learn the social cues. In Toronto she only had Israeli friends. She tried to invite her husband's colleagues from work. "We tried to invite people for holidays; in particular, we tried to get involved with non- Israelis, Jews, and non-Jews. We were not very successful."

In the previous chapter I discussed the commemorative holidays in Israel. These holidays would not have the same significance for Jews in Canada. Not only did she have trouble becoming part of a community in Canada, but she was also cut off from her family and former circle of friends with whom she would have celebrated holidays in Israel. In Toronto, her husband had to spend a great deal of time at his job and this left Devora to spend more time with her children than she had in the past when she worked in Israel. She explained that this situation "definitely strained the relationship." She wanted to continue her education in Canada but then she would have to work as well "if [she] wanted to maintain a middle-class existence." She found it too difficult to juggle "marriage, motherhood, family, teaching, and studying." They decided to return to Israel. Devora felt that it was her responsibility to maintain her family relationships.

The decision to return to Israel did not turn out to be the answer to Devora's problems; she commented:

> I was feeling that my life in Israel was not very pleasant any more. It became intimately known and yet very foreign. And it wasn't intriguing enough for me to dig and find out – to re-establish myself as a rooted person in that place, in that geography, in that history. . . . I felt very uncomfortable in it. I felt really – I felt it had no dignity for the individual. That's a very strong thing to say, but that's how I was feeling.

It was clear to me that Devora felt uncomfortable at this point. She spoke cautiously; she explained that when they returned to Israel after living in Toronto she was not the same person in her "new and old relationships in Israel." Choosing her words carefully, she continued:

> I don't want to glorify Toronto and romanticize it; it was really barren in many ways. People didn't engage, period. But when they did, there was some flow to it that sat well with deep engagement and reflection. Going back to Israel – I guess one forgets that. It came back, you know, the shouting matches. Who yells – the person who is right is the one who can scream the loudest. Initially it was cute. Oh, that's nice. I used to sit there and watch people talk like this. So where do my words fit in? Can we have a conversation here? Again, I saw what I saw in Toronto, but it took me years to see. The rules have changed, or if they haven't, I've changed, or the country has changed. I needed to relearn the rules. And I didn't like it. I didn't like it. I didn't even theorize about it. I just felt a gut feeling was no good.

Then, she backtracked a bit, as though she felt guilty about her negativity toward Israel. She started to talk about some of the pleasant things in Israel, even though I had not asked about that. She said lovingly, "the countryside was beautiful. I was struck by the wonderful food and the beautiful, beautiful land. The land is beautiful. I had always thought so, but now even more so." It was as though she was talking about a long lost family member. Then in the very next sentence she talked about the beauty in Canada. "Algonquin Park was beautiful. We had done quite a bit of hiking and camping and learned to love Canada, but Israel was something else with its layered history and so on and so forth." She seemed to be teetering back and forth. I don't know if she was trying to convince me or herself, but she seemed to be struggling.

Unlike Canada, Jews in Israel are in the majority. Many of the women I spoke with felt the difference. Tali, who has also moved back and forth from Israel to Canada several times, visits Israel three times a year. She explains, "I have to or I'll go crazy. I need to visit, see everyone." She also explained that people in Israel have an unrealistic idea of what it is like to live in Canada and that sometimes they are disappointed.

> They expect, the people that don't know, they think here is like paradise, you know? As long as it's not Israel, if it's America, it's like paradise for them. People live so good and they have a lot of money and everything is so easy and they think it's like – they say the streets in America are paved in gold, you know?

She went on to explain that they find out when they come to Canada that "it's like anywhere else in the world. You have to work hard. You have to give a lot, sacrifice a lot to make something of yourself, right?" She also explained that she did not have these expectations because she spent part of her youth in Canada. However, her husband found that Canada was not what he expected:

> He thought things would be very easy. But it's not that easy. You come here, you have to learn the language. People don't want to take you to work until they see you have some kind of experience here. It's not that easy. Not that you make so much money here. You also have to work hard to get ahead.

She pointed out that it would be different in Israel because "there's a lot of family connections." Moving to a different country and community means building up a new network of allies.

I asked Tali about whether she has made friends in the community. She replied "yeah, we have a lot of friends, but mostly Israeli, from the Israeli community. It seems harder to get in contact with the Canadians." When I asked the reason for this she answered:

> Maybe because they [Canadians] see friendship as something different. I have a few friends [Canadian] but I don't see them. It's not the same relationship as with the Israelis because we're used to, as friends in Israel, to meet every day, to talk on the phone every day. Maybe Canadians aren't that open to that. So

> I meet with them [Canadians], but it's not the same relation-
> ship. I can't say it's friends but maybe because I see friendship
> as something more intense.

I found it interesting that she visits or talks to her friends every day.
There are times when I barely even talk to my children and husband
every day and they live in the same house with me. I asked for some
clarification in this. She responded:

> Yeah. The close ones. Yeah. And when we meet and when we
> have birthday parties it's almost all Israelis. There are some
> Israelis that are married to Canadians so we see them also but
> mostly it has an Israeli connection.

Tali had lived in Canada for several years during her childhood. She
spoke without an accent. I had expected that she would have more
Canadian friends.

I asked her about how it was when she returned to Canada as an
adult. She answered:

> It's always hard to come back. For some reason, for me, I don't
> know, maybe it's because of me, my character or something.
> Every time I go to Israel it's just like I've been there forever and
> I just adjust right in, and when I come here it's very tough.

Tali's family also lives in Calgary, so she has a support system in place.
I asked her what was so difficult to adjust to when she travelled back
and forth between Israel and Calgary. She was very forthright when
she responded, "well, it's a different mentality, different people. It's
quieter. It's the weather. It's cold. It's very cold. You're more inside.
You're more closed in. All of the things that bother you." She seemed to
assume that I would understand what she meant. I pushed further to
see what she meant by "different mentality." She clarified:

> People are quieter. Quieter, less – not less friendly, but less
> open. I like it more when the people – you see people around
> you, people are more loud, more alive. That's what I mean. Here
> you have to be so polite and so quiet. It kind of bothers me. It
> doesn't seem human, sometimes.

I could tell that she was trying not to insult me and I did not take
offense, but I did give some thought as to what she said about politeness being non-human. It made me wonder about how she and other
Israelis viewed me. Her description of what she experiences in Canada
speaks to Schrag's notion of community being life-affirming or life-
negating. For Tali, the quietness and politeness of Canadians is life-
negating. She feels constrained in her relationships with Canadians
and worries that Canadians might find her strange if she were to act
like herself. I asked when she felt this way, and she responded:

> Well, just when I talk. Whatever I want, or say what ever I
> want, you know. People here are more, it seems like,
> programmed. You have to act a certain way. You have to talk a
> certain way. You have to be polite.

I got the sense that when she used the word "polite" what she meant was closer to detached or frigid. She continued:

> Or my neighbor – I just moved into a new house; I tell my neighbor, 'Oh, just drop by for coffee whenever you want,' She said, 'Okay, when? Do I have to call you?' – 'No, just come by!' It's hard for them to understand, you know? Like you have to make them feel comfortable. You have to work hard. An Israeli friend, she would just come by whenever she wanted. Just knock on the door and come for coffee, so you feel comfortable. You don't have to feel that they're [Israelis] uncomfortable and be uncomfortable trying to get them to come.

Tali interpreted this constrained Canadian behavior as unfriendly. She was very much aware of how she had to perform with Canadians.

I asked Tali if her child was being exposed to the kinds of values she wanted. Referring to when she was young and living in Israel, she explained:

> I don't know if it's as good now as when I was a girl. I heard now its getting bad. It's getting very Westernized, too. But we always had values. Respect the older people and family values of being together on holidays and to like your country and to have respect for Memorial Day, Independence Day, for the holidays, to have some kind of a sense of belonging, some kind of identity. Here it seems you're missing something. There you have the army, you have something that is important to you that you have to fight for.

As it appeared to her, Canadians do not have a strong sense of belonging. They do not have strong values. For her the army in Israel signified that Israelis, as a collective, had something to fight for. Tali has mixed feelings about being connected to the Jewish Community. She feels disconnected from the Calgary Jewish community because they do not respect things that she sees as important. She said:

> So it kind of bothers you sometimes that not everyone comes to Memorial Day [Israeli Memorial Day], which is considered very important [in Israel] or Independence Day. Because I understand, it's less important for people here because it's not their holiday. But for Memorial Day and Independence Day mostly the Israelis come, not the – I'm saying there are some things that are kind of hard to connect. They don't talk the same language. It's a different way, because the only thing that's the same is Jewishness, the religion. For me, maybe it's because I'm not that Jewish. I didn't mean not Jewish. I'm not that religious. I don't have that – it's not something so important to me.

By the tone of her voice, she sounded angry when she referred to Calgarian Jews not observing Israeli Memorial Day and Independence Day. I could understand why she might be angry about this. At the Hebrew schools, the Jewish Community Centre and all the synagogues, these Israeli holidays are celebrated. I have sent my children to the Hebrew school and they do observe these holidays and teach how important they are. Tali attended a Hebrew school when she lived in Calgary as a youngster, so she would have the expectation that the Jewish community would observe these holidays. However, she is not far from truth when she says that only Israelis attend the ceremonies (a few Canadian Jews also attend). I think she was trying to tell me that the Jewish community in Calgary is hypocritical. What is interesting is that she was trying to explain what was an emotional topic for her in a very polite way. She tried not to be too critical, but I could tell she was angry. It seems she has learned the Canadian custom of performing in a politely roundabout way.

Raya had lived in Russia until she was sixteen and then moved to Israel where she stayed until after she was married and had children. Russian Jews are often treated differently by other Jews in Israel. Barsky refers to this in "Refugees from Israel: A Threat to Canadian Jewish Identity?" which was part of "a large-scale research project concerning the choice of (Quebec and) Canada as host country for Convention Refugee claimants from Israel, the former Soviet Union, Pakistan, and Peru who arrived in Quebec in 1992."[13] Barsky continues:

> With regard to Israeli claimants, my findings suggest that heightened levels of expectation with regards to Israel (often stirred up by officials of Israel's Jewish Agency – Sochut – who travel to the former Soviet Union to encourage Jewish emigration to Israel), the cumulative nature of persecution (i.e., claimants describe a situation whereby the persecution in the former Soviet Union combined with the discomfort in Israel made them ready for continued flight), and feelings of déja vu among persons of diluted or non-practicing Jewish heritage (i.e., the claimants felt persecuted for the same reason in Israel as had led them to flee the Soviet Union).[14]

I hesitated to include Raya as a participant in my research because she was not actually born in Israel; however, she insisted that she felt more Israeli than Russian. She did not mention whether she felt Canadian. Unlike some of the other Israeli families, Raya's family was happy that she decided to live in Canada because it would offer her and her children a better life. When I asked her reason for choosing Calgary, she explained that her sister already lived here and it was important for her have family. I pushed further, asking why she left Israel. She responded:

> A few things. First of all, and I have to be honest with you, how do you say it 'Security.' And all the things and, you know, the life didn't – it wasn't easier with each year. It just became harder. We were never involved in politics, but it was harder, you know, to adjust ourselves to the life here. Life is very fast in Israel. You have to run after the clock. Okay? You never know when you turn on the TV, the morning, you learned now what happened.

> Bomb here, explosion there.   Your kids go on a field trip and
> you just sit and look at the clock and you wait until they come
> back because you don't know if the bus is okay or something's
> happened on the way. It's very – you know when you live there,
> you can feel it on your skin, on yourself. Maybe when you
> explain and talk about it, it sounds weird.

I told her it did not sound weird, but it was difficult to imagine the kind
of fear she spoke of. I also asked her about some of the difficulties when
she first came to Canada. She answered, "it wasn't difficult but it was
different. Difficult was, first of all, language. We knew zero English." I
got the feeling that she did not want to appear weak to me because she
avoided listing her difficulties.

I also asked Raya about her connection to the Jewish community in Calgary. She explained that she had a job at one of the Jewish
institutions that she loved. She added

> I feel like it's – the Jewish community is split by three parts.
> There is a Canadian Jewish community. There is an Israeli
> Jewish community and there's a Russian Jewish community.
> And each one is polite to another but not more than that. There
> is no interaction between these parts.

She said that she felt most comfortable with people in either the Israeli
community or the Russian Jewish community. With each question she
started with a positive sounding answer, but then the problems would
creep in. I sensed that she was trying to be careful not to insult me,
since I am a member of the Canadian Jewish community. Although she
misses Israel she "loves" Canada: "I like the fact that people respect
each other. At least they show respect to each other. They're patient
with each other. But here we are immigrants, okay?" I wondered if she
really had respect for me or if she was just acting. When I asked her if
she felt she was treated differently because she is an immigrant, she
responded:

> No. Not necessarily. I think we're treated the same way, because
> there is Calgary's policy and there is government rule. Like
> everybody has to be treated the same way. No, differences, but I
> had to – and still, I think, we have to learn different situations.
> Like, okay, if somebody doesn't like me, he wouldn't tell me, 'I
> don't like you. Don't call me anymore.' But there is in between
> lines, that you have to learn how to look at the map. Do you
> know what I mean?

I questioned if that would be the case in Israel as well. She continued:
"No. Not at all. They'll just say, 'You know what? Go and find your
friends. Leave me alone.' And that's it. Here it's different. I'm not
saying it's better or worse. I'm just saying it's different."

I was now starting to understand what Raya meant by "different." Earlier Raya had said that she preferred to have someone be
totally honest with her, like in Israel. Here in Canada it is unclear to
her what it is people want to hear. It was interesting that she was

being evasive with me, especially when she prefers people to be straightforward. In fact, she started many of her sentences with "to be honest with you." However, for her there was a definite dividing line between being respectful and acting as though one is respectful. She seemed to like the fact that Canadians act respectfully but she also suspected they were not being honest with her.

When Raya commented on life in Canada I was struck by her words, "I like the space you know, we don't sit on each other's souls. I love this privacy. Sometimes in Israel, it's impossible because of the lifestyle." It struck me that in Israel they really were sitting on each other's souls. The country is crowded, but more importantly, the history of the country is visible is the many layers of civilization that have built societies, one on top of the other. Canadians do not have to bear the same weight.

When I asked Devora the difference between being Jewish in Israel and being Jewish in Calgary, she told me that her ideas on this subject have changed over time. Like Orit and Meshi, Devora explained that "the lived experience deceptively means that . . . you don't have to think about being Jewish" instead of the assumption that "you're Jewish because you're living in Israel." She also mentioned that for all the area outside of Israel, there is no Hebrew equivalent of the word "abroad." There is no such expression, "abroad." It's outside – *haslet alit*. *Alit* means the country, and, there is only one 'the country': Israel. I realized that *haslet alit* would be a different way of looking at the world. For her there were no boundaries inside the land of Israel, whereas everywhere outside of Israel was defined by its not being Israel. Describing the experience of growing up in Israel, Devora said that when she was young, she believed that Israel was the centre of the earth.:

> Look at the word Mediterranean. Medi, terra, right? The centre
> of the earth, right? So Israel is the centre, Jerusalem is the
> centre. That's a given. Right? Nobody actually says it, but you
> grow up with that, and not to mention the chosen people issue.

As Devora continued it was as though she was trying to convince herself (and me) that there is nothing wrong with leaving Israel. Yet, she was in conflict about her choices. Her ambiguous relationship with community is illustrated by the way she acts in the world. Proud and lonely at the same time she admits that she is different and that she does not fit in anywhere. Her confusion about self is played out in continually moving back and forth between countries. If a person grows up believing that her country and her people are at the centre of the universe, the realization that this story may not be the case may cause her pain. According to Schrag it is difficult to find a positive role for community in the contemporary world today:

> The we-experience and the I-experience are more intricately
> entwined than has been acknowledged by proponents of either

the social doctrine of the self or the individualist doctrine. Whereas social doctrine defines the self as simply an ensemble of societal relations, the individualist perspective argues for a self-constituting individuality that proceeds independently of relations with other selves.[15]

In Israel, the we-experience seems to override the I-experience. Leaving a place where one flourishes as *we*, to enter a social situation where one must excel at the I-experience guarantees a difficult transition. There is a difference in what it means to be a member of a Jewish community in North America and a member of a Jewish community in Israel.

Biale, Galchinsky, and Heschel contend that in North America "Jews constitute a liminal border case, neither inside nor outside – or better, both inside and outside."[16] They further contend that in North America, "to be a Jew, especially at this historical juncture, means to lack a single essence, to live with multiple identities. Perhaps the Jews are even emblematic of the postmodern condition as a whole."[17] This description does not apply in the same way to Jews in Israel. There is not the same need to live with multiple identities and the pressure to fit in. Thus, moving from a country such as Israel, where a Jew is part of the dominant majority, to a country such as Canada, where Jews are clearly a minority, requires an enormous adjustment for immigrants.

> Even the relationship of American Jews to Israel expresses an ambiguity in the Jews' sense of themselves as powerful and powerless: should they identify with Israel as a small, threatened state standing for centuries of Jewish vulnerability or as a regional military and economic power.[18]

It is necessary that the individual overcome the terror of the refiguring stage of one's life if one is to continue the narration of the story which keeps moving. Ilanit revealed that she had encountered some unexpected problems concerning Jewish identity. One of the reasons she moved Canada was to accommodate her non-Jewish husband's career. Her family was not pleased that she had married a non-Jew; however, they did not want to stand in the way of Ilanit's happiness. At some point Jewish identity became more important to her:

> There was a time when we were thinking about conversion. We started the process. The only problem that was with that – I wanted to stop the process. I was the one that stopped the process. The reason is, that the Rabbi wants you to be more with him. . . . For me, Judaism, I like my religion and everything, but I don't want to go to synagogue every week. . . . I don't want to be restricted in everything in my life. . . . I said to myself "no way!" I'm not going to do this. I said to my husband, "I don't want to continue this process here." So my husband got angry.

Her husband was angry because he had invested a great deal of time and energy in the conversion process and Ilanit stopped it. She had not been religious in Israel and she could see that a religious Jewish life in

Canada was not for her. The cultural differences between Ilanit and her husband did not seem to matter until they had children. They do not celebrate Christmas with her husband's family in order to avert conflict.

> The kids understand that their father is Christian and the grandparents are Christian and they know that we don't celebrate these holidays [Christmas]. . . . I didn't think it would be a problem until I had children . . . When you think about how your kids – how will you continue your family you have to think what do you want them to observe, Christianity, or do you want them to observe Judaism. And for me, it's only Judaism, of course.

Even though Ilanit feels very strongly about her Jewish identity, she stopped her husband from converting because she realized she would have to change her way of life. However; it is very important to her that her children are brought up as Jews. Although she had some disdain for the Canadian students who had to "find themselves," Ilanit found that she also had to negotiate Jewish identity issues for herself and for her family. In Israel these issues would have never required a great deal of thought, because Ilanit's Jewish identity would have been taken for granted. It seems that identity issues can appear at any time in a person's life.

Intermarriage

The avoidance of intermarriage has always been a way of controlling the boundaries between Jews and non-Jews. A study of the Calgary Jewish community states:

> Continued high rates of intermarriage and weaker rates of Jewish identity are a challenge posing both opportunities and threats to the contours of Jewish survival. . . . These findings merit serious discussion and should be a priority issue nationally as well as locally.[19]

Several years ago, as my Master's thesis topic, I conducted research on intermarriage among Jewish women in Calgary.[20] Due to the limitations of the present book I will not go into detail on the topic of intermarriage except as it concerns boundaries. At that time I was particularly interested in the topic of intermarriage because I have several Jewish women friends who are married to non-Jewish men. Before meeting these women and then doing further research into the area of intermarriage I had made the assumption that those who marry non- Jews did not value Jewish traditions. My findings were completely the opposite. The women I spoke with for the study on intermarriage were much more aware of both Jewish tradition and religion than I had expected. It seems that the experience of being married to non-Jew had, in many cases, contributed to strengthening their ties to Judaism. I had mistakenly assumed that marrying outside the faith and going against tradition was a way of constructing bound- aries. The women in that study were Canadian and had grown up in a multicultural environment unlike the Israeli participants in my more recent research.

The topic of intermarriage came up in my interviews with Israeli women. Meshi, who has very young children and does not see herself as a religious Jew, commented, "I am a Jew and I'm born into it and I suppose if my children want to get married, I'll have a problem with not-a-Jew." Dafna, who identifies herself as a Jew and a Zionist has older children. When I asked her about intermarriage she responded only to the possibility of marriage to a Russian, even though I did not mention any specific group. She considered marriage to a Russian "who doesn't have proper papers with him" to be intermarriage.

> If one of my kids will meet someone who is not Jewish, it might
> – [matter] for me personally. I don't have a problem with it, but
> it might raise a few problems of where to get married, for exam-
> ple. Many Israelis, today, meet and want to marry Russians who
> don't have a Jewish mother and who are not Jewish according
> to the law. They go to Cyprus and they get married. It's very
> simple. It's not a simple issue within the Orthodox parties.

She went on to explain that she sees the Orthodox view of marriage in Israel as "more a social-political problem." Then I pushed her to make it more personal by asking her if would be a problem for her if one of her children wanted to marry an Arab. She explained:

> It might be. It might very well be. I hope not. Let's say, I want
> to believe that I am a person who sees people as human beings.
> I do, totally, believe in the equality of the citizenship of the
> Israeli Arabs and the Israelis. It might be a very close personal
> problem let's say, because of the different ways of life.

It was clear to me that she would rather think of intermarriage in the hypothetical political sphere. In Israel it is easier to keep these bound- aries separated because Jewish children are not usually raised in a multicultural environment.

Efrat has experienced intermarriage in her family first-hand. Her daughter married the next-door neighbor's son, a Mormon. She explained that it was very difficult for her to accept in the beginning. As she put it, "I was in a panic!" She explained that, over time, as they got to know their son-in-law they came to love him. She complained that the Reform rabbi at the time would not participate in her daughter's marriage which added to an already difficult situation. She made it clear that she feels much differently now and has been able to accept her daughter's marriage. As she described, "I was so afraid about marriage between my daughter and my son-in-law and now I realize that it's not the end of the world." She went on to tell me that she has since become very close to her son-in-law's mother. As Efrat explained, I have a very good relationship with her. Describing the relationship further, Efrat said cheerfully, "she's accepted us and she loves us . . .. This is a very good experience and situation for me as a Jew, you know, living in a very closed Jewish country." Because Efrat had a difficult time accepting her daughter's marriage, she was grateful that her new in-laws were so welcoming. When Efrat first told me about her daughter's marriage, I shared with her that my own daughter had recently become engaged to a non-Jewish man. Like Dafna, I had hoped that I would be open-minded. However, it bothered me more that I expected. I felt that I had somehow failed as a parent, and I worried about what family, friends, and the community would think. I was disturbed by my reaction.

Expectations and Anticipations

It is possible to identify some of the many challenges Jews face in the Diaspora and in Israel. This is not to say that all Jews experience the same challenges in the same way, but there are several typical Jewish stereotypes to which many Jews are exposed. In Israel the stereotypes are interpreted differently so when Israelis move to Canada, they not only have the difficulty of negotiating the everyday practicalities of living in a different culture, but they must also try to decipher some of the more invisible social interactions. Jews behave differently in the Diaspora than in Israel and for the women in this research behavior was often confusing. In terms of myth and narrative, living as a Jew is experienced differently in a Jewish State than in a country such as Canada where Jews are on the margins. Jewish Israelis may not confront negative stereotypes until they move to Canada.

In the new country they may be bombarded with previously unfamiliar expectations. Most of the Israelis I have spoken with make it clear that never have had to question their Jewish identity either in or outside of Israel, whereas in the Diaspora there are many loose ends. By loose ends I refer to those troublesome issues of identity that cannot be comfortably situated in one's narrative identity. Unresolved details can leave gaping holes in one's sense of self. In Canada I do not take for granted that being Jewish is the norm, and to identify myself as Jewish is to place myself in the category of other, multiculturalism notwithstanding. I still feel at loose ends about what it means to be a Jew at the age of fifty-four, and I have not yet figured out who I am in my role as a woman. My expectation was that by this point in my life some sense of peace or satisfaction with my identity would emerge if only through time and experience. Growing up in middle-class Canada, I felt entitled to have the life I wanted. That is what we were taught to expect of ourselves. "You can do anything if you set your mind to it." However, life does not always turn out in the way one expects. Until one has a chance to refigure expectations, this disillusionment may feel like a promise has been broken.

My wording, "what it means to be a Jew" reveals that I must see myself, in some essential way, as a Jew, yet I refer to my female identity as a role. The performance of a social identity is part of the process of the constitution of the self. Performing the role of woman is an acceptable norm in society. I am arguing that both gender and Jewishness can be seen as performances. The idea of role performance, such as gender or ethnicity, carries a negative connotation if one thinks of the performance as pretending and therefore not real. This interpretation is not my intention. As mentioned earlier, Judith Butler questions the extent to which performance is an "act."[21] She explains that the performance must be consistently repeated to become a real-ity. What is important in Butler's description of performance is that the "action is a public action."[22] My argument is that it is easier to avoid publicly being a Jew than it is to avoid publicly being a woman. Although the definition of the performance of "woman" changes over time and in different cultures there is usually no reason to keep this part of one's identity concealed as long as one conforms to society's definition of woman. However, there are many reasons for people to keep Jewish identity hidden.

"Negotiating Boundaries," the title of this chapter, refers to many ways that people tend to build walls around themselves for protection. Specifically I am referring to Jewish people, as well as the fears that I have experienced in my own life. This is not to say that all Jewish people have had the same experience. I have made links between my longings for feeling safety to the sense of alienation I have experienced concerning the constraints of women's roles. Again, these are personal experiences, I can make no claim that these ideas are of concern to other people in their lives. The interpretations and connections I have made with women's roles, Jewish identity, intermarriage, and Zionism may seem unlikely associations to others; however, my experiences have resulted in a type of alienation illustrated in *Zelig*. Like the character, Zelig, I find myself drowning in a sea of possibilities. As time goes on I am getting tired of treading water. People are throwing me life-lines but I do not know which one to grab. In the next chapter I will try to reconcile these perplexing threads.

[1] Bialystok, 290.
[2] Rees, 124-125.
[3] Kaye/Kantowitz, 12.
[4] Gilman, 383.
[5] Ibid.

[6] Ibid.
[7] Kaye/Kantrowitz, 12.
[8] Gilman, 391.
[9] Zborowski and Herzog, xii.
[10] Ibid., xiv.
[11] Kaye/Kantrowitz, 12.
[12] Ibid., 12.
[13] Barsky, 221.
[14] Ibid. 222.
[15] Schrag, 79.
[16] Biale et al, 8.
[17] Ibid., 9.
[18] Ibid., 5.
[19] Torczimer and Brotman, 52.
[20] Fogell, 1997.
[21] Butler, 1999, 178.
[22] Ibid.

Ten

Reconciliation with the Self

Last year on Mother's Day, my oldest daughter, who is married to a non-Jewish man, gave me *Betrayed*, a book written by Stan Telchin. On the cover just above the title was a question: "How do you feel when you are successful, 50, and your 21-year-old daughter tells you she believes in Jesus?"[1] It was clear that she had not randomly selected this particular book as a Mother's Day gift. It would have been easy to perceive this book as a rejection. At this point our daughter, Carie, had been married for at least two years, we could see how happy she was with her husband, and we were happy for her. This does not mean that we were overjoyed at the sight of a Christmas tree in their home, even though they celebrated *Hannukah* as well.

When Carie made the decision to get married she had seemed open to the idea of maintaining some Jewish traditions, and she spoke about sending any children they might have to Hebrew school. She assured us that her husband, Stuart, was not particularly religious as a Christian and that he was interested in learning about Jewish traditions. I never expected that he would convert to Judaism, and I did not think it was necessary. Even Carie's maternal grandmother Belle, a very traditional Jewish woman, accepted Stuart and was supportive of the marriage. Belle died shortly after Carie's first child, Kade, was born, and since then Carie has had another baby, Winnie. During the time since Belle died, Carie has become more and more involved with Stuart's family and their church. Although I may not be pleased with Carie's choices, I accept that they are her choices to make. More im-portant, I love Carie and her family, and I do not want anything to get in the way of continuing a close relationship with her. The situation has been more difficult for Ken and also, surprisingly, for our other children, Daniel, Sarah and Kylie. It is difficult for them not to see Carie's choices as a betrayal. After many years of people giving us their unsolicited opinions on childrearing, Ken and I have gotten used to criticism. Nonetheless, it still hurts. This is one of the many Jewish issues that I struggle to reconcile with myself – being judged by the community.

All of our children had a *Bat* or *Bar Mitzvah* (coming of age ceremony for girls and boys at the age of ceremony). It was never a question for me, whether or not to have these ceremonies. There are many Jews who choose not observe this tradition. In 1964, when I had my *Bat Mitzvah* it was more unusual for girls to go through the preparation and the ceremony. I have good memories of that day. I stood in front of the synagogue congregation and sang my portion of the Torah. It involved a year of preparation to learn how to read and sing the ancient musical symbols. Before that I had attended Hebrew school for seven years learning the customs and the language. Deciding to have my children go through this process required a huge commitment. The North American tradition in contemporary times often includes a weekend of festivities with friends and relatives from near and far. We had this type of celebration for Carie, Daniel, and Sarah in Calgary. These occasions were extremely stressful for all of us. The children were nervous about their singing performances. Ken and I worried about the many details that needed attending to. I was worried about my performance as a mother. I worried about my clothing. I obsessed about the children's clothing for each occasion. I worried about being judged by the community. I was relieved when all the parties were over.

When it came time for Kylie to have her *Bat Mitzvah* in 1998 we decided to do it differently. My parents took us all to Israel and Kylie sang her small portion of the *Torah* at the top of Massada, where Ancient Jews had fought to the death rather than surrender to the Roman enemy. Kylie sang among the ruins over looking the Dead Sea. We were part of an arranged tour specifically for this purpose. We met other families from across Canada and joined them on a ten-day tour culminating in the *Bat Mitzvah*. As it turned out, Ken's first cousin was on the same tour with his family. He also had a *Bat Mitzvah*-aged daughter. It would be an understatement to say the trip was wonderful. I cannot think of enough superlatives to describe this incredible journey with my family. After my first trip in 1995 I went through a period when I wanted to return to Israel. It felt right. I had the same feeling after the trip in 1998. After a while, getting back to our regular lives in Calgary, I stopped thinking about moving to Israel. But now, those feelings about going to live in Israel have returned.

In the writing of this book I have become painfully aware the ongoing struggle in dealing with Jewish identity issues. That is not to say that I have resolved the many perplexing questions with which I have been concerned, but I no longer avoid thinking about difficult issues. I find the pursuit of awareness challenging in a positive way. Clearly, the challenges are not going to disappear.

One issue though, that has become increasingly difficult for me to face is what some scholars refer to as the "New Anti-Semitism."[2] I have found the heated discussions concerning Zionism among Jewish scholars disturbing. It seems that it is no longer acceptable for any Jewish person to express any view that could possibly be construed as anti-Zionist. Specifically I am referring to Judith Butler's essay "The

Charge of Anti-Semitism: Jews, Israeli, and the Risks of Public Critique."[3] In this provocative paper, Butler comments on a statement made on September 17, 2002, by Lawrence Summers, the president of Harvard University. Her statement :

> Profoundly anti-Israeli views are increasingly finding support in progressive intellectual communities. Serious and thoughtful people are advocating and taking actions that are anti-Semitic in their effect if not their intent.[4]

Butler's reaction to Summer's statement speaks to some of my own fears about asking questions. As I mentioned earlier, one becomes suspect amongst other Jews by asking too many questions about Zionism. Butler argues:

> If we think . . . that to criticize Israeli violence, or to call for specific tactics that will put economic pressure on the Israeli state to change its policies, is to engage in "effective anti-Semitism," we will fail to voice our opposition out of fear of being named as part of the anti-Semitic enterprise. No label could be worse for a Jew. The very idea of it puts fear in the heart of any Jew who knows that, ethically and politically, the position with which it would be utterly unbearable to identify is that of the anti-Semite. It recalls images of Jewish collaborators with the Nazis.[5]

In her interpretation of Summer's statement, "he is saying that he, as a listener, will take any criticism of Israel to be effectively anti-Semitic."[6] Furthermore, Butler views Summer's attitude as "the most outrageous form of silencing and 'effective' censorship."[7] There are many scholars who share Summer's viewpoint.[8] One author in particular who takes issue with Judith Butler is Cynthia Ozick.[9] She makes a convincing argument that "the current anti-Semitism" is "accelerating throughout advanced and sophisticated Europe . . . under the rubric of Anti-Zionism" and is "masked by the deceptive lingo of human rights."[10] Ozick then goes on to attack Butler:

> Judith Butler, identifying herself as a Jew in the London Review of Books, makes the claim that linking "Zionism with Jewishness . . . is adopting the very tactic favored by anti-Semites." A skilled sophist (one might dare to say solipsist), she tosses those who meticulously chart and expose anti- Semitism's disguises into the same bin as the anti-Semites themselves.[11]

Ozick's name-calling feeds directly into the labeling that Butler claims "puts fear in the heart of any Jew." Ozick does admit that "one can surely agree with Butler that not all Jews are 'in favor of Israel.'"[12] But then she continues her attack on Butler by pointing out that "her misunderstanding of anti-Semitism is profound; she theorizes rifts and demarcations, borders and dikes; she is sunk in self-deception."[13] Ozick goes even further by accusing Butler of "not merely sophistry; not merely illusion; but simple stupidity, of a kind only the most subtle intellectuals are capable of."[14] Although I can understand Ozick's rage,

I find her method of arguing to be less than productive. I had difficulty reading her words because I too was afraid of her angry reaction. It is clear that conflicting Zionist narratives will continue to proliferate and those strong emotions will abound. I see it as progress that I have come to a place where I can expose myself to disturbing ideas rather than simply dismissing or avoiding them. The fear of being adversely judged by other Jews as disloyal is as powerful as the anxiety I experience as my fear of anti-Semitism. As Butler emphasizes, remembering those who died in the Holocaust is a sign of loyalty — anything less is suspect.

My father suffered from memory loss due to a massive heart attack in 1987 when he was deprived of oxygen. He was able to remember things that happened long ago but he was not able to form new memories. He had forgotten that his mother and brother were dead and each time he was reminded he went through a mourning process as though he had just heard the news. Over several months he recovered enough to go home. The doctors had told us he would likely have to spend the rest of his life in a nursing home. Instead, he went on to live another sixteen years, possibly the most enjoyable years of his life. He found a way to compensate for his inability to form new memories by making the most of those he did remember. In doing so he began a new life. Through his loss we, his family, were also given another chance. The philosopher Kerby comments that, "When asked by others who we are, more often than not we are forced to give some account of our past life, and this will be predominantly narrative in form. Loss of this ability to narrate one's past is tantamount to a form of amnesia."[15] Kerby also explains that "human existence is temporal" and he stresses, "we indeed find ourselves, collectively and individually, embedded in ongoing history."[16] My father found a way to find his place and in doing so he provided us with a relentless optimism.

He always seemed to have a smile on his face so that people greeted whatever he said warmly. He somehow was able to direct most conversations to some topic from his past that he remembered well. He told his stories with such animation and joy that it did not matter if we had heard the same story before. His repeated stories reminded him who he was and also reminded listeners who they were. He made a point of letting the people to whom he was speaking know that he felt honored to be in their presence. He would often ask me, "do you have any idea how much I love you?" This was always a welcome question. This was a question he asked almost every night when I was very young when he would tuck me into bed at night. After we all grew up he rarely asked this question, that is, until after his heart attack when his ability to make new memories was gone. During his last few days of life, I would ask him the same question, "do you have any idea how much I love you?" He would answer in disbelief, "really?" I am not sure if he knew how much he was loved. After his death, I had another chance to remember just how much I did love him and in doing so I got back a part of myself.

In the film *Memento*, the main character, Leonard, has also lost the ability to form new memories.[17] He is able to remember details of his life before his brain injury, but when asked about himself he recites the facts about his life in a mechanistic manner, as though he is reciting his identification number in the military. He is doomed to keep repeating all his actions in the present because he cannot connect them in any meaningful way to his past or to his future. I was struck by the sense of tragedy in this character's inability to tell his story. The only way he could keep track of his life was to take Polaroid pictures of his daily activities. The metaphor used in the film was a Polaroid photograph that disappeared instead of developing. If individuals cannot continue to add to their narratives perhaps their selves also disappear. This did not seem to be the case for my father. He somehow transformed his old memories into an experience in the present and, in doing so, those around him also felt transformed.

In *Memento*, the audience is left dangling, not knowing which version of the truth to believe. We are given several scenarios of various situations, which reflect the main character's state of confusion. I have watched this film several times, and with each viewing I am fascinated by the connection between identity and memory. The main character's constant confusion and his inability to plan ahead seems to erase his identity. Throughout the film he desperately tries to reconstruct his life and his identity as they disintegrate before his eyes. Each new memory is forgotten within five minutes. He is constantly going through actions in the present, and then he forgets this action almost immediately. This magnifies the importance of being able to retain memories of the past and consider actions in the future and its relation to identity. Like the character Leonard, my father would also forget his present actions. Five minutes after dinner he would ask if he had eaten dinner. Unlike Leonard, he was not visibly in a panic over his inability to form new memories. He was able to find peace with his past memories and this gave him his identity. Many of the stories he did remember included details that we would probably never heard had he continued at his earlier work pace – there would not have been enough time.

The expression, "never forget" is a familiar admonition for Jews. Usually it is in reference to the six million who perished in the Holocaust, but a strong component of the whole structure of Judaism is "never forget." Every year at Passover, the same story is told and retold. This retelling of history happened long before the Holocaust. Perhaps this is part of the reason that Leonard's inability to remember strikes me as very significant. His ability to construct himself in the present and the future is lost. His old memories were not enough to sustain him. His old memories actually destroyed him. The directive "never forget" has become the eleventh commandment among world Jewry. What needs to be added to this command is that we must learn to regenerate new ways of being for the present and future. Otherwise, like Leonard we may be destroyed by our memories.

There are still several areas of my life where I feel the need for clarity. This is particularly true when it comes to looking in the mirror. I still engage in the game of "Mirror, Mirror on the wall, who is the fairest of them all?" It is not that I need to feel more beautiful than other people; the challenge is to be acceptable to myself. I had hoped that by this time in my life I could accept myself, accept aging. Instead I may have to learn how to accept myself as a woman for whom the need to be attractive will always be strong. I wish that I could love and care for myself in the same way that I do for my children and grand-children. When I look at them, they are perfect. I love everything about them. If only I could allow myself the same acceptance. Hopefully this will change with time – the sooner, the better. Learning to be more honest with myself is a beginning.

Related to looking at what is reflected in the mirror is the nagging question of being the "right kind of Jew." Does it even matter whether I identify myself as a Jew? Why is it still important to me? Am the right kind of Jew? I am not even sure what that means anymore except that it is about trying to meet the standards of others. However, I am relieved that meeting those standards has become less important to over time. It leaves me with more energy to act in positive ways. I put more of my energy into figuring out what will be satisfying for me in the future as a Jew. Making the trip to Israel has become a priority. I feel the need to spend time there and learn the language in order to feel entitled to an opinion and to feel connected to whatever that opinion turns out to be.

There have been many times over the past two decades when I have wondered how my life would have been different had I never left Vancouver. Certainly there were times when I wanted to return to the lush, green (seeming) paradise. I question my motives for leaving. I wonder if I would have ever had children. What I would have made of myself? I doubt that I would have returned to school especially to pursue an interest in Jewish issues. In Vancouver I would not have had the time. I would be to busy enjoying the outdoors. I would have been too busy networking with interesting people. My agenda was different when I lived in Vancouver.

In this book I have often reflected on the Holocaust. I sometimes wonder why I feel compelled to learn as much as possible about such a horrific part of history. As I mentioned earlier, I have no relatives who were directly injured in the concentration camps. Yet the information haunts me. It feels like a personal loss. I sometimes even feel a sense of guilt that I speak and write about the Holocaust. I feel as if I have no right to feel it as my own injury. I wonder about Butler's notion that "survival is a matter of avowing the trace of loss that inaugurates one's own emergence" applies here.[18] I am beginning to feel a new person emerging. I have survived my own almost clinical analysis and criticism of who I am as a person and, particularly, who I am as a Jew. In doing so, I have attempted Butler's avowing "the trace of loss that inaugurates [my] own emergence." Somehow, keeping the memory of the Holocaust alive allows me to keep growing as a person – to emerge.

Continual loss and rebuilding is a fact of life. On a very basic level the loss of one's youth is continual, and aging requires a constant rebuilding of the self. In his discussion of the way in which loss is constitutive of identity, Steven K. White, a political theorist, suggests that "loss and the ambivalence it entails are not aspects of identity one can simply shed. They set parameters for who I can be and what shape my identity can take."[19] In other words, loss is not something we just get over, but rather it is part of what makes individual people. It is through acknowledging loss that we have the possibility of awareness of how we are called into being.

In the writing of this book, I have also learned to value my emotions at least as much as my ability to think. I do not think that emotion and thought can be separated. The philosopher Anna Neumann also makes connections between identity, loss and emotion in an article describing her father's Holocaust experience. She express-es the sense of fear that accompanies memory and describes her reaction as "the terror of realization and a deep unending sense of loss." Her father's memory is embedded within Neumann's identity. Although she was not actually a prisoner of Auschwitz, her father's memories have had a constitutive impact on her identity. She explains:

> My life has been formed in the aftermath of a horrifying event,
> the Holocaust, and it has been dominated by memories and
> fears and hopes growing directly out of it. I cannot conceive of
> my Jewishness without direct reference to the Holocaust.[20]

She also maintains that these feelings infiltrate every aspect of her life, including how she lives her life "in the academy" and how she sees her "intellectual work."[21] Neumann's observations emphasize the ways that loss, particularly the collective Jewish narratives of loss, can shape one's individual identity. Along with Neumann I believe that feelings cannot be considered as separate from intellectual work.

I feel that I am in a safer place than when I began this journey. Interviewing the participants in this study allowed me to peek into how other women play out their social identities. The tension between Jews in the Diaspora and Jews in Israel has become clearer to me and has shed light on my own anxieties My last conversation with Meshi reinforced my feeling about this tension. She explained that over the past two years she has started to understand how Jewish life in the Diaspora is different than Jewish life in Israel. She mentioned a new awareness of anti-Semitism. She was very distressed about a very public anti-Semitic comment made by David Ahenakew, the former head of the Assembly of First Nations even though Ahenakew made a tearful public apology. Gatehouse, a journalist, commenting on Ahenakew's blunder wrote, "sometimes 'I'm Sorry' doesn't quite cut it. Suggesting that is was a good and necessary thing that Adolph Hitler 'fried' six million Jews in the Holocaust is one of those occasions."[22] Ahenakew has since been stripped of the Order of Canada, along with other honors that had been bestowed on him before he made a public statement of hatred. Like many others, Meshi, a participant in my research, was shocked by Ahenakew's anti-Semitic statement. She found it frightening. I was a bit confused by her reaction because I assumed that growing up in Israel she would be have been used to Arab anti-Jewish attitudes. However, she explained that the Arab hatred is always there so they take it for granted. There is nothing surprising about a situation that has been going on for so long. She was shocked that there was such virulent anti- Semitism outside of Israel. Having grown up in Israel where in a Jewish majority, she had not experienced the fear than accompanies anti-Semitism. She told me this in a very matter-of-fact way, as though it would be obvious to me. Yet, there are many assumptions we make about each; I now see more clearly how much I do not know. Listening to stories about how other women have effected change in their lives has been enlightening, and humbling. So many people have had difficult lives.

In learning more about the lives of Israelis and the many challenges they face, I have realized that there is a definite need for increased dialogue between Diaspora Jews and Israeli Jews. We cannot assume that we have the same values, especially concerning Israel, yet we must recognize that we are not enemies, focus on our similar-ities, and honestly admit our the differences. There also exists a need for open discussions on Zionism and the problems it has caused for Jews and non-Jews; although the polite Canadian context makes honest communication difficult, negative feelings must be aired. Disagreement and pain must not stop Diaspora and Israeli Jews from talking to each other.

The process of researching and writing this book has changed me profoundly. I have recently applied to work in Israel (something I would not have considered before I wrote the book). I believe that I can gain a better understanding of my identity by living and working in Israel and becoming totally fluent in the language. Although Ken does not share my goal, I still feel the need to go ahead. My involvement with Jewish issues has also had an effect on those around me. My daughter Sarah has expressed an interest in coming with me to spend time in Israel. She has also registered in a class on Judaic studies.

I am now more willing to look at my own fear of strangers. I was struck by some of the similarities between my own fear of strangers and a recent book that focuses on the defense of Israel. Martin van

Creveld, an Israeli history professor, discusses a plan for peace in Israel. I found a personal connection to his analysis of the term "defensible borders."[23] Creveld looks at the uses of this term in his discussion of martial strategy with regard to Israel. His study investigates what a strategic defense of Israel "might look like" or "whether it is possible at all."[24] When thinking about my own fear of strangers, the notion of defensible borders is a helpful way to frame the problem. Is it possible to defend oneself against a free-floating fear of strangers? This fear has been with me for a long time and has become more pronounced since the destruction of the Twin Towers. Creveld dis-cusses what he considers the "alleged 'indefensibility' of Israel's pre-1967 borders and wonders how the state actually was able to defend itself."[25] He concludes that "defending Israel within the pre-1967 borders was a very difficult, but far from insoluble task."[26] He offers many plausible reasons. The actual military defense of Israel is outside the parameters of this book; however, the discussion of the defensibility or the indefensibility of borders highlights the preoccupation with the desire for defense. Since the events of 9/11 the vulnerability of all has been exposed. Can this sense of vulnerability lead to reconciliation with the self?

In her preface to *Precarious Life*, Judith Butler along with many others explains that 9/11 resulted in "conditions of heightened vulnerability."[27] The world can never go back to the way it was before: the notion of safety has been forever altered. As Butler describes, "that U.S. boundaries were breached, that an unbearable vulnerability was exposed, that a terrible toll on human life was taken, were, and are, cause for fear and mourning."[28] She points out that this is a time for "reflection."[29] Butler's idea of reflection has always been a part of my own consciousness. Speaking in the first person she comments on the idea of being wounded:

> One insight that injury affords is that there are others out there on whom my life depends, people I do not know and may never know. This fundamental dependence on anonymous others is not a condition that I can will away. No security measure will foreclose this dependency; no violent act of sovereignty will rid the world of this fact.[30]

Butler seems to have accepted that the level of fear caused by violence and injury is now a permanent reality in the world today. I find this thought comforting in that it makes me feel less lonely. There are many people in the world who have been damaged through various types of violence. Butler goes on to suggest that it may be possible to find something positive in the awareness of this situation. She never assumes that there exists a "human condition that is universally shared."[31] Rather, she points out that the question raised for her "in light of recent global violence is, Who counts as human? Whose lives count as lives? And finally, *What makes for a grievable life?*"[32] The reason Butler raises these questions is to emphasize that although there is clearly not one universal reality for all, perhaps:

> It is possible to appeal to a "we" for all of us have some notion of what it is to have lost somebody. Loss has made a tenuous "we" of us all. And if we have lost, then it follows that we have desired and loved, that we have struggled to find the conditions for our desire.[33]

Butler sees the fact that there is a sense of "we" as something positive in the making, for this implies that humanity then has a place to start improving the situation. As she explains, "loss and vulnerability seem to follow our being socially constituted bodies, attached to others, at risk of losing those attachments, exposed to others, at risk of violence by virtue of the exposure."[34] She sees this shared risk as a beneficial tool for clearer communication and perhaps even a way to work towards an effective solution. In the writing of this book I have come to the realization that I am in a desperate search for optimism and along with Butler, I believe that the commonality of the experience of loss may be the place to start. The mourning process may provide hope. For Butler, "successful mourning" does not mean that "one has forgotten another person or that something has come along to take its place, as if full substitutability were something for which we might strive."[35] For me, the notion of loss and mourning can be applied to many areas of life. One can mourn changes of any kind. I remember after I gave birth, and my life was turned upside down by a happy event, I kept waiting for my life to go back to normal. After several months I began to realize that my life had changed forever. I was more vulnerable after I had children because their safety became my primary concern.

Butler's description of mourning provides the possibility of reconciliation with the self and with others. As she suggests:

> Perhaps . . . one mourns when one accepts that by the loss one undergoes one will be changed, possibly forever. Perhaps mourning has to do with agreeing to undergo a transformation (perhaps on should say *submitting* to a transformation) the full result of which one cannot know in advance.[36]

She stresses that the experience of loss is not of our choosing. There is a lack of control that must be accepted. One cannot achieve the "resolution of grief" by simply setting one's mind to the task at hand. I see a similarity in the notion of the "resolution of grief" and the idea of reconciliation with one's self. It requires awareness but it refuses to be forced.

Butler's description of grief sounds much like what I would define as clinical depression, with which I am well acquainted.

> I think one is hit by waves, and that one starts out the day with an aim, a project, a plan, and finds oneself foiled. One finds oneself fallen. One is exhausted but does not know why. Something

is larger than one's own deliberate plan, one's own project, one's knowing and choosing.[37]

I suppose that grief is thought of as a state from which one is healed over time. Mourning involves knowing what one has lost, whereas in depression this knowledge is often elusive. The more Butler describes what she thinks of as mourning, the more I am convinced that it is encompassed by depression. However; Butler sees the state of mourning as a portal, a window of opportunity to understand the Other and ourselves. She continues:

> When we lose certain people, or when we are dispossessed from a place, or a community, we may simply feel that we are undergoing something temporary, that mourning will be over and some restoration of prior order will be achieved. But maybe when we undergo what we do, something about who we are is revealed, something that delineates the ties we have to others, that shows us that these ties constitute what we are, ties or bonds that compose us.[38]

Butler's comments on loss are particularly relevant to what I have written about in this book. I have written about many kinds of loss. The Israeli women I spoke with have been dispossessed of a place and a community whether or not it was of their own choosing. We are dispossessed in almost every life change even though we may not recognize the loss. Sometimes is not until part of us is actually gone that we mourn its loss or even realize that we are now different.

I continue to draw on Butler's ideas here because they have a profound meaning for me. She expands further on the importance of being aware of the process of mourning.

> It is not as if an "I" exists independently over here and then simply loses a "you" over there, especially if the attachment to "you" is part of what composes who "I" am. If I lose you under these conditions, then I not only mourn the loss, but I become inscrutable to myself. Who "am" I without you?[39]

With the recent death of my father, I still see my mother struggling with this question. She no longer has a sense of who she is. All of us who were close to my father felt this to some extent. He was such a dynamic person! Who are we without him? We do not know what to make of our lives in aftermath. In Butler's words, "I think I have lost 'you' only to discover that 'I' have gone missing as well."[40] The thought expressed in this statement feels extremely familiar to me. There have been many times in my life when I feel as thought "I" have gone missing.

The "you" that Butler speaks of, need not always be a particular person. The "you" can stand for a stage in life such as youth. It can represent a projected self that turns out not to exist. It can represent a perceived failure or loss of reputation. Now that I look back on my own story I can see that way that I have been pulled toward loss and mourning, but in positive ways. I was pulled toward my husband, in part, because he was mourning the loss of his brother and sister-in-law. I was pulled toward the children left orphaned even before I met them. After giving birth, I mourned the loss of Robin and Allen, because I had a deeper understanding of who was gone. Mourning is not ambiguous.

Perhaps I was drawn to research Israeli women because I could sense their loss of place, which mirrored a part of myself that had been missing – the Jewish part. I have spent many years trying to find what I perceive as missing in by looking into other people's faces and lives. I hoped to find the missing part mirrored back to me. I do not think I have been looking in the wrong places, but rather I have spent a great deal of time looking without really seeing. Yet, I have hope that my vision will improve.

I began Chapter One with a description of my recurring dream about houses. My home is taken away in a variety of ways. I interpreted my dream as an expression of my sense that I have never felt at home. Now I can also see that I have been looking for a missing part of myself. My definition of home was having a sense of safety and security, feeling at home in my own body, and having a self with an identity I can feel comfortable with. Yet I continue to have this dream.

I also have another recurring dream that has been going on for at least twenty years. I used to be more aware of this dream because it would stay with me throughout the following day. Now it is just part of who I am, and I have not given it much thought for several years, although the dream continues on a regular basis. This dream, which I call the suitcase-dream, has several variations but the problem in the dream is always the same. In this dream I am far away from home in another country. I do not really recognize the specific location of these dreams, other than knowing that I need to get home. The nightmarish part of the dream always concerns getting ready to leave.

Obstacles always get in the way of my departure. The main obstacle is usually that I do not have a proper suitcase. In the dream I am desperate to find a suitcase so I can pack my things and leave. There is always too much to pack. I seem to have brought everything I own on the trip, but I never have enough room to pack everything up again. When I say that I bring everything I have, this includes all of my clothing from the time I was a child, all of my toys, all of my books, and so on. I will have to leave something behind. I have only one small suitcase in the dream, so I have to leave almost everything behind. I agonize having to make a choice about what to leave behind. Hurriedly, I stuff as much as I possibly can in my suitcase. Meanwhile, I have left packing to the last minute and I am terrified that I will miss my, bus, train, plane, or ship.

When I do get to the station, I have trouble finding the departure gate. Often I miss the bus, train, or plane and the rest of the dream is taken up with making alternate travel plans. There are problems here as well. Nobody understands what I am saying, or I try to call to let my family know and the telephone does not work properly. I sometimes try to find someone in the phone book, but nothing is listed alphabetically so it is impossible. The only time I actually make the departure time is when I am travelling by ship. The ship takes me to incredible places and I although I still feel the need to get home, this variation is not as nightmarish as the others. The main problem in the dream is being rushed and having to decide what to take with me. When I wake up I am always relieved.

The feelings I have in the dream are familiar in waking life as well. I am still haunted by the stories of *pogroms*, where persecuted Jews were forced to leave in a hurry. The stories of Jews being deported to concentration camps, taking only one suitcase also feel very familiar. These images are always just under the surface in my waking life. I was never in a concentration camp but I do have the fear that I could be taken away, or that my children will be taken from me. I have done extensive reading about the Holocaust and continue to do so. As horrific as this material is, there is a sense that I am at home with these images. They feel familiar. For me, the desolation I feel when reading Holocaust material reminds of the collective Jewish losses as well as keeping me in touch with personal losses. It pushes me to keep growing as a person and reminds me that I am alive.

My relatives escaped from Poland and Russia taking only what they could carry. They travelled to Canada by ship across the Atlantic. I carry the images of cold, starving, sea-sick people facing an unknown world. They did manage to escape to a different world. Perhaps I am moving towards a transformation. Perhaps I am on my way to a less ambiguous place. I have even had thoughts of *aliyah* (moving to Israel permanently) one day. Interacting with the women in my study along with considering the effect of a shared Jewish memory has made an enormous impact on my life. I feel more connected than both to myself and to others. At the same time I am considering packing my suitcase to spend an extended period in Israel. Maybe then I will feel entitled to my own opinion of Jewish issues. Maybe then I will be able to construct a new Jewish identity that will work for the future.

---

[1] Telchin, cover.
[2] Rosenblum, *Those Who Forget the Past: The Question of Anti-Semitism,* 2004.
[3] Butler, Precarious Life, 2004, 101-127.
[4] Ibid., 101.
[5] Ibid., 103.
[6] Ibid., 107.

[7] Ibid.

[8] Rosenbaum.

[9] Ozick, 607.

[10] Ibid., 602.

[11] Ibid., 607.

[12] Ibid., 608.

[13] Ibid.

[14] Ibid., 610.

[15] Kerby, 7.

[16] Ibid.

[17] Todd and Todd, 2000.

[18] Butler, 1997, 195.

[19] White, 102.

[20] Neumann, 476.

[21] Ibid.

[22] Gatehouse, 37.

[23] Creveld, 6.

[24] Ibid., 4.

[25] Ibid., 7.

[26] Ibid., 8.

[27] Butler, xi.

[28] Ibid.

[29] Ibid.

[30] Ibid.

[31] Ibid., 20.

[32] Ibid.

[33] Ibid.

[34] Ibid.

[35] Ibid., 21.

[36] Ibid.

[37] Ibid.

[38] Ibid., 22.

[39] Ibid.

[40] Ibid.

Postscript

Several years have passed since some of the events in my story. I have lived in Calgary twenty-five years, my children are adults, and, thankfully, I finally feel like a 'grown-up' (at the age of fifty-five). Over time Carie's marriage to Stuart, a non-Jewish man, and her subsequent involvement in Christianity has become part of who we are as a family. The sense of betrayal has long since disappeared. If anything, Carie's involvement with her church has made her a better Jew; she is a fuller human being – a different kind of Jew. To me, she has a new Jewish identity. She has taught me a great deal about acceptance and love. This kind of inclusive thinking is needed in the Jewish community, particularity between Diaspora Jews and Israeli Jews.

In many ways Carie's life choices have made our family closer. Although we each have struggled with our own connection to Judaism, Carie's example has given us the ability to live fuller lives. What once seemed like a betrayal is now seen as one stage on the way to another stage. My son Daniel is planning to marry a woman who was raised as a Catholic, and he also cooked this year's Passover dinner; he displays the new Jewish identity. As a family, we are simply happy that these two people were lucky enough to find each other. Meanwhile, my younger daughters, Sarah and Kylie, have had the courage to leave home in search of who they are. Carie has set an example, showing us how to integrate being Jewish with living in the present.

I have lost touch with most of the women who participated in my study, but I am sure their lives are all different by now. I do know that Devora, who desperately wanted to leave Israel, has moved back and has been there for a few years. Dafna, who could never picture herself outside of Israel has been living in Canada for five years and will likely continue to stay in Canada for at least two more years. I feel more drawn to Israel than I ever have in the past. I can picture myself living there in the future. I will not wait for peace between Jews and Arabs; peace is a state of mind, one that I constantly work towards.

I am making some major changes in my life while embracing the ambiguity that endures. I am moving back to Vancouver. Not only have I finally admitted that I miss living there, but I want to have more time with my mother, who turns eighty soon. Although I am able to venture into new territory, for the time being Ken will remain in Calgary. He has allowed me to lean on him for many years, so I am please to have an opportunity to stand alone and find my Self.

My understanding of the word 'reconciliation' has changed over the course of time. I had hope that it was possible to reconcile ambiguous feelings, but instead I have found that I need to tie up 'loose ends.' Finding a happy ending is not so important, and reconciliation of some feelings may never come. I may be fortunate enough to experience moments of clarity, but nothing stays the same so I no longer wish for absolute certainty.

Reflecting on my life, I know there are many things I could have done differently but now I accept that people work with the tools they have at a particular time. Although I make plans for the future, I know any plans I may have are always contingent on other circumstances. At one time I felt that contingency and ambiguity constrained me, but now I understand that these forces help connect me to the world.

Bibliography

Allen, Woody, writer, Reilins, Jack, & Jaffee, Charles H., producers. *Zelig.* (Movie) United States: MGM Studios, 1993.

Alvesson, M. *Postmodernism and social research.* Philadelphia: Open University Press, 2002.

Alvesson, M. and K. Sköldberg. *Reflexive methodology.* London: Sage, 2000.

Bannerji, H." Popular images of South Asian women." *Returning the gaze: Essays on racism, feminism and politics,* edited by H. Bannerji. Toronto: Sister Vision Press, 1993.

Barnett, M. *Israel in comparative perspective: Challenging the conventional wisdom.* Albany: State of New York University Press, 1996.

Barsky, R. "Refugees from Israel: A threat to Canadian Jewish identity?" Multiculturalism, Jews, and identities in Canada, edited by H. Adelman and J. Simpson. Jerusalem: The Magnes Press, 1996

Beck. E.T. "Therapy's double dilemma: Anti-Semitism and misogyny." *Seen but not heard: Jewish women in therapy,* edited by R. J. Siegel and E. Cole. New York: Harrington Park Press, 1991.

Berger, S, and M. Sutphen. "Commandeering the Palestinian cause." *How did this happen? Terrorism and the new war,* edited by J. Hoge and G. Rose. New York: Public Affairs, 2001.

Bernstein, R. "An ugly rumor or an ugly truth?" *New York Times,* August 5, 2002, p.14.

Biale, D., M. Galchinsky, and S. Heschel, eds. *Insider/outsider.* Berkeley, CA: University of California Press, 1997.

Bialystok, F. "'Were things that bad?' The Holocaust Enters Community Memory." *Delayed Impact: The Holocaust and the Canadian Jewish Community in The Canadian Jewish Studies Reader,* edited by R. Menkis and Norman Ravvin. Calgary: Red Deer Press, 2004.

Blackwell, T., and T. Arnold. "Murder of orthodox Jew in Toronto has hate-crime hallmarks: Skinheads suspected," *National Post,* August 15, 2002, sections A1 and A8.

Blumberg, A. *The history of Israel.* Westport, MD: Greenwood Press, 1998.

Brodbar-Nemzer, J., S. Cohen, A. Reitzes, C. Shahar, and G. Tobin. "An overview of the Canadian Jewish community." *The Jews in Canada,* edited by R. Brym, W. Shafir, and M. Weinfeld. Toronto: Oxford University Press, 1993.

Brown, D. "On narrative and belonging." *Paul Ricoeur and narrative: Context and contestation,* edited by M. Joy. Calgary, AB: University of Calgary Press, 1997.

Brown, L., ed. *The new shorter Oxford English Dictionary.* Oxford: Clarendon Press, 1993.

Buss, H. "Women's memoirs and the embodied imagination: The gendering of genre that makes history and literature nervous." *Paul

Ricoeur and Narrative, edited by M. Joy. Calgary, AB: University of Calgary Press, 1997.

Butler, J. "For a careful reading." *Feminist contentions*, edited by S. Benhabib, J. Butler, D. Cornell, and N. Fraser. New York: Routledge, 1995.

——. 1997. *Excitable speech: A politics of the performative.* New York: Routledge, 1997.

——. *Gender trouble.* New York: Routledge, 1999.

——. "The Charge of Anti-Semitism: Jews, Israel, and the Risks of Public Critique." *Precarious Life: The Powers of Mourning and Violence*, edited by Judith Butler. New York: Verso, 2004.

Cantor, A. *Jewish women/Jewish men: The legacy of patriarchy in Jewish life.* San Francisco: Harper, 1995.

Carr, D. *Time, narrative, and history.* Bloomington: Indiana University Press. Census Nation Series, 1986. Retrieved from: www.datalib.library.ualberta.ca/data/census/1996/nation/index/html

Chase, S. "Personal vulnerability and interpretive authority in narrative research." *Ethics and process in the narrative study of lives*, edited by R. Josselson. Thousand Oaks, CA: Sage, 1996.

Chesler, P. *The new anti-semitism: The current crisis and what we must do about it.* San Francisco: Jossey-Bass, 2003.

City of Calgary Civic Census. Retrieved from: www.gov.calgary.ab.ca

Clifford, J. "Diasporas." *The ethnicity reader*, edited by J. Rex & M. Guigernau. Malden: Polity Press, 1997.

Cohen, R. *Global diasporas.* Seattle: University of Washington Press, 1997.

Dror, Y. "On the uniqueness of Israel." *Israel in comparative perspective*, edited by M.N. Barnett. Albany: State University of New York Press, 1996.

Elazar, D. J., and M. Weinfeld, M., eds. *Still moving: Recent Jewish migration in comparative perspective.* New Brunswick: Transaction Publishers, 2000.

Elliott, J. L., and A. Fleras. *Unequal Relations.* Scarborough: Prentice-Hall Canada Inc.

El-Or, T. "Do you really know how they make love? The limits on intimacy with ethnographic informants." *Reflexivity and voice*, edited by R. Hertz. Thousand Oaks, CA: Sage, 1997.

Ezrahi. Y. *Rubber bullets: Power and conscience in modern Israel.* Berkeley: University of California Press, 1997.

Firer, R. *The agents of Zionist education* (in Hebrew). Tel Aviv: Hakibbutz Hameuchad Publishers, 1985.

Fish, S. *Postmodern warfare.* Harper's 305 (2002):33-40.

Fogell, M. *No-woman's land: Jewish women and intermarriage.* Masters Thesis, unpublished. University of Calgary, 1997.

Foucault, M. *Power/knowledge: Selected interviews and other writings*, 1972-77, edited by C. Gordon, New York: Pantheon Books, 1980.

Gatehouse, J. "No real excuse." *Maclean's*, December 30, 2002, pp. 37-38.

Gergen, M., and K. Gergen K. "Narratives of the gendered body in popular autobiography." *The narrative study of lives*, Vol. 1, edited by R. Josselson and A. Lieblich. Newbury Park, CA: Sage, 1993.

Gilman, S. *Jewish self-hatred.* Baltimore: The Johns Hopkins University Press, 1986.

Goffman, I. *Stigma.* New York: Simon and Schuster Inc, 1963.

Gold, G., and R. Cohen. "The myth of return and Israeli ethnicity in Toronto." *Multiculturalism, Jews, and identities in Canada*, edited by H. Adelman and J.H. Simpson. Jerusalem: The Magnes Press, 1996.

Gold, S. J. "Transnationalism and vocabularies of motive in international migration: The case of Israelis in the United States." *Sociological Perspectives* 40 (1997):409-27.

Goldensohn, L. *The Nuremberg interviews.* New York: Alfred A. Knopf, 2004.

Grossman, D. *Sleeping on a wire: Conversations with Palestinians in Israel*, translated by H. Watzman. New York: Farrar, Straus and Giroux, 1993.

Hamilton, R. *Gendering the vertical mosaic: Feminist perspectives on Canadian society.* Toronto: Copp Clark Ltd, 1996.

Haug, F. *Female sexualization: A collective work of memory.* London: Verso, 1999.

Hertz, R., ed. *Reflexivity and voice.* Thousand Oaks, CA: Sage, 1997.

Hertzberg, A. *The Zionist idea.* Athenum: Temple, 1975.

Hinchman, L.P, and S.K. Hinchman, eds. *Memory, identity, community: The idea of narrative in the human sciences.* Albany: State University of New York, 1997.

Hyman, M. *Who is a Jew?* Woodstock: Jewish Lights Publishing, 1998.

Izraeli, D. "Women and work: from collective to career." *Calling the equality bluff*, edited by B. Swirski and M. Safir. New York: Pergamon Press, 1991.

Jenkins, B. "The organization men." *How did this happen? Terrorism and the new war*, edited by J. Hoge and G. Rose. New York: Public Affairs, 2001.

Joy, M. "Writing as repossession: The narratives of incest victims." *Paul Ricouer and narrative*, edited by M. Joy. Calgary, AB: University of Calgary Press, 1997.

Kafka, F. 1995. "Before the law." *The metamorphosis in the penal colony and other stories*, translated by J. Neugroschel. New York: Simon & Schuster, 1995.

Kaye/Kantrowitz, M. *My Jewish face and other stories.* San Francisco: Spinsters/Aunt Lute Book Company, 1990a.

——. "The issue is power: Some notes on Jewish women and therapy." *Jewish women in therapy: Seen but not heard*, edited by R. Josefowitz, F. Siegal, and E. Cole. New York: Harrington Park Press, 1990b.

——. "Diasporism, feminism and coalition." *From memory to trans-formation: Jewish women's voices*, edited by S. Silberstein, S. Swartz, and M. Wolfe. Toronto: Second Story Press, 1998.

——, and I. Klepfisz, eds. *The tribe of Dina: A Jewish women's anthology.* Boston: Beacon Press, 1986.

Kearney, R. *On stories: Thinking in action.* London: Routledge, 2002.

Kerby, A. P. *Narrative and the self.* Bloomington: Indiana University Press, 1991.

Kondo, D. *Crafting selves: Power, gender, and discourse of identity in a Japanese workplace.* Chicago: University of Chicago Press, 1990.

Kook, R. "Between uniqueness and exclusion: The politics of identity in Israel." *Israel in comparative perspective*, edited by M.N. Barnett. New York: State University of New York Press, 1996.

Kuhn, A. *Family secrets: Acts of memory and imagination.* New York: Verso, 1995.

League for Human Rights of B'nai Brith Canada. 2002. Retrieved from: http://www.bnaibrith .ca/league/league.html

Lopate, P. *The Art of the Personal Essay.* New York: Anchor Books, 1995.

Linn, R., and N. Barker-Asher. "Permanent impermanence: Israeli expatriates in non- event transition." *The Jewish Journal of Sociology* 38 (1996):5-16.

Liptak, A., N. Lewis, and B. Weiser. "After Sept. 11, A legal battle on the limits of civil liberty." *New York Times*, August 4, 2002, pp. 1, 16.

Luce-Kappler, R. "Reverberating the action-research text." *Action research as a living practice*, edited by T.R. Carson and D. Sumara. New York: Peter Lang Publishing, 1997.

Medina, J. "Colleges and high schools to observe 9/11." *New York Times*, July 28, 2002, p.16.

Menkis, R., and N. Ravvin. *The Canadian Jewish studies reader.* Calgary: Red Deer Press, 2004.

Merriman, J. *A history of modern Europe.* New York: Routledge, 1996.

Miller, N. *Getting personal: Feminist occasions and other autobio-graphical acts.* New York: Routledge, 1991.

Minister, K. "A feminist frame for the oral history interview." *Women's words*, edited by S.B. Gluck and D. Patai. New York: Routledge, 1991.

Moghaddam, F., D. Taylor, P. Pelletier, and M. Shapanek. "The warped looking glass: How minorities perceive themselves, believe they are perceived, and are actually perceived by majority-group members in Quebec, Canada." *Perspectives on ethnicity in Canada*, edited by M. Kalbach and W. Kalbach. Toronto: Harcourt Canada, 2000.

Neumann, A. "On experience, memory, and knowing: A post-holocaust (auto)biography." *Curriculum Inquiry* 28 (1998):425-42.

Nussbaum, M. *Upheavals of thought: The intelligence of emotions.* Cambridge: Cambridge University Press, 2001.

Nicholson, L. "Introduction." *Feminist contentions*, edited by S. Benhabib, J. Butler, D. Cornell, and N. Fraser. New York: Routledge, 1995.

Ochberg, R. "Life stories and storied lives." *The narrative study of lives*, Vol. 2, edited by A. Lieblich and R. Josselson. Thousand Oaks, CA: Sage, 1994.

Ozick, C. "The Modern Hep! Hep! Hep!" *Those who forget the past: The question of anti-semitism*, edited by R. Rosenblum. New York: Random House, 2004.

Pellauer, D. "Forward: Recounting narrative." *Paul Ricoeur and narrative: Context and contestation*, edited by M. Joy. Calgary, AB: University of Calgary Press, 1997.

Pratt, M. B. 1984. "Identity: Skin blood heart." *Yours in struggle: Three feminist perspectives on anti-Semitism and racism*, edited by E. Bulkin, M.B. Pratt, and B. Smith. Ithaca, NY: Firebrand Books, 1984.

Probyn, E. *Sexing the self: Gendered positions in cultural studies.* London: Routledge, 1993.

Rees, L. *Auschwitz: A new history.* New York: Perseus Books Group, 2005.

Reinharz, S. "Who am I? The need for a variety of selves in the field." *Reflexivity and voice*, edited by R. Hertz. Thousand Oaks, CA: Sage, 1997.

———. *Time and narrrative*, Vol. 1. Chicago: University of Chicago Press, 1983.

———. *Time and narrative*, Vol. 3. Chicago: University of Chicago Press, 1985.

———. *From text to action: Essays in hermeneutics*, II. Evanston: Northwestern University Press, 1991.

———. *Oneself as another.* Chicago: the University of Chicago Press, 1992.

Rosenau, P. M. *Post-modernism and the social sciences: Insights, inroads, and intrusions.* Princeton, NJ: Princeton University Press, 1992.

Rutty, C. J. 1995. 'Do Something! . . . Do Anything!' *Poliomyelitis in Canada, 1927-162.* Unpublished doctoral dissertation. University of Toronto, Toronto, Ontario, Canada, 1995.

Schrag, C.O. *The self after postmodernity.* New Haven: Yale University Press, 1997.

Shapiro, F. "Learning to be a Jew through the Israeli Experience." *The Canadian Jewish Studies Reader*, edited by R. Menkis and N. Ravvin. Calgary: Red Deer Press, 2004.

Shokeid, M. *Children of circumstances.* Ithaca, NY: Cornell University Press, 1988.

Siegel, R.J. "Jewish women's bodies: Sexuality, body image and self-esteem." *Jewish women speak out*, edited by K. Weiner and A. Moon. Seattle: Canopy Press, 1995.

Silberstein, L. *The postzionism debates: Knowledge and power in Israeli culture.* New York: Routledge, 1999.

Smith, C. *Palestine and the Arab-Israeli conflict.* New York: St. Martin's Press, 1992.

Sobel, Z. *Migrants from the promised land.* New Brunswick: Transaction Books, 1986.

Stacey, J. 1997. *Feminist theory: Capital F, capital T. Introducing women's studies*, eds. V. Robinson and D. Richardson, 54-76. New York: New York University Press.

Sternhell, Z. *The founding myths of Israel.* Princeton, NJ: Princeton University Press, 1998.

Swirski, B., and M. Safir. "Living in a Jewish state: National, ethnic and religious implications." *Calling the equality bluff: Women in Israel*, edited by B. Swirski and M. Safir. New York: Pergamon Press, 1991.

Taras, D., and M. Weinfeld, M. "Continuity and criticism: North American Jews and Israel." *The Jews in Canada*, edited by R. Brym, W. Shaffir, and M. Weinfeld. Toronto: Oxford University Press, 1993.

Telchin, S. *Betrayed!* Grand Rapids: Chosen Books, 1981.

Tessler, M., and I. Warriner, I. "Gender and international relations: A comparison of citizen attitudes in Israel and Egypt." *Israel in comparative perspective*, edited by M. Barnett. Albany, NY: State University of New York Press, 1996.

Todd, S., and J. Todd (producers), and C. Nolan (director). *Memento.* (Film). Alliance Atlantis, New Market, Summit Entertainment, 2000.

Torczyner, J. L., and S.J. Brotman. *Weaving diverse strands: Demographic challenges transforming the fabric of Jewish communal life in Calgary.* Calgary: McGill Consortium for Ethnicity and Strategic Planning, 1996.

Tregebov, R. "Origins: Writing The Big Storm." *From memory to transformation*, edited by S. Silberstein Swartz and M. Wolfe. Toronto: Second Story Press, 1998.

Turley-Ewart, J. "Academics attack Israel for 'atrocities'." *National Post*, August10, 2002, p.A4.

Usher, R. "Textuality and reflexivity in educational research." *Understanding educational research*, eds. D. Scott and R. Usher. London: Routledge, 1996.

Waintrater, R. "Living in a state of siege." *Calling the equality bluff*, edited by B.Swirski and M. Safir. New York: Pergamon Press, 1991.

Warnke, G. "Social identity as interpretation." *Gadamer's century: Essays in honor of Hans-Geog Gadamer*, edited by J. Malpas, U. Arnswald, and J. Kertscher. Cambridge: The MIT Press, 2002.

Wasserfall, R. "Reflexivity, feminism, and difference." *Reflexivity and voice*, edited by R. Hertz. Thousand Oaks, CA: Sage, 1997.

Weedon, C. *Feminist practice and poststructuralist theory*, 2nd Ed. Oxford: Blackwell Publishers, 1997.

Weinfeld, M. *Like everyone else . . . but different.* Toronto: McClelland & Stewart, 2001.

White, S.K. *Sustaining affirmations: The strengths of weak ontology is political theory.* Princeton, NJ: Princeton University Press, 2000.

Widdershoven, G. "The story of life: Hermeneutic perspectives on the relationship between narrative and life history." *The narrative study of life*, edited by R. Josselson and A. Lieblich. Newbury Park, CA: Sage, 1993.

Zborowski, M., and E. Herzog. *Life is with people: The culture of the shtetl*. New York: Schocken Books, 1995. Original work published 1952.

Zerubavel, Y. *Recovered roots: Collective memory and the making of Israeli national tradition*. Chicago: University of Chicago Press, 1995.

About the Author

Melanie Fogell has spent the last ten years in academia as a student and professor. She returned to school after spending several years performing and teaching piano and selling her original paintings.

Recently she has been a lecturer at the University of Calgary in the Faculty of Communications and Culture. In 2006-2007 she will teach in the Women's Studies program at the University of British Columbia.

She has two degrees in Women's Studies and her doctorate is in Educational Research. She is married and has four children. Her future is ambiguous.

5/22